FOR GOLDEN FRIENDS I HAD

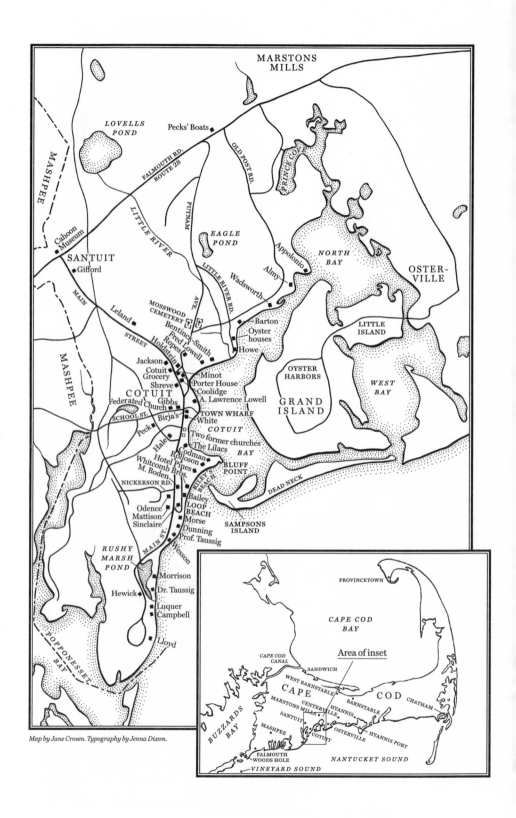

Map by Jane Crosen. Typography by Jenna Dixon.

LEONARD W. PECK

FOR GOLDEN FRIENDS I HAD

An account of a lifelong love affair
with the village of Cotuit

THE BARNSTABLE BOOK COMPANY
OSTERVILLE, MASSACHUSETTS

FIRST EDITION

ISBN 0-9679333-0-7

Library of Congress Card Number: 00-102303

The Barnstable Book Company
P.O. Box 234
Osterville, MA 02655

Copyedited by Linda Lotz
Interior design and composition by Jenna Dixon
Proofread by Beth Richards

Text composed in 11.5/16.5 Miller, a Scotch Roman revival designed
in 1997 by Matthew Carter with Tobias Frere-Jones.

Printed in the United States of America by Courier on acid-free paper.

06 05 04 03 02 01 00   1 2 3 4 5 6

With rue my heart is laden
  For golden friends I had,
For many a rose-lipt maiden
  And many a lightfoot lad.

—*A. E. Housman*

DEDICATION

To Betty, my wife, who asked for it and then didn't like it, I dedicate this book. The text is full of examples of how worthy she is to have something dedicated to her. Writing began Christmas Eve 1997, when I remembered too late that I had found no present for her. She never has this trouble; she makes me something original, something one of a kind, on her stove or her sewing machine. So finally I came out and asked her, and she said, "Write something." She knew I could write if only I would, and for once it worked. That was all it took; the whole thing from that moment came bubbling and frothing out. I wrote recollections of all the local people I have known, most of them now gone, just as I remembered them, which turned out to be not always with affection. "Warts and all!" (Where would we be without clichés?)

Betty said, "I have to live in this town." She was after me from the very beginning to tone it down. "These are your friends," said she. Even called it a "gossip column." Got so bad I finally had to point out to her that *Pollyanna* had already been written. Others, who got a peek at the manuscript-in-process, joined in: our son Geoff, my editor Wally. So this book has been much toned down, the only erotic part excised completely, but I hope it is still not *Pollyanna*. It remains subject to her final instructions: "Please make clear that the thoughts and ideas are yours, not ours."

Okay, Betty? "I'm glad!"

CONTENTS

AUTHOR'S NOTE

INCLUDING THE REMAINS OF A CHAPTER
ENTITLED "A HOPELESS MAJORITY"

THIS BOOK was written in accordance with rules and peculiarities, eccentricities, of the author. While it is presented without apologies, the reader is due some explanation of those peculiar rules. I am a thoroughgoing "word person," lacking almost all numbers. I use numbers hyperbolically, not for definition or quantification, not to give an exact size, time or place, but to heighten an impression. Used for measurement, my numbers are approximate at best. It is therefore a most eccentric history, one in which few dates can be relied on, no measurements are precise except by coincidence.

My method of introducing people is similarly eccentric. It is based on geography of the village, on a walk along the shore or the streets as they were in my childhood, as I first saw them, and as they have since become. The people are introduced as we encounter them along this walk, at whatever age they were when I first met them. So the people I first met are not only of a slightly earlier time than those who appear later, but also my impressions of them are in the early pages more childish than those of characters introduced later. My growing up and the stage of the history where I then was determine the impression I received of each person I introduce. Thus I recount adult memories of people whom I met when I was a grown-up.

I was born in Philadelphia on July 30, 1918, one of the few precise dates and places the reader can count on. I don't remember anything about it, but it's recorded on my birth certificate. (The other date this certain has not yet occurred.) My family and I lived here (Cotuit, Cape Cod, Massachusetts) in the summers only, until I was grown up and starting my own family. I moved that family here after World War II so that my children, conceived reluctantly because my wife insisted on bearing them and my reluctance had not yet solidified, might grow up in a place inspiring such love as I then felt for this village and because this was where I myself chose to live. I loved the place, so I moved here. As marriage is, to the cynic, the cure for love, so living here for fifty years has annihilated love for the place.

For I consider myself a cynic. My favorite philosopher is Ambrose Bierce, author of such profundities as "you cannot stop the wicked from going to Chicago by killing them." Like his contemporaries, Bierce could be wordy and windy, but his short pieces, his one-liners, are marvels of intense heat in a confined space. Like Bierce, I strive to write aphoristically, putting a thought, instantly recognizable, in the fewest words possible. "Marriage is the cure for love" is an attempt of mine to write this way.

My local, personal history, subject of the book, begins with the first remembered journey from Philadelphia. I have always had a singularly precise memory for details of early events but never for numbers. So Chapter I begins with a reliable account of a memorable event, but the date for it is only my best guess.

I have had a lot of fun and gained a few worldly advantages from this "trick memory" of mine. A "trick memory " in the sense of a juggler's or vaudeville mountebank's "trick knee" or "trick finger," double-jointed sort of. I do stunts with it. I memorize things on sight, things, that is, made of words. It does not work with numbers. They bore me. Nor is it all that reliable with people's names. I can learn things like a part in a play in one evening of intense concentration. Even better, I love poetry and memorize it effortlessly and almost instantly. And forever. I could— still can — recite for over three hours without opening the book. My memory got me through high school without the tedium of studying. Also, love poetry has a tenderizing effect on young girls of any age. I don't write much verse, though I can do things like put a sonnet together for an occasion and, without much effort, think in blank verse. I once wrote some double dactyls, amusing, and another time some Spenserian stanzas, as dreadful as this form usually is when essayed by amateurs. These are the closest I have ever come to putting this trick memory to any practical use. I do not regard it as a gift of God — God I have none — entailing any accountability, any reponsibility to make worthwhile use of it.

As I mention in the text, I once went on a year-long pleasure trip all by myself in my classy-looking tugboat, and set out to write a book about it. When I got home I sold a couple of installments of it to a local weekly paper and then was hired as a columnist to write a column a week for that paper. The editor and his readers liked my stuff; friends with connections put me in touch with a New York literary agent, who found me a New York publisher, a great big one, but my talent and my experience were not equal to producing a book of the length I contemplated, concerning such complexities of sex and aging as I was going through. I had half a script and a publisher waiting for the rest, but I petered out halfway through and the book is still unfinished.

A few more details of this part of my life are here and there in this book. It contains, as well, some ideas, thoughts, doctrines which may be of broader interest. First of all there is the phenomenon of "WOE" which is increasing all over the country. WOE is my acronym for "**We Oppose Everything**," and I apply it specifically to the Cotuit Civic Association, an organization devoted to preserving the whole nonexistent village as an unproductive enclave of classy homes for the elderly — for the members of WOE, who were none of them here, but imagine how it used to be, containing perhaps a peasantry who were forbidden to do anything except sit and look picturesque. They seek to make the place as sterile as St. Petersburg, Florida, even as barren as Sun City, Arizona, where nobody is permitted to make a sound.

I am an uncompromising Malthusian, though I reject that part of Malthus' doctrine which seeks to prove by statistics that humanity is going to starve itself to death by breeding faster than the food supply can keep up. I reject most statistics, they are so easy to render deceitful by manipulating the samples. What I foresee is everybody boring everybody else to death by proximity. Nature is full of examples of creatures, lions to lemmings to locusts, becoming savage when crowded. In humans it is called urban crime. The prosperous elderly now spread urban crime by seeking to escape it, crowding into suburbs and seeking to wall themselves into Sun Cities with guarded gates, a form of ghetto. They are walling the crowdedness in with them. No escape. That's what they seek to do to Cotuit.

I call to your attention a phenomenon which I find universal and striking: the nicest guys, whenever they get together and organize, become suddenly a nasty crowd, a bloodthirsty mob, worst of all, now and then, a political party. And the larger and better organized, the nastier they become. Anything two or more people agree on is at once suspect. The more people agree and the more profoundly, the less likely it is to resemble reality. One wise man plus another wise man become two fools. Thus is stated Peck's Generalized Theory of Association. It explains why this democracy we are so proud of usually comes up with unforeseen results, with absurdities. Explains why we agree that profit for a few will insure prosperity for all. If Steve Forbes gets richer, Joe Blow will get richer too, just from being around. Why every one of us, with no evidence at all, is convinced that he shall rise again from the dead. Why so many nice people get together to form the cancer of WOE. For there is no way to control the behavior of people while ignoring their numbers. WOE and all the other efforts to keep neighbors at bay are bound to fail so long as we refuse to deal with population, so long as we continue to assert that even the discussion of population problems is a sin. I savor a quotation, attributed to Voltaire: "So long as we continue to believe absurdities, we shall continue to commit atrocities."

Man is setting himself up for extinction. The sooner the better, before man's technology makes all life extinct. Thurber made a joke of human extinction; I'm serious. Man is destroying his environment. So far he has poisoned the air so it is, in cities, unfit to breathe, poisoned the water, both salt and fresh, to the point of killing marine life. And the ground water, the surface water and even the rain are full of poisonous acid. Even sunshine kills and must be kept off by layers of chemicals.

As a child, I loved this village. As an old man, I have here tried to chronicle its destruction by people who love it as much as I do. They love it so much that they organize to protect it.

Truly, it is in danger only from themselves and the likes of them, and from their numberless children, children to whose service I have devoted much of my life. WOE is a sort of chastity belt, organized to keep our beloved from defloration.

This book, which I first titled *The Underdeserted Village*, tells of a village which is being destroyed by human behavior exactly opposite to that which Oliver Goldsmith saw destroying his village. My village suffers not from too few people but from too many.

First thing about Cotuit for the cynic to feed on is that, in the haunted morass of Massachusetts politics, there is no such place. Therefore do I call it "nonexistent." The law here does not acknowledge that there can be a unit so small as a village. Smallest political unit is the town, and Cotuit is part of the Town of Barnstable, which contains several other nonexistent villages — just how many varies with who is counting. (Legally, there is no Santuit, no Cummaquid, no Hyannisport, the most famous of all. Such places do not exist. Nor Hyannis, even Barnstable village. No such places are acknowledged by the state.) The whole town of Barnstable is part of Barnstable County. Got that? And Barnstable County comprises all of Cape Cod.

The state itself recognizes, by act of its legislature (which it calls a "Great and General Court"), a Cotuit Fire District and a Cotuit Water District. But as far as Massachusetts is concerned, there is a Cotuit Fire Department but no Cotuit for it to protect. With such a foundation, how is it possible to have a view of Cotuit which is not cynical? Our town used to have an annual town meeting. As Bierce might have said, a town meeting is based on the theory that if you put a thousand fools under one roof, out of it must come wisdom. Population growth has forced us to outgrow that absurdity, but wisdom has not grown in its place.

I have a Biercian joke that says, to be effective, abortion must be retroactive. This joke becomes daily less funny, for the response is the organization of Christian mobs to save babies by killing doctors. Thereby seeking to compel the ultimate cruelty: the bringing into the world of another unwanted child.

Centuries of religious anti-education will further blot out all discussion of the true causes of pollution, global warming, poisoned water, poisoned air and poisoned sunshine, loss of habitat, crowded villages. Malthus had it wrong; before the population outgrows the food supply, we will have irritated each other to death by proximity. WOE is just an early, benign example of it, a dignified form of road rage. So WOE may speak for the majority of the people in Cotuit, but its cause is hopeless. So long as sex goes on and it is criminal to discuss it, the population is going to grow, here as everywhere.

As Bierce and a few others saw, you cannot oppose human development while ignoring human increase. Bierce wrote in his *Devil's Dictionary*, "Malthus believed in artificially limiting the world's population but found it could not be done by talking." That, I suppose, is one of the things this book is trying to do: limit population. By talking. Somebody's got to keep saying it, or Cape Cod and this whole underdeserted world will suffocate under people. Each demanding his share of loneliness. The only response one hears is anti-sex and anti-abortion. And anti-discussion of either. Meanwhile, as Housman wrote,

> The signal-fires of warning
> They blaze, but none regard;
> And on through night to morning
> The world runs ruinward.

ACKNOWLEDGMENTS

THIS BOOK owes its existence to many friends who helped me with technical details, first of all Ray Smith, who understands computers and helped me with the purchase of the one now in front of me, staring unblinking back at me as I stare into it. Ray, from way off in his home in Arizona, taught me to use the small portion of its infinite knowledge of everything, to get the words down on the screen and from there to the paper. Ray has always been enthusiastic about my writing, buoyantly encouraging whenever I need buoying up.

Also to Rick Marvin, from whom, with guidance from Ray and from my son Geoff, I bought the enigma machine. Rick kept copies for his own library of every revision every time I had to bring the abominable engine back for error correction. I got encouragement from my old friend Kurt Vonnegut, along with lots of less celebrated friends to whom I vouchsafed a peek at various stages along the way. Thank you all; it's your book really.

I
GETTING HERE

IREMEMBER everything about that first trip except the
date. Early summer 1923 I think; I was about five. My
family—my parents, my little sister Anne and I—lived in
Swarthmore, Pennsylvania, outside Philadelphia, and getting
us here, before we possessed an automobile, was an adventure for a child. It would be a memorable adventure still, even
for an adult. Right after lunch, local Model T taxi to the
familiar Pennsylvania commuter train, change in West Philadelphia to the more impressive on-the-hour New Yorker,
which made the ninety-mile run in ninety minutes (all trains
in this account were pulled by steam, these by the renowned
Pennsy K4's). Yellow cab from Pennsylvania Station to Pier
14, North River, and the paddle-wheel steamer *Priscilla* of
the Fall River Line. All the fanfare, all the ceremony, all the
half-hidden haste of a liner's departure. Details: ship docked
in North River (the Hudson, that is) rather than in more convenient but less classy East River—nearer her destination, less
harbor traffic—purely for prestige; here she was among the

Atlantic liners. All sorts of things for a kid to watch: dropping and shifting of docking lines; much hooting and screeching of steam whistles, police-type whistles, even some bosun's pipes; vibrating and splashing as the paddles turned, stopped, reversed. Being side-wheel, the enormous Fall River boats docked and undocked without tugs and had to fake port procedures of the liners. They put on a great show.

There are lots of arty-type prints, calendar lithos, of these ships in museums. Built for the semiexposed waters of Long Island Sound, they are not at all like the more familiar Mississippi steamboats, not even like the rare side-wheel ones. They had the two tall smokestacks, but they were in line fore and aft, not 'thwartships. There were no gaudy, round paddle boxes; the paddles were recessed into the side plating, and you hardly noticed them. They had to have been state of the art in paddle wheels, for almost unnoticeably they drove the ship at an average of over twenty knots. Ships were plumb-stemmed; the sharp bow went straight up from the waterline to the level of the main deck, but the round stern was carried all the way up to the topmost promenade.

Since then, I have done New York Harbor many times, in boats I was delivering south, but I still do it to the same tune: the voice of my mother showing me the sights: rounding the Battery, Statue of Liberty way off in the distance, Blackwell's Island. Mother had been a nurse there; she acknowledged that it was now named Welfare Island, but I understood that it would always be Blackwell's to her.

Then dinner in the ship's shiny-bright dining saloon. There were, no doubt, restaurants ashore to match it, in places like Paris, London, New York, even Philadelphia. Only we didn't usually move in such circles, certainly not with the kids. If I have to recall just one impression of it, it would be of acres of starched napery, of pirate's chests of silver and polished crystal. So, on these childhood cruises I got a peep at the last of the gilded age. Steamer *Priscilla* and her slightly newer, slightly larger sister *Commonwealth* were almost the last genuine example of it, though imitations, like revivals of the Orient Express, can still be found. Indeed, the ship made, at daybreak, a regular stop at Newport so tycoons could commute to their gilded "cottages."

The staterooms (at least the ones we had) were not gilded. They were like rooms in respectable hotels of the time with the maritime touch of beds arranged vertically to save floor space. Immaculate, I'm sure, or there would have been a reaction from Mother. She went to school in a convent and became a nurse, then a doctor, and her idea of everyday sanitation made our childhood environment a nightmare of constant cleaning. The room had no private bath or toilet; these were a step down the hall, but it had a sink with H and C faucets. Weird; details I have not thought of in seventy-five years return as I write: the H was very H indeed; came out of the faucet with spurts of steam, coughing sounds. Clearly, as my adult learning now tells me, it was heated by injecting steam from the ship's boilers into a tank of fresh water. And, though C enough, the C water was not for drinking. To get a drink, you rang for the stewardess and asked her for "some icewater please," which is still recorded in my father's voice inside my head. She soon came back with a pitcher of it.

Daddy took me to look down at the engine from a landing at deck level made of metal grating at the top of a metal stairway leading down into the engine room, where were tiny, far-off engineering officers doing engineering things. We watched the great cranks as they turned, reaching up for us and sinking back in failure, saying *fwhoom fwhoom*. Years later I learned that *Priscilla* had an eighteen-foot stroke! Crankshaft ran right across the ship and was direct-coupled to a paddle wheel at each end. How they disconnected it in the middle, letting each wheel turn independently when maneuvering dockside, I can't figure out, though I watched the undocking from on deck with great concentration. How much mechanical erudition do you expect from a seven-year-old anyhow? Though I must acknowledge that at that age, my son John would have known the answer, complete with quadratic numbers. He would surely have found out its exact RPM and the operating steam pressure. One more thing about this huge, slow-turning monster to delight a child was its color: rods, wiped with each pass through the packing glands, were polished steel, while cranks, valves, cylinders, pillow blocks were bright red.

I must caution anyone trying to read these memoirs that I write in a special way. Words are precise, accurate, but numbers are only approximate. They have never meant much to me. I am incapable of using them as engineers do, so precise they can be manipulated, like multiplied or divided, raised to powers, have roots extracted like teeth. Recited in loggy rhythms. Don't even assume the accuracy of my age at any time. My numbers are hyperbolic, used to heighten an impression, not to define size, time, place.

Another gilded recollection or two: in the center of the ship, low down, was a place aptly named the "Grand Saloon," furnished with armchairs and sofas upholstered in red plush, so soft I figured this must be that overstuffed furniture I had read about. A kid like me felt as though he sank literally out of sight. The red carpeting on the floors (decks) and stairs (not ladders) felt overstuffed too. Like soft mud. Up from this ornate room there rose an ornate staircase of gilt, white and mahogany, red carpeted. It divided halfway up to the next deck, going both right and left like a square dance, and went on up, deck after deck, splitting between each and coming together again I know not how many times. *Priscilla* had staterooms for like a thousand passengers on four or five decks, all above the hull in the top-heavy paddleboat style. What a floating firebomb that ship must have been, all those wooden upper works and a great open stair shaft right up the middle. Coal-fired boilers. I don't believe there were any bulkheads at all.

Before retiring, Daddy walked with me on the open top deck, where we looked at the path of the moon, made pale by the milky phosphorescent path of the ship across it, both paths leading out of sight over the horizon, and I got sleepy hearing the rhythmic *whoosh* of the engines and paddles, which fell into time with a child's poem by Milne:

> And he sits and thinks of the things they know,
> He and the forest alone together.
> The springs that come and the summers that go,
> Autumn dew on bracken and heather,
> The drip of the forest beneath the snow . . .

Last thing I remember was wondering what bracken was.

I awoke to broad daylight and silence and said to Daddy, already up, "We're at Newport, aren't we?"

"No," said he. "Fall River." So I had slept through Newport and all of Narragansett Bay, and the ship was tied up to a roofed pier shed different from the one in New York in that it was parallel to the shore, not jutting out into the stream. And on the wharf were two parallel tracks, each with a train waiting, one for Boston, the other for Cape Cod. So we had a leisurely breakfast in that most leisurely of dining rooms and made our leisurely way to the train. Not one but two—count 'em, two—steam locomotives, open vestibule (old-fashioned even then) parlor cars (in those pre-depression days the Pecks rode first class) with individual red plush seats which swiveled to face the aisle or outboard toward the huge arched windows. Apart from the open vestibules, the major difference between the rolling stock of the New Haven railroad and the familiar Pennsylvania was that the Pennsy cars were painted red and had green plush seats and the New Haven had green paint and red plush. Air-conditioned trains had not yet been invented (even the ice-cooled kind were still a few years in the future), and each window was expected to be opened and had a screen, and each parlor car had a porter to take care of such things. Each window had also a cinder deflector, a metal plate jutting out beside it about three inches into the slipstream. If it deflected any cinders, there must have been a hell of a lot of them coming out of the stacks, so many cinders still got through.

Aunt Harriet made the trip with us one time and she offered (there was a cousin or two along that year) a princely reward to the first of us to spot a cranberry bog. I didn't know what a cranberry bog was, didn't know what I was supposed to be looking at even when she showed me two, one out either window. I think my smart cousin Dorothea knew, which was all I needed. If Dorothea knew, it was not worth knowing. Like math. I am not over this willing suspension of interest in the cranberry industry to this day; Ambrose Bierce was with me even then.

There was a lot to be learned about the last days of serious passenger railroading on that ride, much of it revealed to me when I was older, but worth putting down before it's lost. The train had two small engines rather than one big one because the sand-ballasted roadbed was not equal to the weight of a big locomotive. The roadbed, hardly used anymore, remains barely adequate today, and such trains as still run, diesel powered, carrying sightseers and a little freight, still go as slow as that one did. Of course, this train, and the Fall River boat herself, ran only in summer, and it was a marginal enterprise even then. They weren't about to lay any new or better track. Around Middleborough the whole contraption ran backward two or three miles, switching from the track between Fall River and Boston and the Old Colony iron for Cape Cod. Also worth knowing is that the boat and the smaller steamers on Long Island Sound, and the trains, all of them between New York and Boston, and all the buses, as well as the ferries to Martha's Vineyard and Nantucket, belonged to the same corporation. God bless the goddamn New England Transportation Company.

So that top-heavy train took us slowly from that top-heavy ship to the depot at West Barnstable. Nowadays, when there is a train, it still stops there, but the station building is today unused, boarded up. Hard to find anybody who will admit to knowing why it still stands and why it stands idle. Somebody told me it now belongs to MIT which, if true, makes the mystery even more intriguing. How did MIT get it? Why did MIT want it? What will MIT do with it? When? Lousy building was absurd even when open. Spanish architecture, curving roof of red tile, pale yellow stucco walls. Perfect for a station on the Santa Fe. Inside, when people were allowed inside, was typical railroad: very dark varnished wood, wrought-iron gratings outside frosted glass ticket windows. Awful stuffy smell, cast-iron coal stove.

Parking at West Barnstable station was cinders over a clay base, full of potholes, and backed up to the depot were a few cars to pick up mail and passengers for the various villages, featuring the one from the Cotuit Transportation Company, a big open touring car of a make unfamiliar to me. I can't understand this memory. At five years old here was a make of car I didn't recognize. With a garrulous and child-loving driver, Henry Robbins himself. Could I have been too shy to ask him? It reminded me of the cars they used to cast in action movies. I remember vividly how the crooks grabbed the girl and the payroll and took off in a Packard phaeton, pursued by the hero and his friends in an open Cadillac, while the cops, in a Lincoln, ran a poor third. These ponderous cars squealed around corners, all the while exchanging pistol fire between members of all three parties standing on the wide running boards. Movies were considered bad for children, so I didn't get to see many, but these scenes were my way-out favorites. And here I was riding a most impressive movie car with a friendly and talkative driver and never found out the make! Maybe a Locomobile, a Stutz, a Stearns, a Peerless. Not a Pierce-Arrow; the headlights were wrong. Gone now. This is what happens to history when you don't pay attention.

Henry made other stops on the way to the Porter House, right on the beach, under the bluff at Hooper's Landing. It's there still. The house at that time had just one bedroom, and how the four Pecks shared quarters there is now lost forever. Evenings were dim, for there was no electricity. The power lines had not yet made it over the bluff, but I can remember the vivid daybreaks in that bedroom. It had one big window, a dormer facing east over the harbor, and the window had a roll-up curtain of bamboo slats. Bamboo has knobby joints so the slats don't fit together quite tight and some light comes through between them. The low roof on the landward side sloped as it rose to the ridge, so what you got as the sun rose

Porter House when it was a smithy, about 1890. The Santuit House Hotel is in the background.

Porter House about 1920. The Santuit House has been enlarged.

was its direct rays, mixed with its flickering reflection off the ripples, all projected in moving stripes on the ceiling. Sound effects of popping as the shellfishermen started their engines to go out to work. An awakening altogether different from sunrise in Swarthmore, Pennsylvania.

Aunts and girl cousins lived in another house just up the hill off the footpath. This equally primitive establishment was called the "House in the Woods." Some of the kids called it, more accurately, the "House in the Bushes," for the woods were almost all undergrowth, so the house was invisible from just a few feet away. It was impossible to see from there to the Porter House, though you could hear talk in one from the other.

The Porter House is right on the shore. High tide frequently comes over the beach and the dirt road and into the front yard, where in times past horses had stood waiting to be shod. Mrs. John Murray, wife of one of the quahoggers I heard each morning, told me all about her grandfather, several genera-tions great, Sylvanus Porter the smith, who built the house. What was the living room in my day was the smithy in his; where now stands a brick-arch fireplace, more recent look-ing, was formerly the forge, still using the same brick chim-ney. Sylvanus lived and raised his family in the rest of the house, beginning in 1815 when the house was built (at least according to a wooden marker nailed onto it by the Historical Society—like most historians and all Bierceians, I nourish a skepticism for the accuracy of other historians). I guess the present kitchen must have been the kitchen then.

I wrote a monograph on this kitchen and the plumbing in it which you can get from the Historical Society, which is join-ing me in publication of this book. The outrageous stair—why do I go on this way? It's still there; go and look. I'm trying to tell about things now gone, before they're lost forever; first of all, things I saw, then things people who were there told me. The big change is that things weren't so crowded then, even in the height of the summer boom of the 1920s. Still, to Sylvanus and his generation, the Cape and the village of my time would have seemed intolerably crowded. My memory is of a lonely, uncrowded place. Same as everybody else's. People have ever since been crowding in to share the loneliness.

II

THE WAY IT USED TO BE

SOMETIME BETWEEN Sylvanus Porter's time and mine, his shop was remodeled into a summer cottage of the Spartan sort then common and became part of the huge estate of the Coolidge family of Beacon Hill, Boston. By 1925 the owner of all this was Dr. Algernon Coolidge, son of Thomas and then or formerly chief of staff, or something equally grand, of Massachusetts General Hospital. I remember Dr. C., a dignified gentleman with a white beard, a white linen suit, a Panama hat and the gentlest manner ever. I remember also Mrs. Amy Lothrop Coolidge, by no means gentle. She was one of those whom I later categorized as a "fierce lady." They were both of them kin to President A. Lawrence Lowell of Harvard. Almost all this part of Cotuit, particularly the waterfront, belonged to him and to his relatives, who all referred to him as "Cousin Lawrence." They administered, in a quiet, understated way, the whole village as a sort of British fiefdom. In this manor I spent most of the summers of my childhood. And in the following manner I approached adulthood, or maturity, without ever really growing up.

All through World War II, I was stationed in the port of Philadelphia running a fire engine in the U.S. Coast Guard, a goldbrick job I attained by a combination of training, experience and influence. In 1942, Betty and I were married; we had known each other all of five weeks. That's how things happen in wartime. Our unique spin on this ordinary occurrence is that we are together still, going into 2000.

I introduced Betty to Cotuit the second day of the marriage, and all the Coolidge family and cousins made her royally welcome and fell under her spell as thoroughly as I. Cousin Lawrence and his wife were recently deceased, his house closed up, but for us his family arranged a private viewing. Singularly unpretentious outwardly, depending for grandeur solely on its superb location, it was high on one of the many wooded blufftops.

Inside it was full of treasures from the past: Wedgwood plates and complete dinner services, even (as at the Coolidges' and overflowing into the Porter House) chamber pots. Many rooms, many guest bedrooms, but only one primitive bathroom. Clearly, the Lowells still lived in the old British way, a chamber pot under each bed, a matching pitcher of hot water brought by the maid to each room every morning and carefully set beside the matching basin on the washstand. Complete Wedgwood protocol. One tub and one flush toilet in the bathroom off the master bedroom; everybody else who was staying like a week or more arranged for a tin tub and additional pitchers of hot water to be brought to his or her bedroom. Altogether archaic, even among Lowell relatives. For the staff, a second flush toilet, but not furnished with even such paltry amenities as partitions around it. It stood right out in the middle of a corridor among the maids' rooms. Far as I could see, for the manservants and the maid-servants both. If any such felt the need to wash, there was the kitchen sink.

My Aunt Lillie Peck, a Coolidge by adoption, was in charge of this tour. She told us that since there were no descendants and the house would cost a fortune to bring up-to-date, the property was to be sold and that it was the wish of the family that, since we were just starting out, we be given our choice of the furnishings for our own home when, after the war, we could make one. We chose an English coaching print in its plain, suitable frame entitled "The Last Change In" and featuring the "York-London Royal Mail." See how one story leads to another? We chose it and it became ours, but we didn't take it with us; we had no home to hang it in. Lillie would see that it was kept for us and taken care of. It was still there, hanging in that empty front room, when along came Cousin Lawrence's sister, Mrs. Ropes, who did not know about our deal and claimed the picture. Aunt Lillie had to break the news to us and she asked us, on behalf of herself and of Aunt Ellen Coolidge, not to say anything. Choose an alternate present. Quietly. So we got instead a set of a dozen hand-painted English dessert plates, each one of a different flower, each one perfect. Then word got back to Mrs. Ropes — not from us; we never told — that the picture had been given to us. She was a powerful woman, not to be crossed, and she insisted that we have the picture. You don't argue with her. So Betty and I now own both. They are bright stars in the firmament we now call home, and we received in addition the right to address fierce Mrs. Ropes as Aunt Alice for the rest of her life.

The Lowell family might have been inbred, as such dynasties are likely to become; certainly, now that Miss Anne, last child of Algernon and Amy, has passed on at the age of over a hundred, leaving no blood issue, such things may be mentioned. Anne had no chin, and everybody who knew her and saw her working at her profession thought her a genius. Her field was mental development of very young children. The degeneration of the Coolidge branch was relevant to my ever coming to Cotuit, for Anne's oldest brother, whom I never knew, was so handicapped, retarded and helpless that his parents, who could afford the best, were forced to hire a full-time attendant.

They got the best; they got my Aunt Lillie, an accomplished young lady with a new degree in social work from Simmons. She accompanied Bunker Coolidge wherever he went, like to Europe, and more important, stayed home with him so his family could go. Aunt Lillie was such a success that she stayed on in Cotuit every summer for the rest of her life, long after that poor little boy had no further need of her love and care. The Coolidges adopted her thoroughly. She became the lifelong companion, and associate in their specialized field of social work, of Dr. Coolidge's sister, Miss Ellen Coolidge, a grand lady, reserved, soft-spoken, full of love. If Betty had given me one daughter, among or instead of three sons, she would have been Ellen.

Ellen and Lillie lived in the House in the Woods I was telling about. It was the estate's former one-room schoolhouse and had stood across Main Street in times when the clan was more prolific. They had moved it to its then present site on the steep hillside above the Porter House, a kitchen and bathroom partitioned off. Bedrooms were a separate building, a prefab one-roomer for Ellen, a lean-to against that for Lillie. They were just a step, literally, from the back door over a bridge two planks wide and not much longer across the foundation dugout. Like the Porter House, it had no electricity.

Running water both had, at very low pressure, for the estate had its own system.

Some summers when Miss Ellen was away, one or two of my girl cousins came to stay with Aunt Lillie. I had four of them, daughters of my uncle Eddie Peck, beginning with Dorothea, my age and haughtily brilliant. Diminishing in age but advancing in beauty were Helen, plump and laughing; Marian, dark, built like a ballerina, good fun to date in spite of attacks of melancholy; and Patty, even as a little child, blonde and statuesque like her mother, Aunt Helen. This House in the Woods was set on the steep and irregular hillside with a hole cut in the shrubbery in front so you could see the harbor from the screened-in front porch. One or two summers when the ladies were abroad, my family lived there instead of in the Porter House. And with the apartment we got the folks downstairs, generations of a family of skunks. Through the bedroom window I used to watch them playing in the moonlight, dancing in a ring, tumbling each other over. On my way to bed one night I came face-to-face with a skunk child, standing on hind legs, front paws against the screen door I was about to open, looking into the kitchen. He contemplated me; I contemplated him; we just stood there. I decided it was a little early to go to bed and when I sought again to open the screen door, the coast was clear. The skunks accepted Lillie and Ellen the same way; in all the summers of my childhood, there was never an incident. They never gave offense, and none of us offered to touch one of them. The symbiotic relationship went on for two generations of humans and like five or ten of skunks. This is part of what I mean by uncrowded.

So Lillie was adopted by the Coolidges, and you might say she moved her whole family in. That's one way of looking at it. But we came not as freeloaders; we rented the Porter House as anybody might have done. Good tenants because we were family friends. For years I saved my allowance and my lunch money to help with the rent, had a bank account we called the Cotuit Fund. The Coolidges wasted no snobbery on us. Possessions had less to do then with gentility, and Aunt Lillie had demonstrated that we were as ladylike and gentlemanly as anybody, even though we were not rich nor related. They took us in as thoroughly as they had Lillie. Dr. Coolidge took us sailing in his huge old catboat *Viking,* first sailboat I ever went out in. To help him handle this ponderous craft he brought along William, "Willem" to Katie the maid, whom he later married. William had started with the family as coachman and was, by that time, chauffeur and gardener. "He had a brogue so rich and sweet!" It was twenty years and more before it struck me that he had a last name (Manning) or any need of one.

Dr. Coolidge had his own style of sailing: deliberate, thoughtful, explaining professorially everything he did. Mother was amused, told about it for years after, by his demonstration and lecture on the use and the awkwardness of the boat hook. *Viking* just suited him; for a catboat of her day she was grossly underrigged. And William's style just suited her, for he had none. He was a horse Irishman who had learned to drive an automobile, but he never became any kind of sailor.

Across the dirt road from our front door was the Coolidge wharf, a ramshackle affair erected every spring for just the one season. It was built of rough planks across two-by-four stringers nailed between pitch pine saplings sunk into the oozy mud bottom. No pretense of getting through the mud down to "hardpan." These seasonal erections, based on trash saplings, were a common form of lightweight marine construction. Planks were taken up in the fall and saved for next year. These and labor, which was cheap, were the only costs. Not only wharves, but moorings and fish and shellfish holding cars, were made that way. Shellfishing scows with one-cylinder engines and light sailboats were moored to stakes instead of to anchors. It added another dimension of skill to sailing into anchorage under the high bluffs, for any of the frequent shifts of wind down there might put you to windward of your stake, where its jagged top would tear the sail.

Dock and pier construction is labor-intensive even in mechanized today, but then it was labor and almost nothing else. Pilings were trash from the third-growth woods and were "swayed down" by a husky man in boots hanging on with most of his weight and swaying the tree back and forth down into the mud. Today they are "washed down" by a jet of water at high pressure from a portable gasoline-powered pump. Not much quicker, though noisier, and the labor is of a less laborious kind. Winter ice took care of pulling the pile up, and if it did not, you got a second season out of it.

The Coolidges had more boats, including three or four stout rowboats dockside, and we had the use of them. Also miscellaneous smaller sailboats. Daddy knew how to row, and he liked to row us about the harbor in the biggest of them, a high-sided affair known locally as an "Amesbury." I quote the words of Dr. Coolidge concerning this vessel: "Its mother was a dory and its father was one of these flat-bottom things." Life preservers were unheard of, whether you could swim or not. I learned to swim quickly, without fuss or comment. Daddy taught me to row, and after that I rowed all around the harbor in a handsome flat-bottom skiff named *Auk*, the unregarded property of Thornton Coolidge. And when the time came, Mother hired for me a college-age sailing instructor, Jim Dunning, who was later dean of the Harvard School of

Dental Medicine and acknowledged by his contemporaries to be the best sailor the Cotuit Yacht Club ever had.

These lessons took place in Miss Anne's old Butler-built sailing skiff *Topsy II*, and in ensuing summers I raced against the other kids, though *Topsy* was too long in the tooth for serious competition. And I was too young. One place our whole family used to sail to, or row to, was Dead Neck, a barren sandbar across the harbor mouth where the beach abounded with soft-shell clams, today called steamers. We ate steamed clams frequently at the Porter House, and Dr. Coolidge himself often joined us. He loved steamed clams; his wife did not. They are messy. I like to think that was as genial and informal as Dr. C. ever got with people not related to him. He wasn't snotty, just shy. And great with little kids.

Thornton, the Coolidges' other child, was, even in the 1920s, openly and arrogantly gay. He had been an Olympic-class figure skater, had a pretty partner named Mirabel Vinson, of whom people who were into skating spoke with awe. Thornton had given up skating by the time I knew him; he seemed to have no interest except to be gay and, like his mother, caustic. Apparently just to annoy her, he went way overboard with it: makeup, lipstick, simpering, the characteristic effeminate way of walking and talking like a tough whore, a series of handsome young house guests. I have thought since that he would have liked to be one of Oscar Wilde's set. Poor Amy put up with it; what else could she do? Finally Thornton killed himself, and his mother ended her days in a lunatic asylum. I'll have more to say later of her long sojourn there.

So, back to being a little kid in those times. I was aroused early in the morning by the sunlight on the ceiling and by those shellfishermen starting their bang-bang engines. Audible in an additional way was John Murray, husband of Sylvanus' descendant, who added his own wheeze on top of the pops and wheezes of his engine. John Murray had asthma and should never had been doing work so exposed and strenuous, but there was a living to be made for the Murrays and for the half dozen abandoned children they adopted. Talk about your quiet, unsung heroes. All those kids grew up to be decent, self-supporting citizens, good husbands and wives. I do not name them because of the sins of their natural parents while I sing the praises of those who took over.

Just as the sun was up, Mr. Milton Crocker, of the Cotuit Grocery Co., came by in his '27 Chevy truck delivering the milk, and I regularly rode around the route with him. He put in a long day; before he loaded the milk, he had to take in and put away the night's delivery of bread, as well as of milk. When I remembered, I took the family two-gallon oil can along in the truck, for the route ended at the store just across Main Street from the big Coolidge house. That's where we got our oil, which is what everybody called kerosene, pumped up from an underground tank under the sidewalk in front of the store. The pump stuck up through the pavement, and I liked to crank it myself. Mother couldn't cook breakfast until I brought the oil, so if I forgot the can I had to walk home, get the can, walk back to the store and then back home with it.

It was a happy walk, however often. Most local transport in those days was by foot, and there was a path, a public right-of-way, straight up the hill from in front of the Porter House, past the lane to the House in the Woods to Main Street, where there was a turnstile, I guess to remind the public that the path was across private property. But I didn't follow that path more than a few yards. Just up from the house I turned right through a gate in the fence and a gap in the high lilac hedge and came out at the foot of the lawn leading up to the main house. I passed first the three-tree orchard, where stood the best and biggest apple tree ever to grow. It produced quantities of small yellow apples, marbled with red, very early, ready to eat by mid-August. I loaded my pockets and the bosom of my shirt or my jacket with a supply of them, fed some windfalls to Aloysius the pig. Aloysius was the Coolidge garbage wagon. He came as a piglet when they opened the estate in spring and departed as a porker in the fall, to be succeeded by another piglet, perhaps named Egbert, next year. His sty was cruelly just beyond the reach of windfalls. They fell instead in the chicken yard, and why they didn't brain a hen I never understood. An apple must be even dumber than a chicken.

On, ever on, up that green lawn toward the great house. The lawn looked, from the water, as well tended as a golf course,

The Coolidge house today, much changed. Taken from just above the Porter House. Here once stood the orchard and the sty.

but up close you could see it was actually a hayfield, mowed with a horse-drawn sickle bar whenever it started to turn brown. The footpaths radiating from the house down toward the Porter House and toward the House in the Woods were the same coarse grass but mowed weekly by William pushing a reel-type mower, thus producing a surface as tough on bare feet as an oystershell road. You learned to put your foot down with a sliding motion to flatten the stubble before putting your weight on it. Ever on, straight toward the front porch of the great house, where nobody was up except the staff; bear right past the porch and some ground-floor windows, out onto the brick pavement outside the laundry and kitchen windows. Katherine, the cook, not to be confused with Katie, the maid, saw me going by and hailed me in rich brogue. "Hello, Leonard. Want a coookie?" Thus I got a pre-breakfast of apple and cookie. Crossed the street, filled the can and lugged it back, replenishing my apple supply on the way. Had my proper breakfast. Not nearly so good; Mother often made oatmeal. Like Crusher Bailey's brother Norwich in the song, "fond of oatmeal porridge." But not till I got home with the oil. And I have to this day my own fondness for the smell of burning kerosene, today mostly diesel exhaust. I'm fond of that!

The dominant force through most of those times was Lowell. Cousin Lawrence himself was a visible screwball. He was very tall and he walked, leaning way forward, very fast, all over town and all over surrounding towns. He owned acreage in Cotuit, in Mashpee, in Sandwich, all over the place. He was usually accompanied by a crony, a less striking but more amiable man named Yeoman (or Yeomans), not notably tall but able somehow to keep up with Lowell's pace. I never actually saw the farmers and villagers touch their caps, but Lowell's passing brings such a tableau to mind. Over the years he spoke to me once or twice, cordial as you please, but there was no indication that he knew my name or who I might be. His wife was even more strikingly screwy than he, and she put less effort into it. For reasons only she knew, she never wore anything more mod than 1890, and she never drove an automobile. Every day or two she drove herself out in a one-horse buggy dressed in the latest mode of thirty years before and driving the trotting horse, who was also dressed in old-style harness incorporating a sort of open-work shawl to keep the flies off. She and Lawrence had no children. Just as well; her maiden name was Lowell too. Over the years, she never spoke to me. Why should she? We had nothing to talk about.

I once, when about thirteen and home in Pennsylvania, gained distinction of a sort with one of Mrs. L's cast-off dresses which Aunt Lillie had sent to us for fun. Wore it at Hallowe'en and won a prize in the local Hallowe'en parade. For me, a satisfying experience, though it failed to give me a taste for going around in drag

Cousin Lawrence drove a car, but in a special Lowell way, as though he were walking across Harvard Yard or around Cotuit, where everybody knew him and got out of his way. People are still recalling the last time he drove down from Cambridge. About 1940, let's say. He smashed up his car in Plymouth, rented another, smashed that one up too before he got here. After that he gave up driving.

All these cousins of Cousin Lawrence had the whole water-front around the center of the village tied up tight. Cousin Lawrence's primitive palace, out of sight on his many acres, was adjacent to the town wharf and to the unpaved road leading down to it from the busy village center. Below his house and nearer to the road he had a little red house which was his study and a big shed with boats in it. Most of them were not even launched in the spring anymore; Cousin Lawrence was getting old. One boat I do remember: *Crab*, an odd-looking hull, tremendous long overhangs at bow and stern—together these overhangs must have equaled in length the unloaded waterline. One year he had her painted—bright red—and put in the water. She carried, like most fast smallcraft in those days, an insignificant jib and a monstrous gaff mainsail. Maybe a gaff topsail; I can't remember. Maybe she was meant to be sailed as a sandbagger; can't remember that either. And I think I was told that she was a creation of the renowned Stanley Butler. Typical of Lowell to subsidize a local genius like Stanley in an experimental sailing bomb to test his theories. I gather *Crab* was an unqualified success for fast, but of no use; nothing in her class to even race against.

Beyond Lowell, heading toward the Porter House along the reedy beach of the sheltered inner harbor, northward and eastward as the shoreline trends, there was a break in the family holdings: the Santuit House hotel, one of several such full-service establishments that were, by the time I came to Cotuit, almost extinct. The Santuit House was closed and out of business by the time I first saw it. The main building had burned to the foundation, and two nondescript annex buildings remained, boarded up. The kids pretended they were haunted.

This hotel possessed a tiny strip of reedy beach bounded on the south by an unimproved, muddy, rocky public boat landing where, just before my time, had stood a substantial wharf. Packet schooners for Nantucket used to tie up there.

And there was once a shop on the wharf which sold ice cream cones. It was no seasonal, swayed sapling construction; that wharf has been gone for the best part of seventy years that I can remember, but you can still poke in the mud and find remains of the pilings—locust pilings they must have been—and the rocks which were in those days dumped under wharves and close alongside them to reinforce the structure. The place is still used seventy years later to launch and haul small boats, and you must know the ground and be careful as you back your trailer in, to avoid the ruins.

Beyond the defunct hotel, Coolidge property began. It extended from the shore right up, with buildings both sides of Main Street, but it had a short waterfront, for the shoreline here took a sharp, a more than right-angle turn from northward to eastward, and the Coolidges' big acreage had only a short strip of reedy, marshy beach where stood their wharf. A sand and shell road came down to the shore, ran between the wharf and the Porter House and continued along the shore to where once had stood the schooner wharf, made a sharp turn and went back up the hill to Main Street. Exactly as it does today except that today it's paved and today two cars, with brave drivers, can pass each other. Here, just beyond the Porter House and across that road from it, was and still is a public landing where local people swim and used to haul their boats. These two uses for the same piece of beach never, in those days, came into conflict. Why should they? They could never occur at the same time. The boats, to be clear of ice, had to be way back from the water, and if some people, for some reason, left their boats on this town land all summer, even year after year, they didn't bother anybody. They just rotted, which makes no noise.

III
SOME CHARACTERISTIC
CHARACTERS

A S I WAS SAYING, these cousins of Cousin Lawrence had all the waterfront and the land behind it tied up for generations, though their hold was slipping here and there. After Coolidges came Putnams, though by my time their holdings didn't reach the shore. Then the beautiful estate of Professor James H. Ropes. On old maps of Cotuit, this sharp turn in the shoreline leading to Ropes land is known as Hooper's Landing after a Mr. Samuel Hooper, a merchant from Boston who was Cotuit's first summer resident. I know no more of him than this; no dates closer than eighteen something. He is to me just a name on old maps, and I intend to let him stay that way. I could learn more easily enough; Professor Ropes' sweet daughter, Harriet Ropes Cabot, lives in Cotuit still, in a little house built to her order high on the bluff at the far end of Ropes land. She is my good friend, a grand lady, a historian by profession, and she knows all about Hooper and is willing to tell, but Hooper is way outside the scope of this memoir. Dead a generation before I was born.

Rather tell about Harriet. At ninety she is still of greater interest. But I've got to approach the Ropeses as I found them when I was six or seven, not sneak up from the rear by dealing with the last surviving child first. I think the house her family occupied until recently is older even than Hooper. A sea captain's house from the eighteenth century, it is crammed from top to bottom with priceless New England antiquities from the China-trading days. Had a weathervane on the barn, solid brass, valuable enough for somebody recently to climb way up there to steal. Or maybe he used a helicopter. The possibility has been mentioned, but the antique has not been recovered nor the perpetrator found.

Most memorable from my childhood is a double set of andirons. In the partition between the living room and the study are back-to-back fireplaces with matching andirons, and on the upright members of these andirons are identical eighteenth-century British soldiers in their red coats, fired tile beautifully colored. My parents took me to call when I was very small, and Professor Ropes asked me if I could see any difference between the two sets. I walked busily from room to room, studied details right down to the expressions on the soldiers' faces, but concluded there was no difference. Then it was pointed out to me that the soldiers in the living room were facing each other while those in the study both looked in the same direction.

So that is my sole, my only memory of Professor James H. Ropes, who was, according to what my mother told me, dean of the Harvard Divinity School. Alice, his wife, was, as you will see, much more vivid. Cousin Lawrence's sister. Big but not fat, like most Lowells, one of the coterie of great dames attending on Aunt Amy, legatee and donor, of the English coaching print now the property of Betty and me. She and the

How Hoopers Landing looked long before I first saw it.

professor owned a stretch of the most beautiful sheltered beach on Cape Cod, equally popular with family friends and with trespassers. This beach is so great that in the more than seventy years I have known it, that part of town has been known not as Hooper's Landing but as Ropes' Beach. If you are asking directions, don't bother to mention Hooper. As I say, it was beautiful yellowish sand down to low water; below that the bottom has always been soft muck with sharp shells embedded in it. At low tide you can't wade out to swimming depth without sneakers.

Both Aunt Alice's children were also Lowells in size; Edward James Lowell Ropes was tall enough to be a pro basketball player in a later age, a huge man without an ounce of fat, with a slight stoop, except when he took thought about it, like Cousin Lawrence. Handsome, with a big, classic Lowell nose. He could be as nasty, as sarcastic, as Amy or Thornton, but he too was seldom that way to me. He was outstandingly mean to his big sister Harriet. Hatta they called her. She too was big but not fat. Timid and never nasty. About ten years older than I. She went to Bryn Mawr, a college for exceptionally bright girls only (cousin Dorothea went there, as did my girlfriend Patsy) and only a few miles from the Pecks' winter home outside Philadelphia.

My parents had Hatta over for Sunday dinner often. She and I never became friends in those days; every visit she saw me being as mean and nasty to my little sister as her little brother was to her. Hatta does not harbor lifelong grudges the way I do; no doubt she believed being mean to one's sister was normal brotherly behavior. Her friendship with me healed gradually. I remember she took my family and some friends sailing for my birthday, tenth or thereabout, in her father's famous catboat *Monomoy*, a Stanley Butler original, about seventeen feet. Seventeen feet of catboat is a lot of ship, being half as wide as she is long, and Hatta kept up a running dialogue with herself all the time about how dismally she was doing. As though speaking her brother's words in his absence. Feelings of inferiority right out of a psych textbook, while handling that handful of boat superbly.

Hatta was married, for a while, to one Ted Cabot, a Boston socialite as grand as any Lowell. There is a rhyme, popular around Yale, about the Lowells and the Cabots, but the marriage didn't "work out," through no fault of hers. She then had a successful career in Boston, where she was for years curator of the Old State House Museum, then retired to Cotuit, built that little one-woman cottage on Ropes property at the far end of the bluff, and in mature life was part of Cotuit's year-round intellectual society, and everybody loved her. After Sinclaires sold out (patience; we're coming to them), Harriet invited the kids of the Mosquito Yacht Club to erect their light wharf, of modified swayed-sapling construction, year after year, on the beach in front of it, although the only land approach for all those kids, and adults with them, was right by her front door, across her lawn and under her kitchen windows. There was no shore approach; Ed Ropes was not in sympathy with all those people crossing his beach, in front of his house. Hatta still lives there and is still as great a lady as her mother and her aunts.

Younger brother Ed stayed on in that superb family house summers, and he and his wife, whose name I think was Charlotte but who was called by a nickname which I spell phonetically "Shyzee," lived what I always considered a decadent life there with a set of loud, sneering, hard-drinking, dissolute friends, some of whom will appear later in these pages. Any time I say so-and-so was a crony of Shyzee and Ed, you will understand that I imply decadence. There was, for example, a very young boy growing up gay and not knowing what it was. He admired their assured, snotty lifestyle, so different from his strict Christian upbringing against which he was in revolt, and they taught him to drink the hardest of hard liquor (he was a "most apt scholar"), got him drunk and made fun of him. Turned him into a buffoon. Over and over, for years, him loving every minute of it. With all this, Ed and Shyzee had three pretty daughters, normal size, not Lowell size, who grew up only marginally eccentric, not particularly decadent and fun to be with. I taught them all to sail, but none of them was much motivated. Hatta is devoted to them; her capacity to love is boundless.

Ed Ropes inherited his father's fast catboat *Monomoy*, but he had not the time nor the inclination to maintain her nor the cash to have the yard do it. She was getting old, as wooden boats will. She had been damaged in 1938 in a hurricane which brought down the Ropes boathouse on top of her. And a cat-boat is frail by nature, with a wooden bottom split in the middle by the centerboard box and the twisting strain of that ponderous mast with all that sail concentrated right up in the bow where there is no place to put meaningful standing rigging. So Ed sold her to Henry Chatfield Churbuck, called Chat, grandson of Thomas Chatfield from Cotuit, a famous captain of sailing ships in Civil War times. I knew the Chatfields well, and there were almost as many of them as there were Lowells. Chat was opening a boatyard in his grandfather's workshop a block up from the harbor, and I was employed there summers in my Harvard days; Chat thought my membership in the summer sailing crowd would bring business.

But Chat couldn't keep up with *Monomoy's* continuing deterioration either; she was bigger than the little sailing and rowing skiffs he was building. He hired the best boatbuilder available, a little man named Merrill Crosby, called Deak, one of the renowned Crosby's of Osterville, boatbuilders for generations and claiming to be the inventors of the cat rig. Deak nearly drove Chat crazy he worked so slowly. He built for Churbuck's eight fine sailing skiffs of the class raced by Cotuit kids, and to hear Chat tell it, he lost money on every one of them. There was never time to turn Deak loose on *Monomoy*; her slow downhill progress continued. Chat had a lot of fun with her, entering her in open class in regattas, where she invariably beat the sticks off modern racing yachts anything like her size. After a couple years he had had enough of boatbuilding, closed his shop and went into furniture manufacturing in Wakefield. Ed Ropes bought *Monomoy* back.

As I say, I worked for Chat summers while in college and learned what little of my trade I ever knew from Deak. I never got as precise as he at fitting wood together, but I soon got faster. Only other thing I learned there was to lust after Chat's underage niece. This came to nothing, but it got the whole village laughing at me.

After Chat Churbuck went out of the boat business, I went into it sort of by default. Had no shop, but I worked on small boats right on the beach around the Porter House and inherited Chat's clientele. I inherited *Monomoy* and her problems too, where she lay hauled out on Ropes land where the boathouse once stood, lying among the beach grass above high water. I was not trained to deal with the structural problems of a planked vessel—sailing skiffs are built more simply, without bent frames and a rigid keel. I did my best, invented some successful and innovative things at deck level, where she was opening up like a pea pod, but I was hopelessly lost down in the bilge where the oak frames and floor timbers joined the keel, everything of oak and everything rotting. I did my best, and the irascible Mr. Ropes appreciated my efforts and was patient and gentle about it, and every year I finally got her into the water, late but more or less watertight. He hardly ever went sailing anyhow.

Monomoy was twice my age, and she was patient and forgiving too. If she were alive, she would today be about a hundred, but finally I lost her in a hopelessly overambitious attempt to replace all the oak: keel, floors, frames and all, in the boatbuilding shop at Barnstable Vocational High School. I was for one year their barely adequate substitute shop teacher while the regular old gentleman was in hospital. I had observed this radical surgery at one of the Crosby yards, but not by schoolboys and an untrained first-year shop instructor. *Monomoy* was in hospital too, a teaching hospital with inadequate surgeons. Like the school's regular man, she never came out. I was offered his job but didn't want it. Too busy building my own business, and anyway, the state, which pays the salaries of "voke" teachers, ruled that my training was not adequate.

The fate of *Monomoy* proves how right the state was. The new man they hired was too smart to imagine that he and the boys could complete anything so grandiose, and the poor old boat ended up in the boneyard. But not a word of reproach did I get from Ropes. I have here been trying to show a complicated man, warts and all. In the end I was as fond of the man as I was of all his aunties. He had too much mind and too much independence to let himself sink over his head in the suffocating morass of family, by his time dying out.

Beyond Ropes, the next summer place was the Fred Lowell cottages—four separate, comparatively small houses so that all the many children of Fred, with their families, could live communally or as independently as they chose. So much wiser, it seems to me, than one big house with all the disagreements of too many strong people trying to get along, living together like Coolidges and Ropeses. Of all the Lowell properties named before and to come, Fred's alone still has Lowells in it. Fred was before my time; his sons and daughters were a little older too, but I remember most of them, some with great affection. There was Dr. Frank Lowell first of all, tall, erect, handsome. He looked like a young southern planter out of the movies. Frank (or Francis) Lowell was president of WOE for several years, so he and I, though cordial, had a fundamental disagreement. He had a strikingly beautiful wife, and their sons are the only Lowells left.

He had two sisters, Dr. Alice and Marianna. I knew Alice Lowell as a customer and friend when I was in the boat business. But Marianna, at least ten years older than I, was my special friend. She had qualities of loyalty and direct frankness to which I responded. Tough and fierce, always she treated me as a contemporary, a member of the family like Aunt Lillie, in on family secrets, a friend whose opinion was worth listening to. Just like the previous generation around Aunt Amy. I once referred to Amy Coolidge as an "old darling," thinking maybe of her special gentleness toward me. But Marianna was having none of it. "She wasn't a darling. She was a nasty mean old woman."

Marianna married a celebrity, the emigré French writer Jacques Barzun, and devoted the rest of her life to bearing and rearing his children (they took sailing lessons from me and she, years later, bought one of my skiffs for her daughter) and protecting Jacques from celebrity-seeking pests, here and in New York. Anna Mattison said of the Barzuns, "It's easy to live in *The House of Intellect* when you have Marianna guarding the door." That's how tough and fierce she was. Her formal name for herself was "M. Lowell Barzun."

One time she did Betty and me a great honor: She had us in to lunch on one of the rare occasions when Jacques was in town—he had no real interest in Cotuit. In preparation for this momentous event—maybe she imagined that we would be an example of her opinion that intellect flourished here too —she lent us a copy of Jacques' latest book, one that purported to teach teachers how to teach writing. And I made an irretrievable mistake: discussed the book with its author with the frankness usual with Marianna, what she had always respected in me. You don't talk that way to Jacques, I then learned. I have forgotten the details of Jacques' book, even its title, but typically I remember clearly my own remarks: Anybody who can benefit from this book is already so learned he doesn't need it. The kind of students most of us get won't under-stand a word. Silence. End of friendship. Her loyalty to her awe-inspiring husband was not up to the stretching required to remain loyal to one who dared criticize him. Who the hell did I think I was? But what I said to Jacques I still believe: after a degree from Harvard in English and a graduate degree there in teaching, I have still never found anything in a book that can communicate the smallest part of the art of teaching, or of writing skills. Teaching texts are not meant to instruct; they are to provide income and prestige for professors.

One thing I miss, that went from me along with the friend-ship of Marianna: she was one of four particular friends with whom I was on a "last-name basis," who always met me or called me on the phone with just the one word "Peck!" uttered explosively. They're all dead now.

Beyond the aggregation of Fred Lowell's was the summer estate of Guy Lowell. This one passed unintentionally out of the family, or so goes the tale I was told. Lowell didn't want to sell, didn't need the money and, when pestered to name a price, named one so outrageously high he figured they'd stop pes-tering him. And instantly he found himself landless and even richer. When I came here, this place belonged to the Bentinck-Smiths. They had built, or enlarged what they found, the biggest house at that time in Cotuit, high on the bluff, with a view out over Cotuit Harbor, Dead Neck and the Sound, almost to Nantucket. They were not, even with their hyphen, aristocrats in the Lowell league. Merchants, worthy burghers of Boston and among the most gentle, most polite, most gen-erous people I ever knew. They seemed untroubled by that inhibition of "old money" that capital must be preserved intact. I'll have more about them when I get old enough to sail.

Truly, the decimation of Lowell holdings had been going on, in bits and pieces, for years as fewer of them were born. About 1920 my father had to pass up the chance to buy, for only ten thousand dollars, what was later known as "the Shreve place," formerly the main summer home of the Coolidges. It included spacious grounds meticulously planted with exotic flora— huge Oriental trees—as well as numerous outbuildings and the formal house. No waterfront; this place was on the other side of Main Street, which may have been part of the reason the family chose to let this part of the estate go. The house was more like one in Salem, oriented to the street rather than to the harbor, though there may have been more view before the timber grew back. It was a showplace rather than the patchwork, nondescript house the Coolidges occupied when I knew them, with its magnificent view over rolling hayfields that looked like lawns, a corner of the tiny farmyard and orchard, hen coop and sty, the Porter House (mostly hidden under the bluff and among trees) and the bay. The family was dying out; the grand house was, by then, one more property than the Coolidges had use for. Algernon was the most modest of men, and Amy had no need to prove anything to anybody. They moved, just before my time, into their last summer house, which still stands. I recognized in the outside wall of the Coolidge dining room an earlier incarnation as a barn door. Not visible anymore. Anne and Ed Moore had the whole house remodeled into a practical, year-round retirement home. Central heat, the works.

The Shreve house, as it now became, was one of the few exteriors in Cotuit that might impress passing tourists—Cousin Lawrence's place had no such pretensions—as everything in it, or around it, was unique, dating back to the time when the

Lowells and the Coolidges owned ships in the China trade. My mother used to go on about the hand-painted silk landscape wallpaper. For all its grandness, it seems to have been a comfortable, livable house. I think I spent part of a summer there when I was an infant, but no memory survives. Anyhow, no way Daddy could have afforded it; his income couldn't have maintained the dining room wallpaper.

But the Lowell facade was showing a crack or two. The new people buying in were no strangers. Boston merchants who, in older generations, respected the same patterns. The Shreves were jewelers in the grand tradition, the Tiffanys of Boston. Mrs. Shreve was as grand a lady as any Lowell, but jolly, interested in me when I was a little kid, devoted to Betty from the time I brought her here, and to our boys when they came, always a good friend to us all. When I was very small, the Shreves had a long, narrow motor launch, state of the art in its day, before planing boats were thought of, before lightweight auto-derived engines were available. She could go, I suppose, twelve knots, standing on her narrow tail and making an ungodly wash. Sometimes they took me for a ride in her. Thirty years later, the Shreves, very old by then, were hiring me to take them for rides in my first motorboat, a handsome double-ended former ship's pulling boat in which somebody had installed a Chevy engine. Even slower than their boat used to go.

And the Shreves behaved like Lowells or Pecks—brought in their relatives. Dr. Peirson, a cousin of theirs, bought a large tract with a fine house on it a block or so north of them on Main Street. His descendants are still here; two of his grandsons worked a summer or two in my boatyard, and one of them married my favorite coed from my sailing lesson and square-dance days, and their kids have kids of their own, so there are still Peirsons growing up here. But the Shreves are gone, the house sold to people I don't know.

Continuing my conducted beachcombing tour, beyond the B-hyphen place, the bluff ends in the marshy mouth of Little River. There is a recent house just on the slope but in my childhood, the next place, on hardened ground in the marsh, was the incongruous house of the legendary Mark Antony deWolfe Howe. Modeled on a Swiss chalet, crossed timbers sticking up in the sky at each end of the gable, and not an alp within thousands of miles. Mark Howe is gone, but his house, as eccentric as he, is still there. You can see it today, from almost all round the compass. It passed out of the Howe family about the time of World War II, and while I know, vaguely, the names of some of those who owned it since, they are not relevant to my history. Howe himself was a Boston character, renowned for his wit and erudition, a renaissance man still sparkly bright until his death at over a hundred. I don't think he was a Lowell relative, but he was of that "set." Like all of them, like a few of us old guys still surviving in Cotuit, they were characterized by admiration of wit and erudition purely for themselves.

I once, at about fifteen, lived briefly in that house. Made a deal with Aunt Mary Lothrop, Amy Coolidge's sister, who was renting it for the summer. Chartered to her my racing sailboat for the use of her nephew Sam in exchange for a couple weeks' board and lodging after Labor Day. They were good weeks; I spent the days sailing by myself or with Sam's sister Joan, with whom I promptly fell in love. At that age I was incapable of not being in love with somebody. Made the same deal with Aunt Mary for the next year, but she made her own deal and, next season, had me stay at her sister Amy's house. Nothing was said, but no doubt she was reducing my proximity to pretty Joan. Flattering but unnecessary; at that age I was grotesquely illiterate about sex. So was Aunt Mary. Maybe Joan too, but no way I was ever going to find out. All this when all I set out to say was that I have lived in that house. Inside it was no different from any other rich summer house of the time; plenty of servants, unpretentious and comfortable. Relatively modern plumbing.

But now I am on the subject of Aunt Mary Lothrop, an old darling in fact. Unlike her sister Amy, she contained no vitriol; it was all concentrated in the other sister. No brains in her either, according to her niece Anne Coolidge. Anne had once, when a very young lady, gone on a trip to Europe with another girl and with Aunt Mary as chaperone, and her response when I reminisced about the old darling was "Yes, but a complete donkey." She was, to hear Anne tell it, so easy for a niece to manipulate that outwitting her wasn't any fun. Anne had even less patience with stupidity than I.

When Aunt Mary moved for the summer into Mark Howe's house, bringing with her a company of nieces, nephews and hangers-on, she brought also her retinue of Irish servants: cook, housemaid/waitress, chauffeur. James, the chauffeur, addressed always by his first name because his last was Dearie, delivered "Miss Mary" from Beacon Street in her Packard limousine. Like "herself," Jimmy was a soft touch. He and the Packard were at the service of the kids, including me, to take us wherever we wanted to go. I took Joan to Hyannis to the movies by limo, and to the Dutchland Farms stand for ice cream afterward. Jimmy let me drive the Packard when I asked, so life at Aunt Mary's was as good as going to heaven. I even dented a fender one time and, advised and urged by Rachel, Joan's lovely mom with the auburn hair,

I confessed to Aunt Mary. She already knew; Jimmy always gave her a full report, but she appreciated my telling her. So that got me only credit, even praise for my honesty.

Things here, as at the home of any Lowell relative, were run according to procedures which changed slowly. The old lady had plenty of voice, and when she was on the phone you could hear her all over the house. Like many people who grew up before telephones, she couldn't get over the notion that when talking to someone too far off to see you must speak loudly, clearly and slowly. Every morning, right after breakfast, she could be heard calling the grocers. E. E. C. Swift's Grocers, in Osterville, not the perfectly respectable Cotuit Grocery, because Swift's was the local outlet for S. S. Pierce Victualers of Boston and thus a little more fashionably expensive.

"THIS IS MISS M. B. LOTHROP, OF LITTLE RIVER, COTUIT." Then the list. Thus you often knew early in the morning what was to be for dinner. The order was delivered before noon in Swift's truck. Some days it amounted to no more than a loaf of bread but Swift's sent it over. At table Bridey, the waitress, offered each dish from a fine Wedgwood platter or serving dish that matched your cup and plate, to each guest in turn, standing at your left elbow. When your turn came and dishes were offered, you took up the serving, spoon and fork and dished onto your own plate however much you wanted of whatever dish she was passing, or you murmured "no thank you" if it were broccoli. The wine was offered but the waitress poured it into your glass for you. Kids were smoothly handled: wine was offered once, and on subsequent passes of the decanter you were skipped, not offered more. All handled smoothly, perfect understanding between hostess and waitress, not a word said.

A last loose end to tie up: what became of Joan? I never saw her again, but Aunt Lillie brought us up-to-date. She went "out" to India and there married an Asiatic of some sort. And when she heard this news, Aunt Mary asked, plaintively, "Do you suppose every fifth child will be black?"

Continuing, in the voice of gentle Aunt Lillie, "And we said, 'Aunt Mary, those are things you just *don't say.*'"

Little River drained Eagle Pond and some cranberry bogs inland and came out to salt water beside Howe's. Little River Road paralleled it and ended at Howe's front gate. That part of town was where the oyster industry was concentrated; in my childhood, there were four oyster houses here—tidy shingled shacks built on pilings out over the harbor. Shell heaps beside them, half in the water at high tide. One year—maybe 1932—there was a polio epidemic in Philadelphia, so my family stayed late in Cotuit, until almost October I think. Missing school, among other benefits. All the summer kids were gone home, the native kids were in school. I don't know what my sister was doing; as little as possible to do with me.

I rented a bicycle from Phil Brackett for fifty cents a week and explored a lot of sand and shell roads. One thing I did frequently was hang out at the oyster houses at Little River. Usually, I went that short way on foot. The oystermen opened oysters and fed them to me. I cultivated a taste for them which proved profitable later in life when I won bets on how many I could eat on trips to the burlesque show in Philadelphia with the firemen of Swarthmore. Once, when I could eat no more, they fed me bay scallops, which were astonishingly different. Tasted sweet and were chewy rather than gelatinous. I ate a lot of them on top of the oysters. Don't remember that this rich diet made me sick, though it might have cost five, even ten dollars in New York. That would have made me sick indeed.

Four separate houses meant four separate oyster firms, each with a sign over its door: Cotuit Oyster Co. (the only one left today), Gifford's, Coleman's and Les Hobson's, which had no sign at all, and less going on. Something went on there one memorable time: Hobson and his sidekick Brad Nickerson trying to row (scull) a ponderous scow while both falling-down drunk. I put these memories in to show that, while this whole place was heaven to me, it was in truth not populated solely by angels. On the other hand, Mr. Coleman was a big, handsome, very quiet gentleman, as striking in appearance as Ed Ropes but much gentler. I used to walk home with him some evenings. He had a cow which he kept tethered all day to a stake, eating a big circle in the grass of the meadow between the House in the Woods and Main Street. I would drop off at the Porter House, and he would go on up the path, unhitch his cow and lead it home for milking, thus getting that grass back liquid. Things here were indeed bucolic in the thirties.

Little River Road, leading up from the shore, passed the summer homes of several smallholders, notably Judge Hitch-cock of St. Louis, who was no Lowell—far from it—but in general it bounded or passed through land of Mrs. Mary Coolidge Barton, sister of Ellen and Algernon and among the nicest and grand-simplest of them all. She's long gone but still treasured and venerated by many who never knew her.

Back from the shore she owned many acres—better meas-ured in square miles—of woodland around Eagle Pond (my father remembered a time when you could still see bald eagles there) intact to this day. After her death (which occurred sometime around 1950) the property passed into possession of her oldest son Otis Barton, the distinguished oceanographer and screwball. Otis worked with William

Beebe, the even more distinguished scientist with a flair for public relations, and it was as Beebe's colleague that he built the bathysphere, the precursor of modern scientific deepwater submarines, and he seemed most at home at the bottom of the ocean. As a kid, before my time, he explored the bottom of Cotuit Harbor in a homemade diver's "hard hat." Otis was very much into conservation, letting nature alone, never saw what is to me so obvious: that nature cannot cope if left alone with human propagation and greed. He lived by himself or with a blond foreign lady in the Corner Cottage (corner of Old Post Road and Little River Road), sometimes called the Peck cottage because my father acted as "straw" for Mrs. Barton when she acquired it.

And with Otis, just before his death, some WOE types made a deal. The woodland was deeded to a perpetual conservation trust called the Mary Lowell Barton Trust or Foundation or something. Mary still had living relatives around here, Hatta Cabot for one, but not one of them opened his mouth. By default, it fell to me to point out to these well-meaning newcomers that there never had been any such person as Mary Lowell Barton. As nonexistent as Cotuit itself. She was a figment (Fig Newton) of their wishful group imagination, hoping perhaps for the prestige of the Lowell name to raise funds. I knew her well; she was Mary Coolidge Barton. So the trust has now been renamed simply Mary Barton. None of these people either knew or cared about the Coolidges. They're all dead, aren't they? This deal was made in the 1980s or early 1990s. Anne was dead; so was her husband, Professor Ed Moore. The Coolidge place, still vast, was divided between their adopted son Nicky, who built a small modern house with an even better view, and Ed's daughter Diane, whose half included the big house. Diane sold her part and moved to

Florida, where she owns *Topsy III*, the only Cotuit skiff in Marco Island. Nicky still owns the Porter House.

That house, much damaged by the hurricane of 1944, was again occupied by Pecks in the late 1940s and early 1950s. I made a deal with Anne and Ed to camp out in it in return for painting and repairs, and Betty, Bill (our first son) and I lived there summers until 1952, while I was in college. It had electricity by then, even a telephone. I missed the smell of the oil lamps and the oil cookstove. And Bill, along with Betty II, his wife, and their children, lived there again in the 1990s. Today it is illegal for Nicky to rent it to anyone like them with small children because I, and generations of painters before me, used lead paint. So Betty and I rented it and subleased to them. "Thou shalt not kill, but needst not strive, / Officiously, to keep alive," saith Hopkins, the latter-day patriarch. Some of us old folks resent the unsolicited meddling of government in our personal affairs, enforcing safety. When we all live forever, where will they put us? Generations of healthy people have grown up in houses while there was no paint without lead. I go by this house almost every day, but I haven't been inside since Bill was there. The memories are too painful. And now, as Bill and Betty II soon found, all the fun of living there has been trampled out of it by hordes of people passing ten feet from the windows on the paved lane and going to the beach that's not a beach just across the road. Sharing loneliness.

I am grateful for the part I was allowed to play in the restoration of the house. High-water mark—debris on the water pipes over the kitchen sink—was higher than my head. The cast-iron kitchen range was smashed to little bits which the receding water carried through the living room and scattered in the front yard. The house still stood, more firm than its restorers. Anne and Ed sprung for an electric kitchen range and even for an electric hot water heater. Hot running water in the Porter House for the first time in history, in about 1950!

A look at the later history of this landing might tell us something. As more summer visitors came here, pressure began to build for more places for them to swim. Most of the decent beaches were private (see later pages for comments on the policies of King Charles II), so the Town Fathers came under this pressure to make better use of the town's limited waterfront. Better use then meant more places to swim. There wasn't space here to store more than a dozen boats anyhow so they paved it for parking, made it a swimming beach and allowed no other use.

This brought the town into conflict with state safety rules, made it responsible for keeping people from drowning, required that the town hire lifeguards for this tiny facility, only a few hundred yards of sand, trucked in every year, with gooey mud from low tide line on out. The state required the town also to construct public toilets—Men's and Ladies'—for this absurd facility. To prevent us from polluting the ocean or something. "The 'P' is silent, as in psea-bathing." Then people bathing there, particularly their children, began to come home with sores from the bites of some marine insects or parasites or things which lived in the mud, which were indigenous, and for which there was no known pest control. People complained to the selectmen, demanded that something be done. Nothing could be done; there never should have been a public beach in such a backwater.

As Archie Bunker said of earthquakes, "It's Saint Andrew's fault." These chigger bites are King Charles' fault. Even in my uncrowded boyhood, ordinary people had limited space to launch or haul a boat. There was a short piece of marshy shore, property of the defunct Santuit House, used by the shellfishermen as though it were a public landing. As I wrote at the time, "to use your boat in Cotuit, you have to trespass." This private bit of shore is still so used today, by yachtsmen as well as by fishermen—another case of inadequate public access to water dating back to seventeenth century British politics. It seems the exiled King Charles II (the Cavalier) gave grants of large tracts of land in Massachusetts (and in Maine, which was then part of it) to anyone who had been kind to him in exile or helpful with his restoration. Specifically, in which they were unique in all the world, these grants ran all the way down to low water. And they are still enforced; every property on the shore in these states is still owned clear down to low tide, and modern rich people, who do not do anything productive on it, who do not even, in many cases, sit in the sun on it, own the only truly private beach land in all the world. In Miami Beach, in San Juan, anywhere in the Bahamas or on the French Riviera, you can walk right down the beach in front of the grand hotels anytime except at the top of the tide, and nobody can stop you. Here, some people who are retired from doing anything else work full-time and for no pay kicking people off beaches they do not themselves even claim to "own." A holy, as well as satisfying, duty.

But the backing and filling that the Town of Barnstable went through reminds me of one more wildly comic, wildly embarrassing bit of Cotuit history. For the state law or something, to prevent pollution of the ocean or something, requires public toilets ashore at public beaches, and that applies equally to the only proper public beach in Cotuit, to what we call "Loop Beach" because the road on land makes a loop here. The town's plan to erect a "sanitary facility" at Loop

Beach encountered fierce opposition from some of the nuts
in the neighborhood (those nuts responsible for there being
so many people as to make such a facility necessary). It brought
on another great schism among those Cotuit people in favor
of public toilets and those opposed, both at the tops of their
voices, in town meetings and in local meetings. Those opposed
were all who were against change of any form, but they were
led by a lady who lived in walking distance of Loop Beach and
who didn't swim anyway. Those in favor of washrooms
included such people as a gentleman whose relation to liquid
stressed the imbibing of it rather than immersion in it. The
story goes that these two people-with-a-message met in the
hallway at a town meeting or a village meeting and that the
gent said to the lady, "Well! Here's old shit-in-the-bushes
herself." The two of them are long dead, but the quotation has
a life of its own. I relate it here to show how pompously the
self-important people here take their pipsqueak problems.
Basic philosophy seems to be: don't make the place attractive
lest it attract people! In the end, the town did the only sensible
thing, the only thing it could do at Hooper's: closed the public
beach, boarded up the toilets, took the lifeguards off. They still
dump a little sand there from time to time, but it is no longer
officially a beach, and you are now responsible for your own
chigger bites and your own drowning. People still swim
there, others still sail off this beach and some just sit there in
the sun and the crowd. There are still so many that they make
living in the Porter House the next thing to living in the city,
and neither WOE's talk of zoning nor my talk of population
control has the least effect on how many there are.

* * *

So I now introduce, by casual one-liners, our three sons who, by imposing my will on Betty before she had quite recovered from childbirth, I called Bill for Shakespeare, John for Milton and Geoff for Chaucer. She was getting used to my ways and to bearing my children and stood firm on the last of them; he is, on his birth certificate, David Geoffrey, after Taffy, her Welsh grandfather. I allowed none of them to be baptized; thought and still think that no defenseless child should be drafted into a church without being consulted. Rejected scornfully the notion of infant damnation which baptism is supposed, like a vaccination, to forestall. Cursing of children by an all-loving diety. Come on, now! If a person old enough to decide for himself wants to become a Christian, I won't object, though I may sneer a bit. But I won't force it on a baby. So, look what happens: all three of them had themselves baptized when they grew up, and it means to me that my ideas are vindicated; I gave them the right to choose, and they chose. And I chose also; I am still unbaptized. Do I perhaps not exist?

I was saying, Aunt Amy's confinement in a lunatic asylum gave me another look at the decline of the Lowell dynasty, for the surviving ladies of her long-lived generation never forgot their duty. Every Wednesday afternoon, two or three of them made the trek from Beacon Street or Cambridge out to the nut farm in Wellesley to visit her. Rain or snow, once in a blizzard. I know all about these pilgrimages; I went along. For the sole purpose of attending to the needs of Amy, her conservators (the State Street Trust Company) hung on to and caused to be maintained the family car, a 1938 Buick of the largest size. I was at that time a student at Harvard on the G.I. Bill, but every Wednesday afternoon I fired up Anastasia in the garage in Cambridge where she was kept and picked up at their homes two or three passengers as instructed by phone, from a list which included Mrs. Alice Lowell Ropes, Mary Coolidge Barton, Miss Ellen Coolidge and other ladies less well-known to me since they did not summer in Cotuit. Most of them Lowell connections.

I felt sort of proud to be chosen for this responsibility. They could perfectly well have brought old William out of retirement. The family's choice gave me the feeling of an old-time feudal retainer or an adopted member of the family like Aunt Lillie, entrusted with its secrets and responsible for all this surviving glory of a time fast departing. Like the curator of a museum. For these were more than just some old ladies; their acute sense of their own responsibility, of rendering what was due, imposed a similar responsibility on me. They expected a Harvard student to know what was going on at least as much as they did, and it behooved me, on Wednesday morning and pretty much all the time, to read at least the *New York Times* and various other publications having nothing to do with my studies, just to be able to converse with them and not look a fool. These were the days of controversy about atomic bombs and all like that. And they were real sharp and capable of a mod point of view. They were interested in what a younger person thought about it all. Knowing them was one of the privileges of my days at Harvard, and the way I was accepted into this close, inbred society is testimony to the greatness of Aunt Lillie. Their esteem for her was also in my hands every Wednesday afternoon.

Amy, the fierce and now altogether wacky old dame, came down to spend summers in her own house with her fierce, aging daughter and daughter's new husband. Guess who lit off Anastasia and brought her all that way? Right! Thank the Lord she was accompanied on these excursions into the unprotected world by a trained psychiatric nurse. To drive her unattended would not have been possible. She got it into her paranoid head that the two of us were kidnapping her with intent to murder. She screamed—I mean screeched—for rescue at every traffic light. She was harder on the nurse than she was on me, but I came in for some of the vitriol. To her, one of the things going wrong with the world was that an upstart like me could now get into Harvard. I must say she could still yell out opinions like this in clever ways. Extempore. Old people, you see, are all alike.

It all makes me think what awful Wednesday afternoons those grand matriarchs must have spent, while I waited in the car. Also it makes me think how much gentler she was to me than to anybody else I ever saw her with. I speculate sometimes on why. How have I deserved such gentleness? All the Coolidges, even Thornton, were thus nice to me, as were some of the fiercer cousins. Anne, too, inherited mucho vitriol, but I never would have known it if Diane, her stepdaughter, hadn't told me. Poor Diane seems to have suffered as much growing up in the stepmother's shadow as Anne herself must have suffered a generation earlier. All the lesser Lowells showed me the same gentleness all my life. Perhaps it was because of Lillie. Aunt Lillie was so gentle nobody could be rough on her favorite nephew. But however this rambling discourse turns out, it isn't going to deteriorate into self-analysis. Apart from being a slightly inside account of the decline and fall of part of the Lowell empire, I am trying to recall what life was like here in the twenties, thirties and forties, to show what I would seek to bring back if I were WOE.

*　　　*　　　*

The Coolidges are all gone. Mary Barton's name, with the Coolidge part deleted, lives forever in the land trust. I remember Mrs. Barton, Aunt Meer the family called her (her family and Aunt Lillie, not I). As grand a person as her brother Algernon and her sister Ellen. She had a Packard too, vintage about 1920 (anyhow, so old that Packards had only six cylinders when hers was built), a seven-passenger open touring car, and I have a memory of a trip with her and a carful of other kids to the Barnstable County Fair when it was a genuine agricultural event held in an enormous wooden building and in the fields around it in Barnstable (the village). Those fields are now crowded with expensive houses, not summer homes anymore but the year-round homes of retired elderly who now dominate local politics but winter in Florida. The big wood building is still there. It stood empty for decades and is now packed with condos inhabited by more of these same tiresome people my age. From Cotuit to Barnstable, seven miles in a straight line, took half a day the way Aunt Meer drove, for she chose a route devious and circuitous to avoid pavement. Never got on blacktop all the way, a difficult achievement even then, requiring close local knowledge and a long wheelbase. Just to show those kids, too soon old—she didn't tell them; she showed them—how it could be, how it had been. She was a sweetheart; no wonder WOE loves her. But saving unspoiled land by buying it rather than by taking its owners to court or by haranguing town meeting, or by passing out leaflets and soliciting signatures in front of the post office and suchlike obnoxious behavior, is the way a truly civic organization ought to act.

The Bartons had a large, unpretentious house—two houses really—with something like a breezeway between. One house was living quarters, bedrooms upstairs, the other contained kitchen, dining room, servants' quarters above. No doubt this memory is inaccurate; there had to be more. Such dwellings had at least two parlors, one formal, the other cozy, but that bare outline is all I remember. There were extensive formal gardens, by my time no longer meticulously maintained nor constantly weeded. I remember a grassy walk between rows of high boxwood hedges whose smell is a big part of the memory. Box smelled to me like piss, and I remember being embarrassed, all inside myself, at the comparison. This walk led from the west end of the house out to Little River Road.

I'm sorry; I don't know who Barton was. This is not a research paper; I'm trying to limit it to things I remember or was told as a child. Thus I protect myself from being responsible for meticulous historical accuracy. So it's wrong; it's a childhood recollection sixty or seventy years old. Write your own! Barton "was dead to begin with" before I was aware of anything, but a person of parts he must have been to have had such a sparkling wife—even as an old lady she sparkled—and such talented children. Four children they had: the aforementioned Otis, a daughter Ellen, another daughter Mary and another son Francis. Ellen was remembered after her early death— late teens I think—to have been singularly blessed physically, intellectually and emotionally. All her relatives, including my aunt, made such a thing of her memory that it can hardly have failed to mark—I don't say blight—the lives of her siblings. But by the time I was aware of them, none of this showed, at least to the eye of a child. I was the age of her sister Mary's (Churchill) children, was acquainted with them but never close. They were clannish and, as a group, overpowering.

But, in passing, I have an anecdote about Mary Barton Churchill, told here to make the point that gentle birth does not always bring gentle manners, that the nobility have pockets in their britches just like the rest of us. This is Betty's tale; I wasn't even there, and to read it you must be subjected to another of my wrenches in time to stay with a person or with a location. This happened many years later; Aunt Meer and her sister Aunt Ellen were several years dead, and finally death came also for Aunt Lillie. So our good friend Anne Coolidge took Betty to the House in the Woods, which she now owned, so that Betty too could have a share of the artifacts the two spinsters had owned in common. No doubt most of the valuable plates and books and pictures were furnished by Ellen; she was far richer, and her family and its possessions went back a lot further (Lillie and her brothers and sister were the first generation of Pecks born in this country), but there appeared (which Betty did not expect) Mary and Pete Churchill, also there to claim their share, more likely to make sure they were not bilked of any of it. And anything Betty showed any interest in, they declared they were sure had been Aunt Ellen's, to the extent that their cousin Anne was embarrassed for them. Seems clear to me that the family's adoption of Lillie was by less than unanimous vote and that this generation of cousins was making a stand. The adoption of Pecks was to come to a stop, not go on with us and our children.

Betty and I are proud of Betty's reaction: she alone kept her dignity, said "I don't think I'm being much help here" and walked away. Seems that Anne was proud of her too. She found, she said, a set of soup plates tucked away in the house and sneaked them to Betty. These turned out to be Chinese, like five hundred years old, and the story of their being "tucked away" was nonsense. We had lived in that house, and if the plates had been there we would have known it. They were from the possessions Anne had inherited from her parents and she had "turned them up" on purpose as a gesture of appreciation.

Betty in 1945. See what I mean?

Like Cousin Lawrence's dessert plates all those years before.

It all goes to show you: either you have manners or you lack them; ancestors have nothing to do with it. Betty's parents were Welsh coal miners and Pennsylvania Dutch farmers, not Beacon Hill Brahmins. Something sure will tell, but it sure ain't blood.

Francis Barton was closer to my age; when his children were the right age, I taught them to sail. Betsy was a little beauty with no idea she was even pretty. Her brother Jim grew into as lovable a screwball as anybody in this screwy family and village. I remember his rendering a drunken parody of "Good King Wenceslas" with wildly exaggerated intonations and gestures. Wish I could hear and watch him do it again.

When these kids were almost grown up, Francis up and walked out. His overserious wife Elizabeth had always been a bit hard to take; her husband abandoned her for a Mrs. Simpson, like King Edward VIII twenty years earlier. Phyllis Simpson was a big, red-headed widow with two or three children who were way too much for her, particularly a fire-topped little boy who was always in trouble. Set the woods on fire, or the house. Things like that. He needed a daddy. Phyllis was always hanging around my shop trying to get me to fix something or just to pay attention to her. Francis came in to get something for Betsy's boat. I introduced them and they "became a thing" instantly. Far as I know, neither of them were ever seen in Cotuit again. Francis' family was tolerant of most eccentricities, but not of anything so middle class as this. They rallied round Elizabeth, who stayed, with her children, in Francis' tiny house on Little River Road and devoted herself to a saintly life after they were grown up.

Mrs. Barton was dead by the time Francis took off. Her daughter, Mary Barton Churchill, and family lost interest in

Cotuit. She and her illustrious husband, Dr. Pete Churchill, one of the best surgeons of his generation, spent their summers elsewhere. Elizabeth stayed right there in her cottage; she visited the sick and ministered to the dying and consoled the bereaved, enthusiastically. Betsy was married, and Jim was too. I hardly see either of them anymore. Betsy tried, for a while, to get her doctor husband interested in sailing, but it didn't take. To please him (I think) she dyed her hair blond, which ruined her beauty. Otis lived on in his corner cottage until the very advanced age typical of Lowells, always concerned with the conservation of everything except his own health, still as nutty as ever. Toward the end he had a blond woman (maybe his wife) with a foreign accent living with him. She was not as old as he, but she was no young bunny either, and she took most loving care of his health and seemed to view everybody who came along with suspicion, as maybe having designs on his wealth. There are, I find, many ways of living too long.

In the barn across Little River Road from Otis' house, Aunt Meer's old Packard sat on jacks for years, increasing in value all this time. I don't know what finally became of it. The barn was kept locked up tight, even with the screws of the hinges rotting out of the wood, but I had access to it because I took care of Betsy's boat. Otis' boats got no care at all; he sometimes smeared on a little paint, but he was too tight to pay for professional work. His mind was, of course, stuck in prewar prices. Like mine when I was paying, not when I was charging. Half of Aunt Meer's house, extensively remodeled, is there still, with strangers in it, from St. Louis of all places. Nice folks. The other half has been moved across Old Post Road to a lot which may once have been Barton land. Don't know who lives there. The breezeway is not part of either. And about where the box alley was, there is, even as I write, a big new house being built. By now you should be able to fill in the next line without my help.

Before ending this tour of how the neighborhood still called Little River was in my childhood, I must mention alternate ways to reach it, ways no longer there nor missed. In the days when the usual way to get about the village was on foot, there were shortcuts eastward, one along the beach in front of Ropes', Fred Lowell's, Bentinck-Smith's, then across the marsh on a hardened clay path, over Little River by a footbridge destroyed in a 1944 hurricane, and thence across Howe's side yard, ducking under clotheslines, right up to his house, turn north close enough to the building to run your right hand along it as you walked, across the front lawn and out onto Little River Road through Howe's front gate. From here you could continue north along the road, or you could turn right, walk down a hundred yards to the shore and the oyster houses. The other way was to go in Ropes' drive, straight in between the kitchen of the main house and the shed, by now the garage, but in my childhood a woodworking shop, on past the little yellow house where the estate farmer lived (all these buildings are still there), past the icehouse, long rotted away, to the limit of Ropes land and the start of Fred Lowell. Here the driveway made a sharp left, past the underground cold storage room where eggs and vegetables were kept, along the chicken house, to the barn. Dolly the horse lived there until fairly recently. She plowed the field and mowed the meadow. Today you turn right here instead of left to get to the house Hatta has since built for herself.

To get to Little River, you left the drive at that turn and walked straight into the woods by a footpath so well worn you could almost drive a Model T through it, straight across Fred Lowell property, straight across Bentinck-Smith property, as the path continued, just far enough back from the shore so you couldn't see these people's houses and could not be seen from them, down a slope to the river, over another footbridge, up the other side of the valley and out through a gate onto Little River Road, just to the south (toward the harbor) of Otis' corner house. I knew these footpaths well; I had friends down toward the Narrows and I liked to hang out at the oyster houses. Best of all was a northeaster, when the fog hung in the woods all day and you got the smell of the pine woods and the sea all mixed together. I know now that the smell was as much bayberry, juniper and wintergreen as pine, but then it was all one, the smell of the woods. And I wonder if it still smells that way. No way now to find out; what was then a public footpath is now all private. I'd get arrested.

A footnote to all this history: My son John was the mechanical member of the family. Always he was fixing something, building elaborate highways for his toy trucks, carrying cargoes in his red wagon. Best he liked fixing real, grown-up things. At the age of seven, he came upon the ruins of this upper bridge, just as the hurricane had left it fourteen years before. Nobody had bothered to repair this bridge; nobody walked anymore, and the new owners of the Bentinck-Smith property were delighted that the public path had in fact been abandoned by act of nature without taking anybody to court. But Miss Polly Hitchcock, unmarried daughter of the late judge, encouraged John to restore the bridge; Polly was of an older generation and still liked walking in the woods. She gave John encouragement; he didn't need much, and he assembled some friends and they replaced the span with what was left of the old one and some windfall logs, better than before. Indeed a marvelous new footbridge on the site of the old. He imagined he had done a public service but it got him into trouble with the new owners of the property, and he was made to demolish his creation. Miss Hitchcock, having encouraged the work, now led the opposition, double-crossed the child, told the privacy seekers who had done this trespass. A sickening experience for the child, an infuriating experience for me.

I was then starting out in business, couldn't pay the rent, never mind afford a lawyer, dependent for trade on the goodwill of these privacy-buying newcomers. But the history lesson in this anecdote is what I am trying to write about: the sudden change in the character of the newcoming rich. Reminds one of the mean, churlish spirit of newly rich landowners shown in the British Acts of Enclosure, which had been going on for the preceding couple centuries. The footpaths to Little River had been "ancient ways" across land of one Lowell after another, never opposed by any of them. Public rights of way which, after twenty-one years of unopposed public use, became legally unclosable. So nobody closed them; the hurricane did, and since local public no longer walked, nobody bothered to rebuild the bridges until Johnny Peck, and nobody cared enough to say a word in their defense. Marching under the banner of WOE, everybody now worships property, even those who have none. Property and automobiles and the law of Charles II.

Once you got east of Little River, beyond Bartons', you passed several classy waterfront houses, more of them today than there were then, naturally, belonging to people of no importance. These homes were sold and resold, lots divided and subdivided to make room for more people who bought and sold, came and went, and had no stability as Lowells think of it. One house among them belonged to the Wellmans, people I never knew, never set eyes on, but whose big Victorian house is important to me because of their three grandchildren, Ned, Tod and Jill Ackerman, all of whom worked for me briefly in my boatyard. By land you are on Old Post Road; in your boat you are entering what local sailors call the Narrows, where Osterville Grand Island, now usually called by the name its developers gave it, "Oyster Harbors," is close to the mainland of Cotuit, with a narrow passage between, through which the tide races four times a day, in and out of wide, deep North Bay, also called Great Bay. A difficult place to sail. Fun. But everything down here has at least two names; the language is as confusing to navigate as the water.

When you reach the Narrows you are pretty well out of Lowell country; you are among the Almys. By my time, there was just one more Lowell-connected family, missing links who had, I was told, Almy connections as well. The Perkinses were vivid people, judging from the only ones I knew, Martha Perkins Wadsworth and her children. She married Bill Wadsworth from upstate New York, a handsome, quiet man who proclaimed himself a farmer. They had four children, three of them enchanting girls and a son, Austin, who worked a couple summers for me. Perky (Winifred Perkins Wadsworth) was one of the brightest stars in the whole Cotuit firmament of beautiful daughters. None of these kids needed sailing lessons from me; the Wadsworths had a chunky sloop named *Albatross* which they really used. Cruised together all over New England, spent more time on her than most yacht owners ever have time to spend. *Albatross* was built by Casey of New Bedford, all of whose works, conservative and underrigged, were regarded as classics.

The Wadsworths, when in residence, lived in the old Perkins place, one of the most visible in town. As odd as Mark Howe's chalet, this one sat high on the very highest bluff looking down the harbor across Dead Neck toward Martha's Vineyard rather than toward Nantucket, which was behind a corner of Oyster Harbors and out of sight over the horizon anyhow. The Vineyard was closer; you could see it on any decent day. The house, I was saying, was odd: Spanish architecture with a red tile roof like the West Barnstable depot, but way up there in the air and two stories high plus that roof. Even way up the harbor that way you could see it—you couldn't miss seeing it—from miles at sea. Perky married Terry Lloyd, scion of another noble family from the other end of town and of the country, and one of my favorite people. I'll get back to them.

On up the Narrows, among the Almys. They had a patriarch of their own, Judge Almy, who lived in a big shingled house surrounded, at a decent distance, by the houses of his married children: the Stanley Cobbs, the Charles Almys, the Percy Bidwells, the Sam Almys. I met the judge once, was introduced and given his hand to shake. He deplored the weak flabbiness of my handshake. He must have been a superb judge; I never gave a weak handshake again in my life.

There was just one family among all those Almys whom I might call close friends: Betty Cobb and her husband and children. Dr. Stanley Cobb had not one but two distinguished careers: led his profession of neurology and then took up and rose to the top again of psychiatry (or was it the other way round?). A wiry, genial man. His oldest son, Sidney, was the unquestioned champion skiff racer of his day. His daughter Helen had beauty sort of ethereal, angelic, and fought this characteristic all her life. When we were all grown up, Betty and I were close friends of Helen and her husband, Lester Solomon, a New York lawyer who worked among poor city businessmen and made a joke, a stock in trade, of exaggerated Jewishness. He was first in a procession of very bright and discerning men who went out of their way to befriend our son Bill. Bill inherited my lifelong fascination with words and language, and Lester was there when I was too busy with boats to pay him the attention such a kid needs. Helen and Lester often had him to visit them in their apartment in New York. Helen is another girl I had a childish crush on. Her slightly younger brother Jock was my particular friend. We sailed together, fished, went hiking in the woods and hung out the way kids do. He lived too far out of town to participate in many of the things Jack Brackett and I did, like on Fourth of July (described in chapter V), but he had a huge imagination and thought up fun activities of other sorts.

The Cobbs, too, had a sailing yacht, the yawl *Pamaho*. To me she looked like the dreamboat of the world, but older, more blasé sailors were critical of her. She might have been a Herreshoff creation; she had certain characteristics of his less successful work. The celebrated Nathaniel Herreshoff's yachts were extreme, experimental, a sharp contrast to the conservative designs of Casey of New Bedford. Some were more successful than others. *Pamaho* was a centerboarder, and the huge board, when raised, split the cabin right down the middle. No elbowroom below, and no headroom either. These things are not important to a little kid. She was flush-deck, no sheer at all; must have been ghastly wet. But beautiful, in spite of her lack of sheer. Black hull, lots of bright varnish, gaff rigged on both masts, all three sails dyed something like reddish tanbark, which they called terra-cotta. I never was taken cruising in *Pamaho*; day sailing once.

Beyond the Narrows, beyond the Almys, you are just about out of Cotuit, coming into the next nonexistent village of Marstons Mills. Here is the property of Theron Appolonio, as nutty as any Lowell or Almy. Appolonio and Ned Ackerman will come up later.

IV
GROWING UP

A ND THAT IS how one segment of the Cotuit shoreline and of Cotuit society looked at the beginning of my memory. I became aware of the rest of the place and of the people gradually: the Jacksons, the Mattisons, the Baileys, the Morses, the Taussigs, the Lloyds, all important members of the Cotuit Mosquito Yacht Club. In my family, I was the only man-child of my generation, and though the Peck name was not self-evidently deserving of perpetuation as if it had been Lowell, still my aunties took special interest in me. Dad's two unmarried sisters, Harriet and Lillie, vied in doing things for me. In 1933 or '34 Aunt Harriet bought for me from Peter Bentinck-Smith his fairly new Cotuit racing skiff, sometimes called a mosquito skiff. Peter was going into racing larger boats, international and Olympic classes, and he chose to get rid of the skiff *Pete*, recently built for him by Herbert Crosby of Osterville. I, in a weird fit of erudition, renamed her *Ariel*.

This acquisition precipitated me, at the age of about eleven, into the center of local sporting politics, which put me ringside in the battle of national and world politics. For among the newer arrivals was the notorious Gardner (Pat) Jackson, a crony of the whole liberal establishment and of the New Deal cabinet when it came to power in 1933. Pat Jackson was a true liberal, right from the heart. He came from Colorado, bringing with him a fortune, most of which he gave away for the defense of Sacco and Vanzetti, wrongfully, the liberals said, accused of murder. The truth of the accusation has never been proved or disproved, but the unfairness of the prosecution, trial and execution is no longer questioned. They were a pair of foreign radicals, and it was for this that they were tried and condemned. All Pat got for his generosity was the enmity of the whole Lowell tribe, for Cousin Lawrence had figured in the case; he had been consulted by the governor of Massachusetts to advise him whether their trial had been fair, whether they deserved gubernatorial clemency, and Lowell had decided no, they merited no such thing. Some of Lawrence's more excitable cousins imagined that Jackson's appearance in Cotuit was the foreshadowing of retribution, perhaps violent action, against Lowell. Nothing could have been less in character than any connection of Pat Jackson to an assassination plot; his passionate defense of the unfortunate Italians was based, in part, on his abhorrence of violence, including specifically putting criminals to death. But Lowell's family didn't know Pat. I knew him, for children, the friends of his children, were welcome in his warm-hearted household, where we met the celebrities you read about in *Time*. Wallace, Frankfurter, Lilienthal, Ickes. To Cousin Lawrence, Jackson was simply the defender of a pair of foreign radicals convicted of murder. But his family considered Jackson a dangerous radical.

Pat Jackson was an amiable, talkative, high-pressure man with an oversize head and a jolly, homely face. He talked to a little boy just as he talked to distinguished men, giving his full attention and showing respect for the child's opinion. That full attention is the biggest part of charm and popularity. He and Dode, his equally amiable but quiet wife, moved in high-pressure circles even before the New Deal, but they were never so busy that they ignored kids. Their own four kids were as friendly and outgoing as they, superenthusiastic about everything, and when one went to play at the Jacksons', one encountered celebrities. When Roosevelt took over the depressed nation, Jackson was among the coterie known as the "brain trust," source of many of the New Deal reforms, and he would certainly have held office except that, with all his lovable virtues, Pat had a flaw: he was fond of alcohol to the point where his associates considered him unreliable with the confidences of government. His uncompromising conscience and his love of booze and of talk were a dangerous combination in high politics.

The four Jackson children all shared Pat's charm and also inherited his outsize skull which made poor Dode's child-bearing extra-agonizing. Gardi Junior was unstoppably talkative and everybody loved him, for like his father, he was personally interested in everybody; Evie's head was a little misshapen, though it did not diminish his intellect, just his self-control. Through most of his life, Evie was the victim of uncontrollable tantrums and a tendency to speak mostly in obscenities. This never quite managed to hide his charm. Geoff was the handsome one, with the appeal of talking with complete frankness, like any Jackon. He was the preferred lover of all the girls his age. Debbie, the oldest, was all her life marked by being the self-appointed mother of these genial, charming little brothers. Her family love of talking keeps her words half a sentence ahead of her mind so you must, to this day, pay full attention to know what she's talking about. Never without at least three conversational balls in the air at once, Debbie uses parentheses as a whole language. She still summers here in Cotuit, along with her husband, Ray Smith, a pleasant and genial guy whose patience is everlasting. Ray taught me enough computese to write this book. Without him, it would never have gotten from my head to the paper.

I am here trying to relate in some sort of order the things that went on around me during the ten years leading up to the outbreak of war in 1939. Relating them in chronological order is self-defeating, for they were all going on at once. While I was inadvertently made aware of national and world politics, I was consciously moving into the local politics centered around Cotuit skiffs and the kids who sailed them. The Cotuit Mosquito Yacht Club was founded by kids in 1906, when a majority of the kids involved were Lowell connections, and among other momentous events which took place before my opening eyes, I saw domination of this outfit move from Lowells to Baileys to Mattisons to Jacksons.

Time now to relate a little about this unique club and its unique boats, the endless dispute over what does and what does not qualify as a Cotuit skiff. The skiff descends, in a direct line, from the boats shellfishermen have used for generations in these shallow bays and embodies special qualities appropriate to the trade. For those who are into nautical nomenclature, it is a local form of sharpie, absolutely flat across the bottom, though with various amounts of rocker from bow to stern, depending on the theories of its builder. The whole idea was to build a boat with maximum flotation right under the feet of the lone fisherman, who had to stand up, lean over the side, raise from the bottom a heavy rake or set of tongs and bring it aboard. The load had to come up, and the boat had to not go down under the weight any more than could be avoided. The side had to be high enough for the fisherman to brace his knees but no higher, so that he need not hoist his load, twice as heavy when out of the water, any higher than he had to. Oystermen-quahoggers used to build their own boats, and some were higher sided than others because some fishermen were taller than others. They all carried similar cat rigs, the mast way up in the bow out of the way, a huge gaff mainsail which was not lowered when the man raked or tonged. That would have put the sail on its long boom right in his way; instead it was "topped," that is, it was left hoisted and the end of the boom raised halfway to the top of the mast by means of a third halliard with the delightful name of "toppinglift." This basic design goes back to the last half of the nineteenth century, maybe further than that, and the shellfishermen competed over the years in creating more efficient platforms to tong and rake from. They are a competitive bunch to this day, even with the shellfish almost gone, and they raced out to the flats and back, no doubt for wagers. So these fishermen, every one a boatbuilder, competed also in building faster boats. Some were very fast indeed.

State of the art in yacht design in those benighted days followed one basic rule: to go faster, you need more sail. Acknowledgment was made of the importance of lightness and sleek shape, but more and more sail was all important. Look at portraits, lithographs of yachts, of Cup defenders, in the last century, with their club-topsails, ringtails, flying jibs. A typical quahog scow of Cotuit about 1900 had a mainsail in which you could wrap the whole boat. And tie a knot! These guys did not bother with jibs or topsails or spinnakers. Just the one huge mainsail with the gaff at the top. To carry all that sail, you had to keep it low; "high-aspect" rigs did not

come until much later and are for an entirely different purpose. But there is a lot to be learned through the gaff rig about
basic sailing; more and finer control of the shape of the sail.

Upon this idyllic scene burst the internal combustion
engine. The typical quahogger's scow of my childhood had no
sail at all, just a heavy, slow-turning gasoline engine. Today it
has an outboard. I used to listen to them starting up every
morning outside my bedroom window in the Porter House.
Along with the reflected sunlight on the ceiling, I'd hear them
start: *Putt. Puttputt. Wheeze. Puttputtputt.* Today they all use
outboards, much quieter, and the typical forty-horsepower
Evinrude weighs less than just the flywheel of a typical 1920
two-horse Bridgeport or Wolverine. The racing skiff hung on,
but only for pleasure, and absent the need to be structurally
adequate for carrying big loads and hoisting them aboard, it
became lighter. It grew a deck and coamings the better to lug
sail and keep the water out when heeled. Here is entry into
what does and does not qualify as a Cotuit skiff. Its commercial ancestry is interesting but irrelevant. The more people
know about skiffs, the more people love them, the more they
disagree over what they are.

As a commercial vessel, the racing skiff has become unrec-
ognizable. And useless, once yachtsmen took over. In the early
days, most racing adults were sailing bigger boats, but their
children flocked to skiffs. They organized the Cotuit Mosquito
Yacht Club. Adults had nothing to do with it; it was a bylaw
from the first day, July 4, 1906, that "nobody older than Mary
Almy may vote or hold office." And just at this moment came
on the scene the man I keep talking about, Captain Stanley
Butler, a fisherman like any other who built his own boats. But
Stanley was a genius; fast boats, and faster, were not just part
of him; they were practically all. His talent was at least equal

to Nat Herreshoff's, but his ambitions were different; Stanley did not aspire to build a big, high-quality yacht yard. He built boats all by himself, even sizable schooners and big unusual-looking trawlers. What the best builders of wooden boats could do, what the last of them, mostly down-Maine, can *still* do, is look at a growing tree and see beneath the bark the exact curve needed to contribute the edge-set to a sharply bent plank, to see in a three-dimensional tree the two-dimensional plank which, when bent just so, will fit into a three-dimensional vessel. They buy their lumber "on the stump," supervise the felling, milling, sticking and air-drying for two or three years and then install it, its exact place held in memory all the while, into the ship when she is finally built. Stanley brought catboat design and construction to a very fine art. His catboats went right on winning against modern racing yachts long after he was gone. The successful racing skiff was largely his creation, and his round-bilge catboats owed something to the skiff, for the best of them had sides straight up and down and bottoms almost flat across, like skiffs. This construction required frames with an excessive bend at the bilge, unnatural, difficult to achieve in wood construction. Frames break.

Stanley's skiffs had a different problem, for he was an experimenter, never would build two boats alike. Each one had to be faster than the last, or he considered it a failure. And there were some. Although none of Stanley's competitors, amateur or professional, ever succeeded in building a skiff that could beat the worst of his, Butler boats became obsolete before they wore out. Building class racers all alike, to an inflexible set of plans, didn't interest Stanley, who didn't work with paper plans anyway. So, to stay competitive in skiff racing, you had to buy a new boat every couple years, and even for the children of the rich, it got expensive. Even when you could buy, built to order, a new skiff for under three hundred dollars, it got expensive. And worse than the expense, for the parents of these kids, was the idea of paying an artist whom your money couldn't control. Stanley Butler was an independent Yankee, "the kind who made this country great." Yacht racers like it the other way; all boats in a class to be as nearly identical as possible, so what the race is testing is the skill of the skipper, not of the designer or builder. So that the rich sailor can buy no advantage over the poor one. A noble ideal, hardly attainable in wood and cordage and cloth, hopelessly beyond reach in a design which began in working vessels built by a hundred different craftsmen, each with ideas of his own, a hundred years ago.

When they failed to make Butler conform, the parents of the skiff racers, many of whom were tycoons of one sort or another, hired a naval architect to measure what they agreed was Butler's most successful all-round creation, Stan Nickerson's *Scamp*, and draw up a set of plans to which all skiffs built forever in the future were to conform if they were to be admitted to the racing. Stanley washed his hands of us, moved to Nantucket and went on building boats of various sorts, including some Cotuit skiffs, which evolved through his experiments into boats not even recognizable as skiffs at all, some longer, wider, some narrower, vee bottomed, Marconi rigged, with jibs, Lord knows what. But, to get anything so radical as standard skiffs accepted, the tycoon fathers had to permit existing boats to continue racing as long as they lived. Starts for boats impossibly old, those by inferior builders, the new "standards" (skiffs built to the new plans) and the most recent Butlers (before standardization) were given handicaps, three minutes at one extreme and a minute and a half at the other. That's how the races were run when I first raced.

So goes the world; parents are never long able to overcome the impulse to complicate the lives of their children. Anyway, the kids continued to control the meetings, which occurred on land, and to elect the officers from among themselves. Wisdom came; it became apparent that Mary Almy grew a year older every year, so the by-laws were changed from the name of a person to a number. Typical adult behavior. Instead of "nobody older than Mary Almy," they said "nobody over 25 or married" shall vote or hold office. Anyway, there were now, in poorer times and times of more expensive boats, as many adults as kids racing skiffs. The kids were generous; they allowed adults to race on weekends. And to help with the bills.

An unsurprising amount of rancor was generated by the addition of adult rules to this kids' sport, and some comic scenes. When that naval architect, J. Murray Watts, known locally as J. Worry Lots, went to measure *Scamp*, he found that her centerboard was actually an off-centerboard; it was an inch to port of the centerline. No mistake; Butler wouldn't have made such a blunder by accident. He had observed that most of our racing, in the prevailing southwest wind, was on starboard tack, so he built a boat superior on that tack. Seems incredible, but it is a fact; I can vouch for it. Years later, old *Scamp* passed through my hands for repairs, and I measured her my personal self to check, so I know. This oddity was drawn out of the plans Watts produced. In any case, J. Murray was an incompetent designer. I learned when I was working at Churbuck's that if you try to build a skiff in strict conformity with his plans, you end up with your deck an inch in the air above the hull at the stern. You have to interpolate, and even a jackass boatbuilder like me knows enough to do that. Plans were redrawn in 1946 by Ned Mairs, a better draftsman, and many of the superfluous features which Watts had dreamed up, things never seen on any Butler boat, were eliminated, and we got a decent set of standard plans. For better or worse. There is a lot to be said on both sides of the question whether skiffs should or should not be all alike, even if they could be, and the whole argument gets so emotional that it is easy to lose sight of the truth: to all the rest of the hungry and crowded world it is insufferably trivial.

The Cotuit Mosquito Yacht Club was founded in 1906, but as I have said, skiffs existed and raced before that. I have in my attic a bronze trophy inscribed

COTUIT SKIFF RACE

1905

WON BY FROLIC

Stan Nickerson, who had a memory something like mine, recalled that *Frolic* was sailed on that occasion by Roland Nickerson. I remember *Frolic*, an old Butler, long past racing. She lay unregarded in the Coolidge boathouse all my childhood. She remained rotting there until 1944, when the hurricane demolished the boathouse. I remember Rolly too. He had a daughter whom for a time I admired and also an old double-ended ship's pulling boat in which somebody had half-assed installed a Chevy engine. A handsome craft which I later owned; she was my first *Big Wheel* when I went into the Committee Boat business. Rolly was a nice guy; must have been quite an age to have been winning races thirteen years before I was born and to have a courtable daughter about my age in the 1930s!

In 1906, annual dues in the CMYC were set at fifty cents; by my time, they were up to a dollar, and now they are five. The insidious encroachment of adult inflation on a kids' sport. But the kids still ran things, allowed adults to race on weekends and to pay the bills, which were way up. Adults brought inflation; let them pay for it. In spite of the resistance of the children, and those of us who insist on remaining children, the parents invariably got control early in the fifties, part of the drive to control others, which is what such organizations as WOE are all about. Strangers kept renting, buying, building summer homes faster than quaint local traditions could be absorbed, part of the process of destroying what they came here to find. New traditions, handed down from the distant top, crowded in. Like the mad modern quest for safety. Here is an inherent conflict, for a sport must have some danger or it ceases to be fun. You can't have the thrill without the risk; they are the same thing. When I began racing, the only concession to safety was that to join the club you had to be able to swim. No skiff had ever been known to carry a life preserver (a personal flotation device, or PFD, the bureaucrats call it) or an anchor or any safety gear except the bailer, and that was optional. But we somehow became aware of new laws compelling boating safety which we were expected to obey even though we were here first.

Philosophically it has always seemed to me that the words "boating" and "safety" are a contradiction in terms, an oxymoron. Boating is inherently unsafe, or we wouldn't do it; the risk is inherent in the thrill of any sport. It is getting away from the regulation and safeguards of ordinary life. If it were all that safe, we wouldn't bother. Less trouble to sit home and watch TV, which still has no law requiring a PFD, though the regulators, humorless adults, go way too far in censoring its content. A PFD in a skiff is as sensible and as tyrannical as a helmet on a cyclist.

But this tirade about safety began with talking about how the kids of Cotuit lost control of their club to their better-

organized parents. For the new families who moved here in
such crowds after World War II had no maritime background,
and when they got a look at the social structure of the place,
built first of all around the children and their little boats, it
looked dangerous. Because in fact, it was dangerous, to anyone who had not grown up in a seaside environment. And
rightly or wrongly, before I was old enough to become a seden-
tary philosopher, I was right here to cash in on their concern.

The first solid, gold-bearing example of this concern on the
part of parents who didn't know any better came just at the
time of my introduction to skiff racing, an example personi-
fied in Mrs. Marian Bentinck-Smith, a grand matriarch and
at the same time as close to achieving real rapport with kids
as a rich lady can hope to get. We all loved her; she addressed
every child with adult respect. Her approach to boating safety
was direct: she hired Captain Bill Nickerson with his rum-
running lobster boat *Sally Moran* to follow every race and
rescue any kid who capsized. She paid him, would never have
thought of soliciting contributions from other parents. Just as
well; the notion that their kids needed any sort of baby-sitter
while sailing would not have received much sympathy from
people who grew up racing skiffs themselves. Another gift
from this lady's bounty was the Little River Yacht Club, a program for very young kids, for beginners, which ran supervised races from her pier and never went outside the harbor.
After the death of Mrs. B-hyphen, all these safety programs
lapsed; nobody was about to pick up the tab. We went back to
unchaperoned racing for another generation.

In their day, the Bentinck-Smiths had a profound effect on
the sailing-oriented life of the children of Cotuit. Mr. B-
hyphen, who had been, I was told, a clergyman, was dead by
the time I got here. They had four kids: Bill, who inherited

his mother's gentle voice and her influence on everybody while making no noise at all, and Pete, who sold me his boat. He had the loud, brassy voice stereotypical of gays before he could have known what gay was. I speculate that when he found out he shot himself, but I have no entry to his mind. Shoot himself he did, in I think about his seventeenth year, and a lot of us missed him. He was cynical and caustic, but underneath he was as kind and gentle as all of them. John, the third brother, was shy, as in the cliché "painfully shy." Pleasant but full of his own insecurity. I sailed with him once or twice, and he kept up a running commentary to himself about how badly he was doing. Just the way Hatta used to do.

All three boys had their own skiffs—the *Bill*, a Butler masterpiece; the *Pete*, later renamed by me; and since you can't call your boat the *John*, John called his *Jolly Roger*. Like their owners, each of these little boats had its own personality. And there was Joan, a few years younger than I and, as a child, shy as her brother John, always accompanied by a nanny out of a British novel. The nanny's name was Miss Towle, but Joan called her Towie. In time they reversed roles and Joan took care of Towie, a doddering, uncomprehending old lady. Joan's hobby was horsebackriding; she had a horse named Tubby. Joan still lives in Cotuit. After her mother's death, that huge house and estate were sold, owned by a succession of rich men, and Joan built a cottage for herself on a corner of the estate back from the water. She was all her life a teacher of children with the euphemistic requirement known as "special needs," reputedly outstanding at it. She was sure to be; she has the same intelligence, the same loving gentleness and soft voice they all had. John is, I am told, a veterinarian, also good at his work. He never comes here. Bill was editor of the Harvard Alumni Magazine. I used to hear his voice now and then in restaurants around Harvard Square. You couldn't mistake him; gentle, perfectly modulated Harvard accent but with incredible carrying power. Never raised his voice, but it was always heard. Quiet now.

There was another Bentinck-Smith too, no relation but important. Stanton Nickerson was employed by Mrs. B to "brat" her three boys every summer, to be their full-time tutor for what seemed to one as small as I forever. He was part of the scene, of the landscape, unchanging. He was perfect, a local boy anyway, with a world-beating skiff of his own and a way with boys like I have never seen. In addition to his regular charges, he had half the kids in town at his heels all summer. The B-hyphen boys owed much of their popularity to his magnetism. He organized games, taught us songs, told long, fascinating stories extempore, showed us how to knot and splice and row and make our skiffs perform. He was the technical knowledge of the Little River Yacht Club as well as an officer of the Mosquitos. His versatility was always a step ahead of all problems. In the winter of four of those years, he went to Harvard.

I have a memory of a game of "hare and hound" which Stan organized. In case you don't know, this is played by any large number of kids who are divided into two teams. The hares are given a five-or-ten-minute head start and a sack of torn-up paper and take off leaving a trail of paper behind. The hounds take off later and try to find them by following the paper trail. When they run out of paper, the hares scatter and hide. So this time, I hid in a long-abandoned house somewhere near the corner of Old Post Road and Little River Road. And in that house I made a historic find: in a trunk I found an old newspaper with headlines and copy announcing the defeat of the Spanish at Manilla Bay. I was aware that it was important history but had no idea what to do with it. In the end, I did nothing. Left the paper right there and went away and forgot about it until today. That house isn't even there anymore.

We got along fine without any rescue boat for the ten years or so after the loss of our benefactress, until in the prosperity following the second war, we had an invasion of WOE material. People moved in, spent money and thought they should control the place. One particular influx originated in Cleveland, nice people, generous, enthusiastic, genial, competitive, athletic. They wanted the best for their children, and this yacht racing for kids was it. One Cleveland Rotarian told another, and first thing you knew, you didn't amount to anything in Cleveland Heights unless you summered in Cotuit.

But here came a watershed of a different kind. The new summer crowd did not winter in New England nor own large summer estates with barns, workshops and sheds. Part of growing up in skiffs was painting and fitting out one's own, but these people had neither the time nor the elbowroom to maintain skiffs that way. The part of learning to sail that comes from maintaining your boat was lost. And that's where I came in. I was already giving instruction, particularly in skiff racing, to half the summer kids in town from age eight on up. I was a good teacher always and the kids loved me; guess I sort of filled the boots of Stan. Parents called me "the Pied Piper." In the couple weeks between the end of classes at Harvard and the inrush of the summer crowd around Fourth of July, I got many of the boats ready, served as broker for renting the boats whose kids had outgrown them, gave sailing lessons all day and ran square dances all night until Labor Day and then put all the boats away for the winter and went back to Cambridge. I hired prep-school and college kids, whose school year was shorter, to help get the boats painted and ready and to haul them in the fall, but the sailing lessons were a solo operation. And I now branched out into safety, bought a motorboat (that same double-ender that had belonged to Rolly Nickerson; then to Tom Fisher, a Chatfield descendant; last to Bucky Botello). I renamed her *The Big Wheel of Cotuit*, and with her I started and finished all the skiff races and followed them closely all round the course, counting sails not only until everybody was across the finish line but also until every kid was back at his mooring with his sail lowered. For a guy who secretly believed that safety was the ruination of sailing, I did an overly and overtly conscientious job. And I sold life preservers in my store. Every skiff was now required by law to carry one per passenger.

In the 1950s skiffs took off; the whole fleet numbered sixty-five boats, and we sometimes got thirty-five of them across the starting line. I took personal responsibility for every kid and adult, ostentatiously so that parents could see, could not fail to see, that they were in the best of hands. They had to be pleased with the service; they were asked to chip in to pay for it. But, as the church found out centuries ago, free-will offerings are never more than barely enough, even with me handling most diligently my own PR. No way I could levy tithes.

So some of my friends, people who sailed with me when we were children, organized a brand-new charitable corporation to "promote the safety and welfare" of the Cotuit Mosquito Yacht Club. They did it well; some of them were hotshot city lawyers, but they were led and inspired by Ben White, a doctor, not a lawyer. I owe him lots of gratitude. The Association, as we call it for short, underwrote most enthusiastically any innovations I thought up to make the racing safer and more fun, paid me what I asked for my services as Committee Boat, hardly ever made any demands or questioned my judgment in return for all the money they raised and spent. Like my salvage pump, which I belted off the front of the engine. It could pump out a skiff-full of water in about a minute, so capsizing no longer required towing the swamped boat to the beach and passing to the kids enough buckets for a fire brigade. The Association was formed, in large part, to bail me out in appreciation for all I did for their children, and I appreciate them in return. I bought a larger and more reliable workboat, navy surplus and also named *The Big Wheel,* which I usually hired someone to operate so I could sail in the races myself, and in the end I had a beautiful one designed and built (we built much of it ourselves) in part for the yacht club work.

By then I had become a full-scale little boatyard with hull shops and engine repair facilities. Betty ran the office, and our three sons worked for us part-time in winter, full-time in the busy season. Bill became a brilliant small-boat carpenter, John was the engine man—he was born knowing more engineering than I could ever be taught—and Geoff was a number-one salesman. With all the plusses and minuses of a family seeing so much of one another, most people would call our life idyllic, and, thinking back on it, I have to agree. I told people that I was the nearest thing they would ever find to a happy man.

Our shop was outside of town on the highway, for by then, under the leadership of a fierce real estate lady named Helen MacLellan, WOE had the entire village zoned residential. To make your living was now illegal anywhere in Cotuit! Those already in business were "grandfathered," which meant granted a monopoly so they did not oppose on principle such high-handedness. They were allowed to stay but forbidden to grow; that's the way zoning works. It did not affect me; Cotuit waterfront, or any land in Cotuit, was way beyond my means, and zoning prevented somebody with more capital from moving in between me and my customers. I rented land and buildings just outside the village, technically in the next village of Marstons Mills, still not zoned, from my neighbor Bob Hayden, dealer in secondhand buildings and building materials. Hayden used me better than anyone could ever deserve. I'll have more to say about him when I get to that part of my story. This brief paragraph summarizes years of cordial relationship between my customers and me. We kept things cordial by careful, tiptoe regard for one anothers' feelings, for of course the members of the Yacht Club Association were such stuff as WOE is made of; all religiously opposed to the eyesore of anything productive on the horizon. But there was the feeling among these folk that without me their children's whole society might crash. In addition to the sailing, I was putting on square dances for the kids.

That is, one mother or another would give an evening party which consisted of nothing but refreshments and square dancing. I didn't call the dances. What I did was walk the kids through each new number, make them do it without music until they had it cold, then put on the record (78 rpm in those days, apt to jump grooves if anybody walked heavily on the porch near the record player) and they would dance it. Required a good-quality machine, loud enough to hear the calls. The kids got so good they did the dances perfectly and added features of their own to liven them up. Cotuit square dancing soon ceased to resemble the decorous ritual seen elsewhere. Active, almost violent, all with extra frills and features the kids made up to outdo one another. It was all done barefoot out on the grass, and after a session, the lady had to get the landscapers back to build her a new lawn. One number called for the two head men to go "round the set." My dancers went round the house while they were at it and were back in place for the next call. I didn't teach them that; they made it up. We sometimes got eight sets going, sixty four kids all dancing at once, if the lawn was big enough. A Cotuit set needed a lot of room, and in my day I was thought to be indispensable. I not only taught them the figures; I kept them in order while I participated. Danced with one pretty teenager or another, every number. We had five square dances a week all summer long.

Might as well finish it right here, recount the end of the square dancing. The police raided it! The kids and their sailing might have local priority, but overall, the power in the Town of Barnstable, and all over the Cape, had shifted to elderly, retired people who expected an environment like St. Petersburg. They were paying for it. They sought to make being young against the law, prohibited noisy parties, prohibited renting of quarters to people not related to each other, prohibited any noise at all after ten. Playing records loud enough for sixty-four kids to hear while shouting with glee is a noisy activity and some old fart who wasn't with it called the cops. They came and ordered the noisy activity stopped. Right now, in the middle of a set.

This was a perfect moment for me to take on the cops and the whole busybody town. What a court case I could have made about shutting down a healthy outdoor activity for kids, harmless, "keeping them off the streets." I can still taste my courtroom speech. Only one thing wrong with it: the boys were like boys anywhere, strutting, ballsy teenagers. They pretended to be reluctant to dance, so the hosts bribed them by making cans of beer available among the Cokes and lemonade in the tubs of ice around the periphery. A rare and laudable attempt by grown-ups to tell it like it is. But the beer attracted hard-case native boys who didn't dance and didn't intend to, though I was proud when I could cajole one into joining and watch him secretly enjoying himself. But making beer available to teenagers would surely come out if I went ahead and made a "federal case" of it, and the hosts and hostesses might even go to jail. Nothing for me to do but close the dance down as ordered. I never put on another, gave the records away. The square dancing stopped forever. But I still taste my unuttered speech.

I remained scornful of busybody regulations. Scornful of life preservers in skiffs while stocking my store with such things. Scornful of fishermen who wouldn't buy a yellow artificial lure because the latest big bluefish was caught on one that was identical but blue, although one of the few sure things known to science is that a fish is color-blind. Lures, I used to say, are not to catch fish; they are to catch fishermen. I learned, and taught myself, to build boats. Eighteen skiffs I built in the fifties, and every one of them won something its first year. Today mine are considered heavy; they have been outbuilt but are acknowledged to be the stoutest wood construction ever seen in skiffs. You can now get a new one made of fiberglass, for almost exactly ten times what I charged.

Late in the fifties something new came along: the Optimist Pram, designed to be sailed single-handed by kids eight to twelve, who are group-taught to sail in a program so organized it is almost bureaucratic. The whole program, along with a couple of the little boats, were brought here by a Dr. Chesney and his family from Coral Gables. They rented a skiff, and all of them, parents and kids, won races right and left, demonstrating how good a start you get when you begin in prams at seven or eight. All the Chesneys were so charming and the tiny boats so delightful that Cotuit bought the idea. The family excelled in everything. Barbara Chesney was racing her rental skiff single-handed and the wind blew up a squall. Barbara, at maybe twelve, was, as Damon Runyon wrote, "about knee-high to a flivver and weighing maybe as much as a dime's worth of liver," but she brought the boat in right side up, lying stretched out on the side of it and reaching one leg in to steer. None of us veterans had ever seen such a performance.

We now had an Association, and the Association had money. It organized a complete pram program for next season, which would be like 1961, hired a corps of college-age instructors, and Optimist Prams were off and going on Cape Cod. Gerry Henderson, Geoff Jackson and I organized a corporation to build prams and market them. I flew to Miami to learn how from a guy Dr. Chesney knew who had a one-man operation something like mine, had him make for me a form and patterns. To be sure, an eight-foot pram is not hard to build for one who has built skiffs, but lightness, down to the ultimate ounce, is critical, and I thus got my hands on years of experience when I began.

I built almost fifty of these; yacht clubs in several other villages started pram programs too, and some of the plywood prams I built, along with all the skiffs, are still being raced by grandchildren of the kids I built them for. Feels good. An eight-year-old can race a pram single-handed; two eight-year-olds can pick one up and carry it. By contrast, at least one aboard a skiff has to be like twelve just to be strong enough to steer and handle the lines. Prams are always raced single-handed; there is no room to carry a crew of any age. So many kids all of a sudden; all part of the unrestrained population growth I rail against. Most fun I ever had in my life was the first annual parents' race. The boats are so small and light (we kept the weight under seventy pounds) that an adult weighs one down. They maneuver so abruptly that when you tack, change sides, find the tiller with the other hand, the pram has jibed and tacked again. This race, I still remember, was won by tiny Debbie Jackson Smith, the littlest parent of all.

With the prams, there got to be races every morning and every afternoon, and hiring me and my boat to follow every one of them got to be a strain on the most benevolent Association budget. And it got to be a strain on me; with all this time on the water, I tended to neglect my business. We built the new tug in 1968, and she was too big to work among prams. An outfit this active is better off with its own equipment. The Association now owns not one but three fast, open boats and employs a whole staff of college-age kids every summer to teach and run the program and the skiff races too. Not without problems; nothing is without problems, so old-timers like me look back regretfully, but it works. And I have left my mark: all those skiffs and prams I built. And the yacht club's smooth, coordinated activity whenever a hurricane threatens, which has at least twice saved undamaged every skiff, pram and other small craft of every club member. All the result of a procedure I put together in 1955, which now works almost automatically (but not laborlessly) and "swangs into iction" at every hurricane warning. I used to boast, when I was in charge, "I can make one phone call and put a hundred men to work." And afterward, "My customers and I didn't lose a dime." Few who now participate even remember that I had anything to do with it, which is the greatest triumph of all.

But one thing appears: the kids have lost control of their own club. It isn't anybody's fault and no deep, dark plot has been hatched to put the grown-ups in charge. It has just happened, the result of there being too many of us and this silly preoccupation with safety for every last one of us, whether we want it or not. The law requires it, so those of us who purvey it charge an inflated price. The kids haven't the money, so the parents have to finance it, and no adult is going to put such money into anything he can't control. *(Afterthought: except on Wall Street.)*

V

A NORMAL CHILDHOOD

So HERE IS where I grew up, at least every summer, among the oysters and cranberries, cordwood and pond ice. My first friends of my own age, when I wasn't hanging out at B-Smiths' sharing Stan, were kids from the village, kids my snobby mother disapproved of, the same sort of kids I knew in public school back in Pennsylvania. Many of them are now dead, but dead or quick, I recite their litany: Jack Brackett, his brother Harrison, their cousin Phil known as Sippy, Pret Fish, Eddie Hoxie, Nelson Nickerson, Roger (no relation) Nickerson, Wally Rapp, Bob Dottridge, Weston Gifford, known as Wheels. They all helped me, which was more than any summer kids did, to get *Ariel* painted and rigged and in the water, and they all, by ones and twos, went sailing with me and crewed for me in the races. Change goes on; today year-round kids (natives, they used to be called) take part in yacht club activities regularly, but in the twenties it was unheard of.

So thus deviously, like Mrs. Barton going to the fair, I approach the subject of the natives and what they did in the twenties and thirties. One thing I am compelled to say: like Lowells, they showed signs of inbreeding. A couple of my friends were chinless, showed traces of albinism, brilliance, cleft palate. Times were hard; commercial oystering was dying out, the world-famous Cotuit oyster was becoming extinct. Oysters have not bred here in commercial quantities since (I was told) about 1900. Seed oysters from Long Island, Jersey, Chesapeake were brought here by the schooner-load, dumped into the harbor over that part of the bottom granted to this or that oysterman, who had chartered the schooner and bought the seed. A seed oyster may be of edible, even of marketable size, just brought here to clear themselves of pollution or take on that good Cotuit flavor. Often perfectly edible when they got here.

Most of what I know of the trade I learned, laboriously, from Foster Nickerson. Laboriously because he was so hard to understand; Foster had cerebral palsy, and to listen to him required intense concentration and a shower bath. He mumbled, exploded, repeated parts of words, spat and sputtered. He had enormous patience, incredible good humor and would repeat a statement over and over until you understood. What he said was always witty and informative, but it took a while. His father was captain and owner of the last of the two-masted coasting schooners that traded among these little ports, and seed oysters was one of the commodities he carried. Foster told, with delight, a tale of Ezra Gifford, a stiff-necked, stiff-collared (like President Hoover), solemn Yankee waiting for Captain Nelson (Nickerson) to arrive with his long-overdue seed oysters aboard the schooner *Tansy Bitters*. Ezra sculled out to meet her in his dory, took half a barrel of seed and dunked them in the harbor, headed up the barrel and shipped them to his impatient customer. "Label says 'From Cotuit Waters,'" said he." Foster's delight in this story got everybody wet.

What became of that schooner reveals a little of the older history of Cotuit and Cape Cod economics and everything else just before my time. Along with seed oysters, her most important bulk cargoes were coal eastbound and cordwood going west. All the first-growth timber along the coast had long since been cut for lumber and a generation later the second-growth was being cut again for rich people's fireplaces in New York and Westchester. The *Tansy Bitters* was carrying cordwood that voyage, in the early twenties, when she caught fire spontaneously while anchored for the night in Tarpaulin Cove, Vineyard Sound; flashed into flame so quickly that the captain and his one-man crew barely got over the side, so quickly that one account I heard of her loss said she "blew up." I guess much of that cargo was pitch pine, which exuded sap containing volatile material, the stuff from which turpentine is distilled. Lucky poor crippled Foster wasn't aboard that trip. So all that remained of her was her name, *Tansy Bitters*. That name was given to a racing skiff which belonged for a while to Gardi Jackson and was regarded as one of the fastest of Bigelow's "standards."

What this shows is that at that time (about 1920) one of Cape Cod's major exports was cordwood and that the coasting schooner played out at about the same time as the cordwood did. In fact, halfway up the Narrows there is one of those narrow landings at the foot of a lane into the woods called Cordwood Road. From the shore, this road meandered through the woods and round the head of Eagle Pond, much of it no longer passable by my time, till it came out at Hayden's property on the newly built State Highway 28 near where I later built my boatyard. Cordwood seems to have been what once passed here for an "industry."

So what became of Cotuit oysters? Nothing became of

them; you can still buy them in discriminating restaurants, but they have gotten very scarce. They all still come from imported seed, and today they must be harvested when still not fully grown, before they catch an oyster disease which kills them. For Cotuit and all of Cape Cod were shoved out into the Atlantic by the most recent continental glacier, which dragged across hundreds of miles of land, scraping up whatever the ground was covered with and leaving it in one long ridge, a moraine, where it stopped advancing and began to melt back. (There are other, more complicated, steps in the process, but I leave them out; they will not add light to the dark history of the oyster.) And the pile of glacial drift that is Cape Cod has been ever since sorting itself, the more fertile parts nourishing plant life of every sort, becoming ever more fertile in the process, and the glacial and the new topsoil washing continually down to the sea. As the meltback began, great chunks of ice remained buried in the "outwash plain" and, melting slowly, formed ponds and the fringe of harbors.

The new land supported whatever form of life was appropriate, and the ponds and bays and sounds did the same. But it was all transient, one form of life replacing another. The bays, Cotuit Bay among them, supported life also, oysters among other things, but the process is favorable to oysters only in one stage, for the ponds and bays were silting in, plant matter washing down and decaying where it came to rest, and being buried under more silt. The sailor observes that in just one lifetime the bays are getting shallower and muddier. Some day they will all be dry land. For perfect example, we have Cowyard Bay way up the Narrows, so named no doubt for farming on the land beside it. In the very few years that I have owned a boat with an echo sounder, this bay has shoaled from over thirty feet to less than ten, to no more than the depth of the surrounding waters. The ice is long gone, and the deep hole above where it lay has filled in with silt, with stinky mud.

Everything that lives is temporary, but some things are more temporary than others. The poor oyster is among earth's most temporary forms. It is, for one thing, locked in one place all its adult life, not free to move a single step. An oyster in heaven, where there are no predators, would be fastened to something solid and permanent just below low tide, for it cannot climb out of the mud, and it can take no action to avoid a predator except to close its shell. Then the predator has unlimited time to work on the oyster, pry its shell open or gnaw through it. When buried in silt, the oyster suffocates. It is prey to whole genera of specialized predators—from starfish to toadfish to many kinds of crabs, worms and drills, evolved only to eat oysters—and to special oyster diseases too, for if its environment is polluted, it can only stay where it is and die. Even a clam can wiggle its shell and move about a little to escape starfish. I have seen them do it on my TV. A scallop can flap its shell and fly under water. The oyster is stuck. Lucky predators. I speculate that without man's intervention, oysters might never have made it into the twentieth century at all. We are now making progress in culturing oysters in artificial, protected environments. For profit. Lewis Carroll was the only writer who had true empathy with his distant cousin the oyster. Until I came along; now there are two of us.

As temporary as the oyster is the oyster business. Where there were, at Little River, once four oyster houses there remains only one, the Cotuit Oyster Company. No more Coleman's, no more Hobson's, and all that is left of Giffords, once the most successful of all, was the right of my contemporary, Weston (Wheels) Gifford, to continue putting on Gifford's celebrated clambakes in the one surviving oyster house as long as he lived. Wheels is gone now, and the clambakes are gone too. So, as I was saying, oystering was, in the twenties and thirties, a doomed business. Though it was labor—most strenuous labor—intensive, most of the men engaged in it were elderly. Henry Robbins, who drove the movie car that brought me here the first time, was the youngest man among the four houses, and he was an employee, in the pay of the out-of-town corporation that owned the Cotuit Oyster Company, and it employed him because the law required that a grant of bay bottom on which to grow oysters could be made only to a local resident.

But in the 1920s, Prohibition came along, like a blessing from heaven, to take oystering's place. The sons of these hot-shot old watermen went into rum-running. They laid up their fathers' ponderous dredge boats, designed to plod along as slowly as possible so the dredges wouldn't plane up, towing a couple of wire mesh, steel-framed dredges along the bottom. Now they bought or built fast craft of the lobster-boat type, designed to carry a small load fairly fast in the open ocean, and they went out to bring in booze. You didn't need to go terribly fast to outrun what the Coast Guard could bring against you; their larger, deeper craft, capable of going to the assistance of ships in distress in storms, all the boats they had when the duty of enforcing the liquor laws was dumped on them, were too slow, above all too deep, for the shoal waters of the twenty or thirty intricate harbors on the Cape, and their officers lacked local knowledge of the waters and the landings. Large boats, owned by city gangsters, went way offshore to meet the great ships coming in from Canada, Europe, the Caribbean, loaded up and headed fast for rendezvous off the lonely beaches. If the Coast Guard or hijacking rivals got on their tails, they dumped the booze overboard. It was all in burlap, a case to the weighted bag.

Some local yachtsmen got into the act, dragging not from skiffs but from sailboats only slightly larger. Local boys went out and towed grapnels, steel rods with treble shark hooks spaced along them, brought up cases of Old Log Cabin bourbon, Overholt rye, Ambassador scotch, even champagne, and sold them to bootleggers ashore. Some of them made underworld connections and bought it from the ships direct. All the romance of smuggling was there: defiance of authority, a popular product unpopularly suppressed, danger braved in a popular quest. The danger was real enough; two local young men whom I knew were shot, one fatally, in a hijacking attempt not far from here. A young man who became my good friend when I grew up was arrested by local cops with enough contraband to send him to jail for a long stretch, held up the police station with his revolver, took off in his Packard and hid the evidence, then came back and turned himself in. The analogy to today's "War on Drugs" and "Zero Tolerance" is so plain that everybody sees it, but nobody this side of Hugh Hefner suggests doing anything different.

I was too young to be directly involved but old enough to be aware, in detail, of the traffic. It was easy to tell who was in it; the sign of affluence was acquisition of a fairly new and ornate Packard phaeton with a tonneau windshield, huge searchlights atop chrome-plated masts on each running board. Late adolescents here were no different from young men anywhere: ballsy, flaunting the accepted symbol of masculinity whatever it might be. I myself am not immune; I have as many calendar prints of classic Packards on the walls of my bedroom and office as I have Playmates.

*   *   *

Here is the place to tell what it was like around here at Fourth of July, all over the country a time of excess in celebration. Back in Pennsylvania, the volunteer firemen turned their hoses on each other in water fights. I had an eardrum pierced, or a passage blasted through from my ear into my sinus that way, so that for a brief time I could truly blow cigarette smoke out my ear, but it healed itself by strict neglect in a week or two. Before fireworks were banned, they were on sale in profusion like today's displays of trash at Hallowe'en and Christmas. Festivities here began as soon as the year's shipment of fireworks arrived, a week or so before the actual holiday. Every store was overflowing with explosives, every shop a bomb! In "downtown" Cotuit were two variety stores across from each other. School Street intersects Main in a tee, and one of the two, Birja's, fronted on Main Street and looked straight up School. It's a real estate office today, one of three in a quarter of a block. That will tell anyone like me, or Bierce, what business has sunk to around here, for, for a reason I can't understand, the real estate business is exempt from zoning, WOE-proof. Maybe because it produces nothing. The other fireworks store, Gibbs' Sandwich Shop, was a couple of doors up School Street. It's there today, known as the Kettle-Ho.

Each of these establishments had its adherents, not quite so formal as a team but something of that idea. They threw lighted firecrackers at each other all evening, working themselves up to more dangerous exploits as the night went on. Birja's was more vulnerable; the front door opened directly into the line of fire. To fire into Gibbs' you had to venture down the block. Right inside Birja's two swinging screen doors was a long display table piled with fireworks. Why the place didn't explode from the barrage aimed at these doors whenever they opened was a wonder of its day, but it never did.

In those days, across School Street from Gibbs', where now stands the defunct gas station, there was formerly a little wood commercial building where at one time Herb Long had a produce market. In those simple times, Herb had no telephone and no back door. Time to close for the night, Herb couldn't get out to bring in his fruits and vegetables, displayed on the sidewalk in their crates. Minute he opened his door, he was met by broadsides from both directions. Herb had an impediment in his speech or maybe his false teeth didn't fit tight, and when agitated, he spat and sputtered worse than Foster Nickerson. We kept him in there all night.

As it got later and spirits grew higher, the exploits became more daring. Popular with Birja's team was to prop a skyrocket against the curb, lying flat instead of pointing at the sky, and fire it straight up School Street, along the gutter which passed Gibbs' front door. If there were any cars parked on School Street, it zipped under them, shooting sparks till it burst in front of the church at the corner of High Street. As good as a rocket was a Day-Go Bomb, a daytime firework which fired straight up in the air hundreds of feet, then went off with a tremendous explosion and boom. The special use for this high-power blast was to fire it up the street so that the explosion took place at ground level, between the church and the school. The danger of someone blundering around the corner unaware was taken care of by hoping nobody did. It always worked.

Rockets and bombs were expensive, some as much as a dollar each, and without rum-running money, Fourth of July in Cotuit would have been tamer. The unprecedented supply of cash formed the leavening to raise the spirits of the local young to this explosive level. (A case of the dough providing the yeast!) For the younger kids, lacking this income, there were things like Roman candle fights. For people who grew up after fireworks, I explain: A Roman candle does not make a bang; it consists of a cardboard tube with a fuse. You hold it in your hand, light the fuse and point it away from you, being particularly careful to aim it in such a way that a backfire will miss you, not fire up your sleeve or into your shirt. If it worked as it was supposed to, it shot out balls of different-colored fire, roughly toward what you aimed it at, discharging six or more puffs of fire at intervals of about a second. They hissed and flew about twenty feet, burned out and fell glowing to the ground. Used as intended, you held it aimed up in the air at a slight angle so that spent fireballs would not fall back on you, and everybody admired the puffs of colored fire. Or you stuck it in the ground, lighted the fuse and helped watch. A dull amusement in a crowd so fired up. Roman candles were unreliable, for they were handmade in China, and a coolie is not famous for precise workmanship in measuring unstable chemicals; then they crossed the Pacific in the damp hold of a ship, crossed the country, desert and prairie, in a boxcar. Just being in the same room with one was hazardous. So we dueled with them. More dangerous than pistols were in the days of duello! Two kids holding Roman candles faced each other at about five paces, in the middle of School Street, and each tried to set the other on fire while everybody watched and cheered. Bet and took bets. The weapons, which weren't cheap either, were furnished by the rum-rich sailors.

Explosives were the essential ingredient in every man's mixture for weeks before and after the Fourth. I hung around, usually around Birja's, for the early evening, but I took no prominent part. By local standards, I was a timid child, but I discovered an inborn talent for dodging fireballs when I failed to dodge the challenge. Jack Brackett and I each sported an outsize cigar, like a foot long, for lighting fuses. We threw Chinese firecrackers at each other and at everybody. Chinese crackers were cheaper, just as loud but came with primitive fuses altogether uncertain in timing. Might burn quickly and go off in your hand or hesitate till you got close to see what was the delay and got it in the face. Often would burn out, so you had to break the paper cylinder open and get the powder out to see it hiss and sputter in the open air. Two such defective firecrackers, broken open and laid to form a cross and thus lighted, jumped around and hissed, and this was called a "cat 'n' dog fight." The "black powder" in there was dark gray, but if you got burned by a cracker going off in your hand, it left a brilliant silver stain on you. It happened with a big "salute" (a large firecracker) to Lee Crocker, but he recovered the use of his hand in a day or two. We bought and set off in innovative ways such explosives as we could afford, learned which were the best bargains and watched the antics of bigger, richer boys.

Cap'n Merrill (he's still alive, over ninety and still as active as ever) drove up in front of Birja's in his Packard, leaned out over the right front door to talk to Jiggs Condinho (long dead) about who knows what. Real purpose of the stop was so Merrill could slip a four-inch American salute into Jiggs' hip pocket. He got away with it because Jiggs was engrossed dropping a string of Chinese crackers, their fuses braided together the way they come, into the back seat. Which of them was more surprised is arguable, but Jack and I and some other kids saw what was happening before it happened and were satiated with delight. This sort of thing went on without end for night after night before and after the holiday.

The wild, fierce young men got more and more into the spirit of hazardous recreation, worked themselves into orgies of barn burning, setting fire to boats hauled out on the shore, all sorts of illegal, expensive and dangerous deeds. There were no radio-dispatched police cars out of Hyannis. Law and order in Cotuit were embodied in the person of Mr. A. Seabury Childs, a solemn and dignified little man who had one qualification which made him perfect for the job: he knew his village. He knew, personally, everybody in town, winter and summer, the M.O. of each potential delinquent even before he "delinquized." And they respected him. He was village fire chief as well as deputized town police. Fire chief was an elected office, and Seabury was reelected year after year. The on-call firemen were paid by the hour when on duty, so Seabury appointed some of the more restless youths to the fire department and paid them to stand by all night at the firehouse. His public money could not, of course, match what rum-running paid, but these were younger men, not boat owners, cash was scarce and fire department duty was a distinction.

During the day, Jack and I set up a battery on the beach to repel an invasion fleet. Guns were short lengths of iron pipe from Dr. Coolidge's boathouse, supposed to be rollers to move small boats over land. We buried the landward end (the breach) in the ground, muzzle-loaded by dropping a lighted firecracker down the open end. We found an unpretentious American firecracker called an "electric flash report," not cheap but as powerful as the better-known cherry bomb and waterproof. You lighted the protected fuse, threw it in the harbor and when the fuse burned down it made a satisfactory explosion and splash that could raise hell with a paper boat. We invented some realistic effects, but none, of course, as exciting as what went on "upstreet" at night. Fourth of July was a long time coming and longer going, but at last Birja and Gibbs sold out their stock and the celebration petered out for another year.

On Main Street, between Birja's (now Oyster Realty) and the lane leading down to the town wharf, was a great hole in the ground walled in with the masonry foundation which was all that was left after fire destroyed the big commercial building that had stood there until a year or two before I can remember. This building had once housed the Cotuit Grocery, along with numerous other commercial enterprises: a tailor, even a jeweler, they say. And out of the hole stood for years Cotuit's only billboard telling the whole record of Cotuit's history and geography. Today we have a Historical Society which seeks to do these things. It is graciously helping me get this book published. But in my childhood, history was preserved only on this billboard. I quote, from imperfect memory, some of the things it said: "Formerly the Indian Village of Coatuet, or Long Fields. Purchased in 1639 by Miles Standish for a Brass Kettle and a Hoe." Another line went "Around 18 [I forget the exact date] a Sea Captain Came from Every Family in This Village." In the top north corner was an arrow pointing "Hyannis and Points Down the Cape." The sign faced west, straight up School Street, just where we shot off the bombs and rockets, so people coming into town from Falmouth could see which way to turn. Route 28 had not been built, and people heading "downcape" along its south side had to go right through the center of Cotuit, Marstons Mills, Osterville, Hyannisport. They had to make a sharp left turn here or drive into the harbor. And a sharp right a quarter mile north in front of the grocery store in its new location.

Other things went on. I won my first trophy in skiff racing —the booby prize. In competitive sailing, I turned out to be the slow learner of the world. I was told years later that the Bentinck-Smith boys admired my determination, coming in last race after race, and bought this pretty little bronze cup to show their regard. It was eighteen years before I won a race, but then I caught on, got a faster, Butler-built boat and won them all.

And my acquaintance ashore grew as I got older and my legs got longer. I have mentioned some of the friends I made; here are some more as this book turns into a list of "dear hearts and gentle people." First of all Henry Robbins, who has already come up twice, the driver of that big car that met us at the depot, later the resident manager of the Cotuit Oyster Company, the only commercial oystering operation in business today. He was one man no child could forget. Oystering, even in the good old days, was always slack in summer because of the belief that oysters are not wholesome in months not spelled with an "R." Any truth in this myth reflects problems in refrigeration, not zoology. But it resulted in oystermen having leisure time in summer, which many of them used in the service of yachtsmen.

Oystering could never, in any case, have kept Henry too busy to talk and work with children. He helped us with our sailboats, and we all adored him. I knew him for over fifty years, even after he had retired. He developed an allergy, as Alice, his heroine-ic size wife expressed it, to "anything a-comin out o' the sea." Ironic, what? His hands got scabby and swollen when he touched his dredges, so he had to give up oystering. The company, in the late forties I think, brought in a younger man from Rhode Island. Meanwhile, Henry helped the kids with their boats. In depression times, when I was lucky enough to have a full-time job, he acted for me as ship's agent. Brokered *Ariel*, renting her out for the summer, launching and rigging. I always found a week in the spring to "get down," paint her and fit her out and usually got down again in fall to do a little sailing.

I was saying that Henry helped me, a poor working lad from Philadelphia, afford to own a sailboat. He was involved in my maritime affairs for years. In my teens, I was usually employed and usually broke both at once, for the kind of pay a teenager without experience could earn was not enough to live on, and my tastes were expensive. I couldn't even have fed myself, but fortunately, I never had to; lived at home with my parents and we never went hungry. Daddy earned a good income as a salesman all through the Depression, but never without acute worry and therefore never without grouchiness. He walked everywhere, all over Philadelphia, to save the seven and a half–cent trolley fare. I dropped out of high school of my own choice and had some job or other, also by choice, to avoid being sent back. Hated school, resented being told what to do even by the parents who supported me. Developed a technique of listening in class without seeming to, and memorizing what the others had sweated to learn. Never, on principle, let myself get caught paying attention. My pattern of never doing homework started out as indolence and became inflexible policy, and I developed a technique based on talents, mostly verbal, of passing scornfully, with the highest mark, any examination the stupid teachers could write. It made them furious, which was my major objective.

Back to Cotuit and Henry Robbins: he had a peculiar speech pattern found among a lot of Yankees which I can only describe as "phonetic pronunciation," speaking in written form, pronouncing any word exactly as it is spelled: Town of Chat-ham, a Ware-ham boat. Andy Post, the Tiverton oysterman who was brought in to help Henry run the company as

his health began to fail, and who took over the oyster operation when Henry had to retire, quoted Henry's description of
the '44 hurricane and its aftermath, "Utter dee-vas-tation.
Deb-riss all over everything." Sometimes it required close
concentration to know what Henry was talking about.

Though he was no skilled yacht carpenter, Henry could fix
anything, quickly, but not prettily. And he charged what a kid
could afford, what a skiff's season rent could cover. Another
thing about Henry was what Frank Minot called his "cheerful
pessimism." He expected the worst and passed on bad news,
impending doom, like any disillusioned old man, but with
open delight. He developed a strain of Bierce. Unique about
Henry was the jolly Pollyanna way he recited ill tidings of
great grief. One day in the post office he met a local hypo-
chondriac whose father had been dying of melancholy and
complications for years. He inquired, of course, after Joe's
father, but he didn't wait to hear the answer. Henry went
merrily on, "Well, it didn't take old Borden long to go when
he took sick, did it?" Henry Robbins died soon after his
forced retirement, predicting his own death in the same jolly
way. It was painful to watch.

Life went on. There was a legend in town that every fall
President Lowell gave a check to Milton Crocker of the Cotuit
Grocery, to be used at Mr. Milton's discretion to make sure
that certain families did not go hungry in the winter. All
Cousin Lawrence's relatives denied most vehemently that
any such arrangement was ever made or considered, and I
believe them. It wasn't necessary. Milton gave unlimited
credit to every family in the village all winter, on his own. He
and his wife were like that, and they kept it up long after

Lowell was gone, and their son Harry carried on the same way throughout his life. They were always paid off out of the cash that bloomed in the spring, though payment of interest was unheard of. Meanwhile, they did a good business when few people had automobiles to drive to chain stores in Hyannis or cash to spend there. They lived simply, for years right over the store. For a time we had an A&P in Cotuit, and people who had cash shopped there, but there could not have been many such, for the A&P closed. Cotuit Grocery survived and prospered, and Mr. and Mrs. Crocker went on carrying half the village all winter.

The Crockers and their store were an essential part of village life and an essential part of my own life, early and late. I have told of my own daily walks up the hill from the Porter House for something my family needed. You could get amazing things there, for it was a bit of a general store. Even had hardware; a folding wooden ruler such as boatbuilders use, jackknives, chisels, oyster knives. In 1950-something, Betty even got a new glass chimney for one of those old-time kerosene lamps which she was polishing up for use in power outages, and found also new glass chimneys, clear and red, for kerosene lanterns. I forget why she wanted one, but Mr. Milton had them tucked away and remembered where he had put them.

When I was a little boy, he gave me a job, for ten cents a day, and I made typical child's long strides memorizing where various stock was located on the shelves. You used to stand at the counter of a grocery store, independent or chain, and wait your turn to tell your wants, read the list your mother gave you to the clerk, who brought your groceries to you, wrote the prices and added them up on a paper bag in which he then put your purchases. The bag became your itemized

The grocery store as it is in 2000, just like 1928.

receipt, and he either wrote the total on a slip for the book-keeper to charge to your account or took your money and counted out your change.

I do not mean to follow the history of the Cotuit Grocery beyond the Crocker family. Milton and Nellie's son Harry ran it for another generation after they died, and he acquired a packaged liquor license. He no longer drove the milk run, but he worked as hard as his parents had. His sons and brother had no interest in working that hard all their lives, and the business passed out of the family after Harry dropped dead in the store. The new owners make no attempt to run it as the Crockers did, trying to stock every item you can find in a supermarket. Cotuit has changed; there is now a supermar-ket just outside of town, next to Pecks' Boats, where groceries are cheaper. People have gotten used to paying cash, and we now have credit cards. The store is no longer the center of the community, except for the kids, but the new owners, the

Goulds, must be doing something right; all the kids, the teenagers, hang out there. This is where Cotuit has changed the most; when I came here, it was oriented entirely toward kids. Today the village has no recreational facilities at all. Now, the way things have been going, kids have to be driven to Hyannis to do kid things. To the mall; to the Kennedy ice rink.

But I want to relate two or three more anecdotes of the Crockers. The first recounts a conversation I overheard when I was very small, between Mr. Milton and Freeman Nickerson the plumber. There was nothing particularly confidential about it, and such a small kid was ignored. Crocker was ordering work on the store's pipes over the winter. It tells a lot about the place of cash in the old-time Cape economy, for Milton wound up with, "And if I have a good season next year, I'll pay you." Only half in jest. Years later I went into business here that way myself.

The other story concerns Miss Nellie and a child, maybe five years old, she had hired to help her, much as her husband had once hired me when I was a lonely child, to give the poor kid some feeling of usefulness. She was the youngest (or perhaps the only) girl in a long string of boys, each of whom worked at being the toughest, and they were as cruel as kids are to their little sister. Called her "Meatball," and the name stuck all over town. And I, now a grown man who should have known better, said to her as I passed by the register on my way out of the store, "Bye, Meatball."

Miss Nellie said to me, as icily as Amy Coolidge at her haughtiest, "This is Miss Nancy Parker." A lesson which, as anyone who reads this page can see, I never forgot.

I don't exactly have an anecdote about Harry, but not because there aren't any. Rather, there are too many; he was gifted with language, appreciated all sorts of wordplay. Conversation was always his delight. He should have been a writer; his joy in putting words together was something like my own; he would have been a better writer and, with his diligence, more prolific than Michener. I always saved good word games to tell him. One he was still chuckling over years after I had forgotten concerned a bumper sticker I had seen:

IF YOU DRINK DON'T PARK

ACCIDENTS CAUSE PEOPLE

Cotuit had another large building, Sears' (no relation to Roebuck) Department Store, two stories plus the basement, a big central staircase with varnished oak bannisters, merchandise on all three levels. Everything you could conceivably want except food. Paint, tools, nails, overalls and yard goods, furniture, harnesses, cosmetics, oil and electric lights, needles and thread, buckets and shovels, matches and toothpicks, sledge handles, ice picks and ice tongs, scythes and lawn mowers, feed and fodder. Sears' closed in the thirties and the building survived, parts of it occupied for a while by the post office, by Manny the barber, by the A&P, by a poolroom. It's torn down now, and the ground is park.

Also in Cotuit center were some little buildings along School Street: Charlie Harlow's butcher shop, Charlie Fred's barber shop (these buildings are still there, both today real estate offices!), Handy's Variety Store which sold quaint things called "notions" in those days. Sometime in the twenties, I went with Mother to the closing of this establishment, the first auction I ever attended. We found nothing to bid on, but I remember two quaint things offered: a child's game called "Magic Dots for Little Tots" in which I was faintly interested but didn't dare say so, and an item which amused Mother because it was even then so old-fashioned: a large box of ladies' hairpins, each one as big as Mother's thumb, made of tortoiseshell. There were no bids on these at all; finally some joker muttered, "Ten cents." With an auctioneer's quick wit, the man held the box out to him and said, "Here. Take 'em!" Years later that building still stood. It was the one in which Herb Long the greengrocer spent the night of Fourth of July. Years later still, Walter Scudder (his friends called him Monk) opened a gas station there with as little capital as I had when I went into the boat business. Like Milton Crocker, he expected to work, did work as hard as anyone I ever saw, and always with the most incredible good humor. Nothing was ever too much trouble, even the crazy, inconvenient tasks the summer people, particularly the ladies, expected of him on short notice. Routine with him was winter custody of the keys to many summer homes, so craftsmen, the police, the firemen who had work to do there had to get the keys from Walter.

I have a Walter Scudder story too, though I was away in the service when it happened. It is Betty's story; she was "down" in Cotuit with my nutty sister Anne staying in the House in the Woods, and the two of them had tickets and a train to catch out of here. But Anne couldn't cope with fitting all her possessions into her luggage. She collapsed in fits of giggling, and even the stalwart Betty could not recall her to a sense of time and duty. Walter arrived to take them to the depot in his taxi—a station wagon by now, no longer a phaeton—and persuaded them to get in the car. "I'll finish your packing and send the stuff on to you," he promised. This was the sort of thing Walter would not only do but volunteer to do. For nothing; you don't tip your neighbors.

Walter was as generous with credit as Milton was. Such

pleasant diligence was sure to succeed, and Walter kept rein-
vesting, expanding automotive service, fuel oil delivery, and
he soon outgrew that silly shingle building and collided
head-on with the zoning regulations which the blind zealots
of WOE had imposed on us all. They had pushed through
town meeting a zoning bylaw which classified all of Cotuit as
"residential." Nobody could ever put up a business building,
not even downtown, and if one burned down, it could not be
rebuilt. There was, of course, some fine print specifying what
proportion of rebuilding might be classified as repairs, but
I'm not, at my age, going to start talking in numbers like a
computer. Walter found a loophole in the fine print which
allowed him to build a two-bay service station right over and
around that silly shingle store. When it was up and doing
business, he tore down the old building and carried it out the
door. Ingenious, but one result has been that he had to put
the new building so close to School Street that it fouls up the
parking. Local businesses changed hands, changed buildings, changed proprietors, but struggled along in spite of the
trend to drive to Hyannis once Route 28 was completed and a
car became a necessity.

So, from people to places and back again to people. I have
described the northern and eastern property and shores of
the village in terms of which Lowell relative lived where and
owned what, but the southern and western end of town lacks a
single unifying family to write about. A few very grand Boston
and Cambridge families were represented in more or less
grand houses, but between them were rich families of no
social significance, and so beneath the notice of a Lowell
retainer like me. Cousin Lawrence's house was on a point and

the shoreline trended away from it toward the north, where we have all this while been and also toward the west along the short walk to the town wharf and the narrow road leading down to it from the village center. There was west of the house a low, reedy place on which stood Lowell's boathouse, which I have mentioned, and other outbuildings: the barn where Mrs. L. kept her trotting horse and her cart, and an ice house.*

But, as everybody knows, the major industry on Cape Cod through the twentieth century was cranberries. I said, very early in this account, that I was turned off cranberries by an intellectual triumph of my cousin Dorothea, but I could not have lived in the middle of all these cranberries without becoming aware a little bit about them. Jack Brackett's father and his cousin Phil's father, too, were owners or bosses of cranberry bogs. I liked eating them well enough with my Thanksgiving turkey (Don't get me going on the sin of

*Pond ice was an important commodity as recently as about 1920. It was cut on the freshwater ponds which occupied the kettle holes and was stored in these little buildings, mostly underground, insulated with sawdust, kept for the summertime uses for which today we have refrigeration. There were all sorts of special tools for handling it, things like great long saws to be powered by the hands of experts standing on top of the floating ice and, with artistic skill, kept cutting in a straight line, hand tongs and tongs on the end of a rope for handling the blocks. Once the ice was cut loose, it went right on floating, and the techniques for handling floating blocks of ice were similar to those used in lumbering. Except that a log won't melt. And nobody is fool enough to try walking across a pond by stepping from ice block to ice block. Much of the ice was shipped south by schooner and this practice was an important reason for the demise of schooners. Salt water is good for a wooden vessel — helps preserve the timbers — but fresh water, full of mysterious algae, that comes from melting pond ice, devours wood almost before your eyes. A wooden vessel that took on such a cargo was marked for death. The work of these wood-eating algae is mistakenly referred to as "dry rot" because of the residue of very fine wood dust, but it originates in dampness and is retarded by ample ventilation. Dry rot is also inhibited by salt; one technique used in building large wooden ships is salting,

Thanksgiving turkey. It is worse than pride, far worse than gluttony; it is blasphemy), but I never got in any way involved with their production. My mechanical son John, who showed signs of workaholism before he could walk reliably, helped Phil on his bog before John was old enough to be legally employed. Phil paid him off in crates of fresh berries which Johnny brought home, making for his mother a problem of what to do with them. She couldn't throw them away when Johnny had worked so hard and was so proud of his earnings, and anyway, Betty was a country girl herself, and she could cook and sew and do all manner of things. One thing a girl cannot do is throw away anything usable, but the uses of cranberries are limited. She even tried to make wine of them, but it didn't work. Cranberries contain less sugar than almost any fruit that grows on ground. Cranberry vinegar we had for a few years.

packing the space between the planking and the ceiling with rock salt. As every sailor knows. But salt and ample ventilation as you work south both melt ice. A dilemma: destroy the cargo or destroy the ship?

But before economical mechanical refrigeration, all civilization more or less depended on pond ice. The railroads used tons of it to bring fresh produce to market, and they had elaborate and fascinating machinery to handle three hundred–pound blocks of it at cartop level. They were skidded along catwalks and dropped into hatches in the car roofs. The first air-conditioned Pullman cars blew air over ice which was carried in great iron chests under the car floors. Low, battery-powered ice carts were part of the summer landscape in any passenger terminal. They ran along the platforms, all among the boarding passengers, carrying the big blocks which were slid into compartments under the cars. My very fat Italian barber in Swarthmore, Pennsylvania, used to set a fifty-pound block of it in a tin tub on his second chair (Frank employed no second barber), drape a towel over it, set up a big, noisy electric fan to blow over it directly at him and thus endure the heat of the Delaware Valley. All over the cities, all over the suburbs, house to house and store to store, in stout two-horse wagons moved the iceman, on the box or walking alongside, uttering his harsh cry. In Cotuit, cutting, storing and shipping ice was winter work for hardy men.

To begin at the beginning, for readers who are as ignorant as I was when I first came here, cranberries need sandy soil, so Cape Cod is perfect for them. And they don't ripen until very late in the fall when the chances of a frost in the night are high, and freezing kills cranberries, or at least makes them soft and of short shelf life. Therefore are they grown in bogs. In the evening when the skies are clear and frost by morning is to be expected, Mr. Grower puts a board or two across the flume in his lower dam, maybe takes one out of his upper dam, and floods the bog. His berries spend the night underwater, where they are protected from freezing. But they don't ripen underwater, so in the morning he drains the bog and lets them resume ripening. All this isn't exactly easy, but it requires no special intelligence. But, as with any crop, the earlier you can bring it to market, the better price you get. So the smart grower waits until the last moment to flood. Stays up all doubtful nights with one eye on the thermometer and one hand on the flume to just barely anticipate the freeze, flood at the last moment. He designs his dams and flumes for swift action. It makes cranberry growing a gamble with your whole year's income. I can see how cranberry growers get that way.

Modern growers also flood their bogs at picking time. A new-fangled machine cuts them loose from the vines underwater, and they float to the surface and are skimmed off. This technology has made the old long-tooth wooden scoops obsolete, so now they make more of them than ever before, to sell to tourists who take them home, set them on the hearth to display magazines. The same technology has also made obsolete the bouncing-berry sorting; only sound berries float.

There was, when I was growing up, a local cranberry tycoon named A. D. Makepeace who thought to own, or at least control, all the cranberries in the world. He brought in docile employees from the Cape Verde Islands. (Earlier generations of these people had come to this region as whalermen, though harpooners are not remembered for docility.) Makepeace bought up every bog that came on the market, but he had no chance of owning them all; just the notion that he wanted to was enough to make the cussed Yankees hang on. What he did do was organize the growers in an association as reactionary as WOE, with the purpose of restricting production to keep the price up. This gang forced many small growers right out of business, took marginal bogs out of production, became petty local racketeers. They had a bank in their corner and played real rough. One grower who wouldn't play took them to court and I think he won, but he didn't win enough to much more than pay his legal expenses. Ended up out of business, but the bank was shaken up pretty good.

I have just one personal anecdote about big-time (what passed for big-time in this small-time industry) cranberry growing. It happened after Makepeace himself was dead and gone and the operators of the Cranberry Association were pipsqueaks playing at being bigshots. To sell cranberries, they dreamed up a beauty contest among high school girls in cranberry-growing regions: New Jersey, Wisconsin and Cape Cod. I was a teacher at one of them; had the proper degrees from Harvard and taught English to support the family so the boat business could reinvest and grow, and this contest came at a time when our principal was in hospital. Two older teachers were taking over for him, and they were busy doing their job and his, so they delegated to me the chore of managing the entry from our senior class. We wasted no time on the formalities of choosing which girl she should be; we had plenty of pretty ones, but only one fit to play in this league, possessing extraordinary sophistication and poise, at home before an audience, a born model or starlet.

She won the title of "Cranberry Queen" of course. Her poise, the way she stood, so at home with her body, would have beaten most high school girls even if she had not been pretty. Pop and Andy, the double-duty teachers, wouldn't have bothered entering the contest if we had not had such a walkaway winner. She didn't need me for her manager to win, but she needed me and my wife and both her parents to get her out of there intact. Final award was presented at a banquet in a classy restaurant off-Cape, and there the old goat (name withheld, though he's been dead for like thirty years) who was executive secretary or some such thing of the Cranberry Association took one look at her and began to slobber. I thought he'd drown. With the help of me and my wife, the young lady's parents got her out of there, and I'm not sure to this day but what she could have handled him without help from any of us. The guy was dumber even than President Clinton, who never hunted among high school girls as far as is known.

Not all cranberry growers were made in the same mold as this old goat. One of the old native families of Cotuit was the Ryders, many of whom had roots in bogs. Malcolm Ryder lived across from the grocery, next door to Coolidges. On Ocean View Avenue, across from the Pines, lived the Bertram Ryders, prosperous burghers who owned bogs all over the place. Bertram was a quiet, reserved small-town potentate, vice president and director of one of the banks. He had a daughter who went to Washington as Congressman Gifford's secretary and a son Richard, who was my age and my friend. A serious racer of the most all-out modern sailing speedboats, but too Yankee-tight to own his own.

All these Ryders were exceptionally tight. As laid-back and

understated as his father, Richard Ryder had a Yankee wit, told delightful tales of Cotuit characters. I remember one which took a quarter hour to tell, about some strangers in an automobile lost in the wilderness of Cotuit, seeking directions to get out. Asking the way to Falmouth, of three nuts in a row. First Foster Nickerson, who knew as much as anybody but with his handicap could communicate practically nothing to a stranger. Brought his wheelchair to a stop, heaved himself around to face them and began "Ah ah aah spt ur . . ." till they took alarm and drove away. Next they tried blind Chet Baker, walking confidently up the sidewalk he had known all his life. To their question, he too heaved himself around to face them and said, "Which way you headin'?" Then they tried a local idiot whose name I never knew, though I had seen him all my life. His reply was incomprehensible in a different way, though I am unable to reproduce it in typescript. Sort of long, drawn-out "errrrrr." That was one of Richard's most popular tales. Another concerned a different stranger who was being introduced to local celebrities. He was introduced to Polly Hitchcock, Elaine Mycock and Rhoda Cocks. He too took flight. There was a punch line, but I forget it. The tale doesn't really need one anyhow.

My other acquaintance with the berries was a result of my boat business. I used to rent unused farm buildings to store boats in when all boats were wood and suffered from exposure to winter. Among other sheds, I rented a boghouse in one part of which were some brand-new, never-used cranberry-processing machines, the property of the rich Mr. Pemberton Whitcomb. He bought property all over the place, much as Cousin Lawrence used to do in his day, and some of what he acquired included working bogs. Whitcomb put in machinery to process his product but found it cheaper to send the work out. To process the berries he would have had to hire men who knew how to run the machines, and Pem couldn't bear to pay them all year for a few weeks' work in fall. He was the scroungiest millionaire I ever heard of. I'll tell of his ghastly death when I come to it.

Anyway, I rented that boghouse from him, set up scaffolds to store skiffs two high and moved them into space left open to store boxes of berries in process. The intriguing machinery fascinated my dilettante engineer's eye. So much of it was made of wood and cordage and fabric, very little metal anywhere. I never had more than a vague idea of how it worked, what it was supposed to do to the berries. Thus, vaguely, I can explain that one step in processing is to bounce them off some kind of surface, harder than a trampoline but not so hard as a plank floor. Bruised or overripe berries won't bounce, and this machine bounces them, thus sorting sound berries from non-bouncers. They did that, but don't ask me how. Never saw them work.

Only other time my path intersected those of cranberry men was over trailers. In Kingston, just the other side of Plymouth, there was the shop of a clever machinist who made certain machines of his own invention to work in the bogs. His was not a custom, one-off process, not a job shop. He was into repetitive manufacturing of a certain few products. Fred Carlson was a real hard-ass, crusty old guy, but somehow we became friends. To even out his plant's seasonal production, he made a line of inexpensive boat trailers, little ones only, just right for the little boats I dealt in. And cheap. Customers, having persuaded themselves to spend the price of a boat, always want to save on the trailer. I brought ideas to Fred from boat shows: an inexpensive kind of waterproof (when new) wheel bearing; having trailers galvanized to retard rust-ing. Anyhow, his main output was those strange-looking machines with little gas engines on high, bicycle-type wheels, which worked waist-deep in bog water.

Back again to Cotuit, I rail on against the work of WOE, but time and change confound me. Going into business for yourself today means buying a franchise from McDonald's or Blockbuster or Kentucky Fried Chicken or CVS or Ace Hardware, and I confess I would be as reluctant as anybody if a row of these were to open in Cotuit. They operate on the principle that you hire the cheapest help you can find in the knowlege that the average customer is stupider still. I'm not yet ready to lobby against them or take them to court, but the notion of opening a small, independent business has changed since I opened one, and I must at least acknowledge the change.

VI
MORE PLACES,
MORE PEOPLE

I WAS TELLING ABOUT the shore and who owned what.
You see how one thing leads to another? Back to the town
wharf; note in passing the significance of the word "town."
The wharf belongs to, was paid for and is maintained by the
Town of Barnstable. This is important; it signifies that the
people of Cotuit enjoy no privileges there above those of
other taxpayers and residents of the town. Keeps WOE from
kicking them all off. Fortunately for WOE, the state isn't in
the act, or anybody in Massachusetts would have equal rights
to park there. For these privileges apply only to the land — to
the parking lot. The federal government has its hand in the
wharf itself; the Corps of Engineers' permission is required
for anyone to build, maintain or extend a wharf over navigable water, and the Corps decrees that any vessel may tie to any
public wharf and local people may not restrict its use by outsiders except as they restrict its use by themselves. I am not
quoting law here; don't know how it is written, only saying
how it applies.

Since all waterfront here is private and zoning prohibits marinas, the ancient wharf has far more users than space. And since the majority of users are yachts with pristine topsides, nobody ever ties outboard of anybody else. The town restricts dockage to twenty minutes, loosely enforced, and supplies a water connection for washing down and filling tanks. They discontinued supplying electric hookup; people were lying there half the day charging batteries. Three or four commercial fishermen unload there in spring and into the summer, but they are little boats; no deep-draft trawlers can get into Cotuit anymore, and these fishermen, many of whom do not speak English, are more careful to clean up and get off the pier promptly than are a lot of yachtsmen.

There is an old photo of the shore at some early time — earlier than mine — showing a wharf at this place with a coal elevator on it. Schooners used to unload in Cotuit when the harbor was deeper and the entrance straighter, and the coal they brought was distributed by the wagonload all over the Cape. This picture was copied by artists working for the New Deal's WPA during the depression and has since been restored. It formed the curtain of the tiny stage of Freedom Hall (patience; we're almost to Freedom Hall) and was seldom unrolled, basketball being more popular than theatrics. The coal tipple was long gone by the time I got here, and since then the size of the wharf has been doubled and an ell built onto the end of that, and there still isn't room for all the boats. There are the four dinghy floats, and there still isn't room for all the dinghies needed to get back and forth to all the boats moored in Cotuit Harbor. Tommy Hadley's launch service absorbs some of the pressure during the hours and seasons when he operates, but access to your boat in Cotuit is still inadequate, and marine traffic is necessarily concentrated on this little wharf when it would be better spread along those miles of empty shoreline.

It is all the fault of WOE and of King Charles and, more than either of them, the fault of all those who think to keep people out by passing laws. The only politician who ever did anything about population was Chairman Mao. In easier times it made no difference; people like Lowell and kin felt neither crowded nor threatened; they made room for fishermen and even yachtsmen to pull their dinghies up on their beaches and leave them there. The tradition died with Lowell's generation. New millionaires pay higher and higher taxes the closer to the shore they own, and they resent people who don't share the cost but expect to share the privilege of passing over the beach. And most of these "trespassers" aren't there to earn their living but just to enjoy nature. Without paying for it! Cotuit is no longer the friendly place I write about. When people, like animals and insects, feel crowded they get hostile. Chairman Mao, I miss you.

Also painted on that theater curtain is the shore and harbor seen from Freedom Hall before intervening houses were built. It shows in the foreground a shipyard with schooners under construction. That shipyard stood on a low piece of flatland, probably filled-in marsh, at the foot of a steep bluff, and by my time this land had become part of summer places, a row of them along Main Street at the crest of the bluff, each with its narrow lot reaching across what once was shipyard to the water, a couple of them with private wharves.

One of these homes was year-round, the home of Congressman Charles L. Gifford, Republican, who for years represented the whole of Cape Cod. There are a lot of stories about Charlie Gifford, but none are concerned with my childhood. As well as that home on Main Street, he had an office built on a stone jetty out into the harbor right beside the town wharf. He bought and sold properties all over this part of the Cape, sometimes renting his main house and living in one or another of them. Some of the real estate deals of Charlie Gifford are comically casual, careless. Hilarious but not part of this account. They are appropriate to his time, when most land was almost valueless. Years ago I was asked by the Historical Society to give a talk, write a paper about him, but I declined. Didn't want to dig up the inevitable dirt about a man whose family was good to me. And dirt was surely not what the historians wanted to hear and read. They got somebody else to do it. Where would I come off writing about him now?

Where the lane (paved now) down to the town wharf comes up to Main Street, as I mentioned when recounting the Fourth of July celebration, it continues as paved (even then) School Street, passing Gibbs' and other small businesses like Herb Long's, passing between the new church and the new school (new in those days meant less than a hundred years old) and leading by the homes of various residents, mostly year-round. Henry Robbins lived out here, and one house, the remaining half after the last main Coolidge house had been cut loose and hauled (I am told on oak skids over the snow by teams of oxen) to its present location, was the home of Florence Rapp, a notably eccentric real estate lady and my good friend. Flossy was tiny but utterly fearless. She'd take on anything in the world. I used to take a room with her when I came down in the spring to paint my boat. Her husband was dead, and she fearlessly brought up her two very active little boys single-handed. She had so much pep and energy that the boys partook of it. She managed everything she came near. Tried to manage me into a relationship, tried to set me up with the beautiful Barbara Hale, an acquaintance I would probably have shunned out of shyness without Flossy's encouragement. But with Flossy to back me up, I did establish a sort of relationship; Barbie and I used to date somewhere between occasionally and frequently. Flossy's surviving son still lives in her house. He is an MD specializing in X rays and I am told he is pretty good at it.

Continuing out Main Street, we pass in front of those houses overlooking the site that once was shipyard. Next house after the congressman's I called the Irish place because it was occupied, in succession, by Higginbothams and O'Keefes. Each of these families had a boy near my age with whom I had a superficial acquaintance but nothing close. Then came a larger house, belonging at that time to B. V. White the elder and wife and their daughter and two sons, all half a generation older than I. Ben Junior was away at college or medical school, but the younger son, Boyd, was around. Boyd couldn't walk; I think he'd had polio or something, and he got the kind of treatment the crippled son of a very rich man might expect: a classy mahogany Hacker speedboat named *Dipper Duck* and a husky college-age young man with a deep southern accent to attend him. This man's name was Roy Williams, and most of what I saw him working at was carrying Boyd piggyback between the house and the boathouse (which involved a steep flight of wooden steps) or lifting him in and out of the driver's seat of *Dipper Duck* or, once in a while when there was a race in very light weather, the cockpit of the White's fast Butler skiff *Scaup*. The kids all called Roy "Wawhoop" because of a wild rebel yell he gave when he had drink taken; he was a terror among all the teenage girls, setting a standard for littler boys to aspire to when they got old enough. Boyd White couldn't walk, but his jaw wasn't paralyzed; he knew more dirty songs and stories than anyone I, up to that time, ever met. I think now how awful it must be to be so horny and paralyzed! Jack Brackett hung out at the White's; they were friendly and hospitable and liked kids, but I was shy around grown-ups, and when I was there I took care not to show too much exuberance.

Boyd's brother Ben was a quiet but extremely accomplished young man, the only kid in town who built his own skiff, *Banshee*. She wasn't exactly like any other skiff, certainly no match for a Butler except in very light weather, but as Dr. Johnson wrote about something else, "we are surprised that it is done at all." Having built eighteen of the foolish little boats in an equipped shop, and having swapped gossip with other commercial builders, I will testify that it cannot be done in wood in less than three hundred hours. I built only to order, charged a thousand dollars per boat the first year; five years later the price of the last one was only twelve hundred fifty dollars. I didn't expect to get rich building them; worked for prestige and because I loved them. Today lots of grown-up kids build their own, and a complete set of plans and specifications is available.

If you want one commercially built, it will be of fiberglass and cost you around ten thousand dollars. And to keep its weight comparable with the weight of a wooden boat, so the two can race fairly, ballast is built in, and this incorporation of lead is a source of endless trouble. They build a few every year of these expensive, outmoded, unstable craft. I puzzle why and conclude it is because the competition is so keen. You could be sailing bathtubs, but if the racing is good, and the company, people will flock to get aboard. There is at least one cocktail party every Saturday night and another Sunday in which the day's skiff race is resailed over and over, and if you were not racing yourself, it is unbearably tiresome. For me it gets harder every year to remember how important these races and these discussions once were to me.

Ben White endures, an important part of the past, around ninety by now, always understated, always erect, still a bit lean. He it was who first came out with the idea of a Yacht Club Association, first purpose of which was to bail me out. I was giving such superb safety coverage of the races, teaching all the children to sail and to square dance and going broke doing it.

Ben had four sons, the brightest boys in the village, all of whom worked at least one summer at Pecks' Boats. Lunch hour there in those days was an excitement the Harvard Faculty Club might envy; competitions in parodying T. S. Eliot, brain games like that. Only Ben's pretty little red-headed daughter escaped. Ben's second son, Jim, was the most challenging intellect I ever met. He went on from Pecks' to Harvard Law, where he was head of the *Harvard Law Review*. Then taught law in Chicago. His book *The Legal Imagination* is overwhelming. Much of it is too erudite for me, yet it is all light and fun.

And talking of Jim White puts me in mind of the girl he married, Connie Southworth. She was one of the series of pretty girls who ran my office after Betty gave up, a striking little blond with great musical talent. Her father, a lawyer from Cleveland, was a strong supporter of mine. I built a skiff for Connie and an outboard runabout for one of her brothers. And to her father, after his first devastating heart attack, I sold, without meaning to, a marvelous motor yacht, formerly a thirty-eight-foot Coast Guard cutter which had been listed with me for sale. This boat I took to Florida for him, and aboard this boat he had the second heart attack and died. Jim

White and Connie Southworth both raced skiffs and square danced and knew each other; they didn't meet at my boat-yard. But they noticed each other there. She was intellectu-ally his match, which he was reluctant to acknowledge in anybody, so their marriage didn't last, but I loved them both and still do though they don't come to Cotuit anymore. Before she took up with Jim, Connie had a crush on me, and I must confess, or maybe boast, I had one on her. But nothing came of it. She was far too smart even at sixteen.

After Ben's wife (also named Connie) died, he was a good husband to two lovely women in succession. First of these was my old love Helen Cobb, by then a widow too. She got Alzheimer's and died. Ben was an outstanding achiever with-out ever raising his voice. And for Ben's idea of a parents' association I will always be grateful. The Association's taking over in later years what the kids used to do for themselves and do better is inevitable, the future made manifest. It is the result of the refusal I keep coming back to, the refusal of peo-ple to take responsible control of the number of their chil-dren while insisting on controlling their behavior.

Next place beyond White's (the elder Whites sold it after Boyd's death, moved to Hyannisport) was a lot smaller than theirs but also reached from the water to Main Street. Owned, when I first knew the area, by Alan Crawford, who was not related to Lowell or to any other of the old society families. Alan was a printer from around Weymouth, work-ing class and talked that way, a no-nonsense guy with whom I, wearing my harbormaster's hat, had at first many disagree-ments. He didn't approve of the things I let boat people, some of whom were my customers, get away with and specifically of what I let myself get away with. He frowned on the way I so often kept my boat tied up all day and all night to the town wharf, of which I was in charge. Admittedly, I should not have done so; it was just easier, I was so busy and used the boat so often, and rowing out to my mooring as everybody else had to do took so much time, of which I had so little, that I just let myself do it. Justified it as having a rescue boat quickly available, like a fire engine. True, but only an excuse. *The Big Wheel* and I did actually save a couple boats that had chafed through their moorings in storms and were headed for the beach, but nobody else thought keeping my boat there was justified. This was the closest to corrupt I ever got, and partly because of people like Alan, I soon gave it up. I was still growing up, and I hope I grew in integrity too.

Thereafter, Alan Crawford and I became good friends and he became a good customer. He bought a new boat from me, among other things. On the small lot, in the days before WOE, he built no fewer than three houses, two of which were for summer rental and my memory of him as a great guy survives. He felt things intensely; he and two of his three children all died relatively young. But Alan died a rich man; bought a tract of undeveloped land on the Cotuit side of Popponessett Bay and put in roads and house lots.

Beyond Crawford's (back again on Main street, Cotuit) the bluff got even steeper, the grassy foreshore dwindled quite away and the beach at the foot of the bluff was very narrow. The next place, a huge house on a tiny lot, was further enlarged and turned into a modern resort hotel and classy restaurant, went through a series of owners, all undercapitalized. The last of them was put out of business by WOE when they got too greedy and put in public dockage. WOE got a court decision, and they had to demolish their new, very classy pier. I would have been with them in this nasty public washing of local linen and against the moneyed machinations of WOE, but the innkeepers were so arrogant and nasty, as well as reputedly crooked, that I held my tongue. Not that my tin sword would have made much difference in this battle of the pipsqueak giants.

And now we come to the premises of the two former churches, called even in the 1920s "Freedom Hall" and "Mariners' Lodge." Of these churches is told one of the funniest stories of all about Cotuit. I do not vouch for the authenticity of the funny details—Betty says ain't a word of it true, but my wife has become a pillar of the church while I remain more like a bomb ticking under it—and we can neither of us vouch for the verity of events which took place in the preceding century. An atheist is just as human as a Christian; he will believe and pass on a story because it is beautiful or funny, regardless of its truth. I pass it on as authentic.

These two churches, the Methodist and the Congregational, stood side by side and they couldn't agree on anything beyond the inspired absurdity of Divine intervention. So, when the preacher in one was preaching against this or that sin, like adhering to the wrong denomination, the organ and choir in the other were inspired to drown him out. Him and his false doctrine!

Years went by with the village split by this great schism. Progress progressed. Change changed hands, and the division of one congregation into two warring factions side by side was costing everybody money. Debts were more and more expected to be paid in cash rather than in quahogs. Finally a Methodist spoke to a Congregationalist and got a civil answer, and they agreed to federate, each yielding as little as possible. Nobody went so far as to agree to meet in the other's building; they built a third building in another part of town and all moved into it. The whole theological fracas, of course, fills a village atheist with exceeding great glee, even though it happened before I was born.

The two churches, side by side, still stand, no longer consecrated. The one to the north, the first one you come to in this tour heading south parallel to the shore, is the Freedom Hall I keep referring to, property not of the village, which still does not exist, but of the Cotuit Fire and Water District, the meeting place of this village which, in the face of all evidence, still believes that talk is essential to government even when there is nothing to govern. Go figure. It has folding chairs, basketball hoops of regulation height at each end, steel mesh over the lights in the high ceiling, a tiny stage with the curtain I mentioned. In the smaller, handsomer building, the one with the steeple still standing, Mariners' Lodge of the Masonic Order meets, its membership smaller every year.

As with churches, so with fraternal lodges. Cotuit once supported not one but two. In Santuit, way at the north end of Main Street, is another hall, the Grange. Being composed of and devoted to the needs of farmers, the Grangers are all dead. The hall was for a while taken over by a third such group: EPAC Grotto, Nobles of the Mystic Shrine, affiliated with the Masons but separate. That lodge is also defunct and the building seeking new owners. Fraternal groups have run out of young men eager to pay into the treasury for the privilege of learning a secret language in which to communicate secret nonsense to each other. All these groups make a big deal of never asking anyone to join, but I have been discreetly invited to join all three. I should be proud.

So Cotuit's two warring churches (reminds me of Omar's "two and seventy jarring sects") joined into one, but the ancient feud breaks out occasionally. For years they agreed to choose ministers alternately from the Methodist and from the Congregational (who now call themselves something silly, nondescriptive) ministries. They now, nondescriptively, call themselves the Federated Church, so used to the title that Bob Hayden's youngest daughter, Cindy, one of the most outspoken and energetic children I have ever seen, once said of herself, "I'm a Federated." The feud breaks out when least expected, most recently in a failure to agree on what hymnbooks should replace the worn-out ones. Methodist hymnbooks or hymnbooks from the other sect? Betty was right in the middle of it, trying to settle the fracas before it defederated the federation. For a while there were two different hymnbooks in every rack, a red one and a blue one, and worshipers were directed from the pulpit which one to use this time. I'm not sure how it worked out; think some anonymous benefactor paid for a set of one or the other out of his own pocket, so those are the ones they chose. Free is free. I'm not sure about this; I go into a church only when one of my friends is being married. Or buried.

Still, I have to give this church its due: it had for years a black minister, an immigrant from Africa itself. And it has today an even more astonishing minister: a pretty, red-headed lady. Incredible in a congregation of elderly conservatives in rural New England. They're doing something right! My wife Betty was influential in both these choices.

Across Main Street from the two former churches stands a far more significant building, for years devoted to the care of our bodies rather than of our souls, whether more successfully or less so I leave to those less prejudiced than I. For here was the home, office and dispensary of Dr. Don Higgins. Don carried on an old-time practice right up to the time of his retirement, I think in the 1960s. It still operated the way medicine was practiced when few patients had automobiles and few considered the option of going to the tiny hospital in Hyannis, the time before the Cotuit fire department had an ambulance or thought of needing one. Dr. Higgins saw patients in their homes or in the office in his home. And rather than leaving his office with a prescription on paper to be filled at the drugstore (there was none), you came out with the medicine itself, from the doctor's extensive stock of remedies and placebos. By the time I knew him, he had begun to acknowledge more up-to-date practices, was on the staff of Cape Cod Hospital, no longer so tiny, where he specialized in anesthesia and delivering babies, including two of our three. But right up to the time he closed his office, gave the house to his son for his growing family and moved himself and Mary into their summer cottage halfway down to the beach and began wintering in Florida, he kept right on filling his own prescriptions. For a while, right into the second half of the twentieth century, Dr. Higgins maintained the strangest medical practice seen this century: nothing but house calls; no office hours at all. You could have an appointment at his office in the hospital, which nobody did, or you could wait till he came to your house. He always came.

Don Higgins was Past Master of Mariners' Lodge, and it is fitting that his summer cottage, halfway down the bluff, was in the shadow of the lodge. Even more fitting that his son Reid and his wife have likewise moved out of the house on Main Street into this cottage to make room for another generation. Life insists on going on.

Dr. Higgins' medical theory was based on just one demonstrable fact: something is always better than nothing. For the villager with persistent aches and pains, persistent fainting spells, a persistent cough, he had a persistent remedy: sugar pills. If white ones don't help, try pink. So much of what ails one goes on in one's mind that the patient's mind is where he applied the cure. So the doctor's treatment is no greater and no less than the parson's; both are treating infirmities of the mind, both relying on faith.

Perhaps it was because of this attitude that the doc failed for years to diagnose my chronic appendicitis until it became so acute I diagnosed it myself. Just in time. Dr. Higgins, once alerted where to look, got the troops together in the middle of the night. Called in Dr. Chute the surgeon, got the damn thing out, saved my life. I might go on, like any old man, about my appendix. It has comic elements, and all the doctors at Harvard missed it as absurdly as Don Higgins, but it has really nothing to do with my growing up in Cotuit. But before I continue down Main Street and down the shore, I must recount the end of Dr. Chute.

He lived in Osterville, not in Cotuit, but how he died involves this village. It is, after all, still a fishing port, and jolly, good-natured Dr. Chute went fishing off here with a friend and the friend's young son late one afternoon in one of those lightweight wooden fishing boats then popular, factory built by a firm called "Lyman." These boats are constructed of plywood ripped into planks which are put together, like shingled or clapboarded houses, so that each plank overlaps its neighbor. Thus each seam becomes a sort of girder, two planks thick and riveted together. The longitudinal strength thus achieved takes the place of a heavy keel and rigid framing. The "long ships" of the Vikings were built (though not of plywood) in just this way for just this reason.

Just off Cotuit, in Nantucket Sound, there is a popular fishing spot known as "Horseshoe Shoal" where the water, in one place so far out you can't see land, is less than a foot deep. Just south of this spot lies (or did then, about 1950-something) the wreck of a sizable vessel which the army used for a target to train fliers during the war. This wreck was marked by the stump of a mast at low tide but by nothing at all most times. Now, following the well-known disregard of fishermen for anything farther than the end of the line, Dr. Chute and party ran over this mast and punched a hole in the bottom of the Lyman, which sank so quickly they barely had time to get off one radio call for help. So everybody at once put out for Horseshoe in whatever boat he had. All except for Dick Pierce, who was captain of a ponderous wooden motor yacht in Osterville, who stood out into the Sound in another direction, doing, I suppose, instinctive math in his head, figuring the precise set and drift of the swift current at that hour of that day.

Three hours later, in total darkness, he came to the sole survivor, the boy clinging still to the engine box. This was long before the invention of precise navigation by satellite; it was the result of precise knowledge of local conditions and precise handling of the vessel, a feat I have never known surpassed. I make a sort of hobby of reading about rescues at sea, but nothing I ever heard of touches this for precision. I pay Dick Pierce the respect he deserves in this account of life in Cotuit. I have never heard of anything like it.

Next to the Higginses dwelt the Lenares and then my irascible friend J. Goddard Wright. These three seem to have lived on little parcels of shore, all reached by a common unpaved lane over the bluff and along the edge of it, mountain road building among miniature mountains made of soft sand bound together by tree roots. Cut down a tree and you may lose the road next year. Then the bluff ends and is succeeded by a spot of true salt marsh where what rain falls on the low land behind the bluffs makes its way finally to the sea. There is no recognizable stream or watercourse, but here there is a low place between the hills and Main Street takes a small dip, and this marsh indicates where the fresh water ponds up and marsh grass grows and the water is brackish.

Nobody lives on the bay side of Main Street except in one house so close to the road it seems to be practically under it, but before that comes a gap where it is actually possible to see the harbor from the street. Sometimes. I don't know who owns the northern part of this marsh, but there is a little turnout where you can park and look across the swamp at the water. Sometimes. Succeeding owners have planted, uprooted and replanted a row of evergreen shrubs to prevent anyone who does not pay taxes for the privilege from enjoying this view. Successive owners have successively planted and uprooted these. All according to the whim of the owner. Botanists ought to develop a row of such plantings joined together in a strip, sort of like Christmas decorations, to be set in place if the owner feels grouchy at breakfast and dug up and stored if he feels better after he hears from his broker.

Across Main Street, on the inland side, was once the home and studio of Reggie Bowles the painter (that is, the artist—Cotuit has always had plenty of house painters), who seems to have specialized in flying ducks. He had a considerable cult locally, but I always thought his ducks looked like flying decoys, carved out of wood (so I've become an art critic yet). Next along, at the corner of Piney Road, was the home of Arthur and Ida Hale and of their daughter Barbara, the blond of the world. No relation to the Hollywood brunette of the same name, Perry Mason's sidekick; our Barbie was far more beautiful, as all our swains would proclaim. In the Hales' parlor was a life-size, full-length portrait of Barbara by Reggie, much the best thing of Reggie's I have ever seen, with Barbie looking her loveliest in this incredible likeness of features and expression. Sexy without trying or even aware. Except for a season when she went steady with Bob Bramley, she dated anybody who asked her out and treated us all the same. Above all, stressed having fun. Fun she was; only time I ever saw her disconcerted was when she forgot to pay attention and let me drive her one-armed through Cotuit center right past the two village gossips, old Link Sturgis and his contemporary, Julius, whose last name I never learned. Every daughter in town knew not to drag her reputation in sight of these guys, who always sat in front of Birja's all day and half the night waiting for a character to ruin. I might have taken pride in being known to be that close to a girl that beautiful, but honestly it never entered my mind. Barbie was, as I say, fun to go out with. But not for sex; sex was no part of a date with the princess.

But poor Jack Brackett, my mate on *Ariel*, my Fourth of July gunner, wasn't having fun. He was more in love than any of us, hopeless of course. Jack was singularly unbeautiful, and he had no fortune. No more chin than Andy Gump in the funny papers. He spoke with just a trace of cleft palate. He was blond, almost albino, though his eyes were blue, not pink. He was always doing something crazy to amuse us all. Never seen without a bottle of beer. He was bright, one of the smartest of the kids I grew up with, so long as his wits weren't addled with hopeless love. Or beer. Bright enough to realize his hopelessness and get clear. He left Cotuit and never came back, made a fortune in heavy equipment during the war and drank it all up as fast as he could.

Last I heard of him was a series of phone calls, more or less drunk, from California. These were recent—late 1960s—when I was thinking of selling my boatyard and retiring at not much over fifty. Jack was evidently so far gone in alcohol that he only heard that part of a conversation, or of a rumor, that he wanted to hear. He would sell out in the West and return to Cotuit to buy into my business and become my partner. I hadn't invited him, hadn't heard from him in like twenty years, and the way he sounded over the phone, I didn't want to be in business with him nohow. But I couldn't get through to him; he was on his way.

Then I heard no more till I got a call from his more serious brother Harrison in Florida, I think, asking what I knew of Jack. I told him the facts, not the feelings, of those phone calls. Harry called me back a few days later: turned out that poor Jack was dead; he had indeed withdrawn all he owned, in cash, and had been rolled and robbed on some sleazy street in Los Angeles.

It all shows the awesome power of beauty. None of it is in any way Barbie's fault, but because of her Jack went off the rails and never got back on. If she had been charitable and married him, he probably would have turned out a drunk just the same. (Alcoholism, we are told, is not caused by circumstances, but the tendency is inborn. Genetic or something.) She would only have ended up with a drunken husband, which she had not asked for, done nothing to encourage or deserve. Gentle and understanding always, she had treated Jack no differently from any of her many suitors. She is an example of my notion of Aristotle's notion of the nature of God: the unmoved mover, the object of affection. She moved Jack profoundly and was unmoved herself.

VII
LOVE AND COMMERCE
IN THE OLD DAYS

BEFORE GOING ON, I think I must pause and do something about *when*. If I am to call this book "history," and expect readers to put up with my contempt for numbers, it will get more and more confusing. I began in the 1920s but here I am suddenly up in the 1960s. I jump around this way, organized not by time but by where a person lived or an event took place as I work my way southwest along the shore of Cotuit Harbor. My story begins where it does because I landed first in that part of town and my acquaintance spread first northeast and now west along the shore.

At Hale's, Main Street forks and Ocean View Avenue goes left and follows, very approximately and not very close, the curve of the shore. And the first house on the shore side is called the Lilacs. It was for years the residence of my particular friend Bob Hayden, dealer in used buildings and even more used building materials and in antiques and near-antiques salvaged from demolished buildings. Bob and Libby Hayden and all their five children loved land and real estate as much as they loved antiques. Libby hung on to antiques too, but they both hung on like barnacles to land and were reluctant to let any of it go. Their daughter Jane (or does she spell it Jayne? somebody I know does) still lives in the Lilacs, as Bob's father, Dr. Hayden the dentist (before my time), did. Bob and Libby, many years ago, built themselves a large homestead of selected preused lumber, fir paneling from a church Bob had demolished on the army training camp after the war, colorful roof of used flat stones, all sorts of good used stuff, and Libby started her life's work anew, filling the basement and every hidey-hole with old treasures from Bob's work or from auctions to which she accompanied him. But they hung on to the Lilacs, renting it summers until Jane and her two beautiful children (her husband was killed in Vietnam) needed it to move into. She lives there still, but her kids are now grown up and in residence only for visits.

Bob had a store, a service area for his trucks, a used-lumber yard, on the state highway just outside Cotuit. He called it "Treasure Highland," and in it he had for sale things like stained-glass windows from demolished churches, carved granite or marble cornerstones from demolished banks, postal scales from demolished post offices, hand tools from defunct crafts—I bought there an old-time ship's carpenter's adze—all cumulative evidence of the Hayden vision, which saw value beneath any old surface.

Hayden had been to college, and in him, as in me, it came out in a fascination with words. Only he specialized; liked his words polysyllabic. Never use a short one when you can find a long, abstruse, archaic one that will say it just as well. This was one of his ways of turning loose all the things churning in his mind, things like the unhappy state of the world, the frailties of man, the inevitability of suffering, the politician's transparent efforts to clothe in decent garments his true motives, on and on. It all came tumbling out in a polysyllabic stream. To him, my beard was my "hirsute appendage." Conversation with Hayden was, as I said at his funeral, an adventure.

To give this part of my story a proper date, I was in 1952 trying to carry on my business on Coolidge property. I had put in the foundation of a boatbuilding shop on the site of the former boathouse, demolished in the hurricane of 1944. But Aunt Amy was still alive, nuttier every day, and all her property was held by a Boston bank — State Street Trust Company, no less — as conservator. It is the duty of a conservator to conserve, that is, the bank said, to allow no changes during the lifetime of the incompetent he represents. The bank put down its heavy banking foot. Anne and her husband, Professor Ed Moore, had given me permission and support, and they were in line to inherit the whole works. But not yet; not until the old lady was no more. They approved of my quiet, community-interested way of doing business. They loved my wife and our three boys. But from the financial point of view, my plans were of questionable value to the estate. Its land intersects the curving shore on a front only a few hundred feet long, though there were who knew how many acres fanning out from that short bit of shoreline; what I wanted to do would have changed the whole nature of the place from summer residential to village business, as in the days of Sylvanus Porter. My new building had to be up and operating right quick before the new zoning kicked in. Which could not now be done.

Anyhow, I went on doing business. About 1950 we moved into the Coolidges' dirt-floored four-car garage, a block up the hill and round a corner. We were growing every year. I bought from Churbuck some obsolete, heavy woodworking machinery. I was teaching at a local high school in winter, hiring more and more kids to help get the boats out and commissioned in spring and put away in fall. I recall a scene from before we moved, 1949, my senior year in Harvard: boats, mostly Cotuit skiffs, everywhere; kids, boys and girls both, sanding and painting on them while I supervised from the front porch of the Porter House, book on my lap, reviewing Chaucer. The scene had a happy ending: got an A on the exam, which consisted entirely of spot passages, for identification and comment, from *The Canterbury Tales* in Middle English. It might have been written just for a mind like mine, which Professor Whiting had. And all the skiffs got in the water on time for the opening race on Fourth of July.

So, in 1952 I approached Bob Hayden, who had no more cash than I but who owned acres of land all over the place. Would he set up and rent to me a secondhand building out on the highway near Treasure Highland, technically outside Cotuit, out of reach of WOE and its zoning zealots? It took a while; money was not a necessary part of any deal with Hayden, but discussion was. But with all the discussion, Betty and I were unable to find out what the rent would be. Hayden didn't know, but he wouldn't come out and say it that simply. Mumbled about finding time to figure his costs. We agreed that if things went well, I would have the option to buy the place if I ever got the money. A site was chosen, two and a quarter acres next door to Bob's own establishment, and Hayden's men (he employed like twenty) set up foundation piers a suitable setback from the road. Then, one spring morning in 1953, Hayden's biggest truck, a bright red war-surplus International with A-frame crane and huge winch on the front (it's running still) rolled in behind a flashing blue police escort, towing the former Sandwich freight depot on a set of Hayden's wheels, the roof cut into four panels and laid flat on top to reduce overhead clearance. Two of Hayden's heroes were up there to push up utility wires so the building would go under, laughing and singing as they came, the load filling Route 28 pole to pole.

They stopped, still tying up the road, right in front of the site, and turned into the site. This involved more of Hayden's daredevils underneath, reaiming the wheels, repositioning the truck. Then a utility wire hooked under a corner where the eaves would be. One of the young men on top leaned over with a wooden pry and got it loose. It said *boing* and sprang up and back like a piano wire, took the boy's hat off. If he had been standing erect, his head would have been in it. That boy stood up there, roared with laughter and danced a jig on the roof. That's what it took to work for Hayden.

Railroad buildings, like railroad everything, are singularly overbuilt. As Dave Leland used to say, "Hell for stout!" There wasn't a stick in it less than two inches thick. They moved the wheels out and jacked it down onto the foundation, set the roof back up, did some minimum finishing, doors and partitions to my specifications. Show windows cut into the wall to fit a couple of used pieces of plate glass from Hayden's stock. One of them came out of a former post office and had "U.S. Post Office" lettered across the top edge. To avoid confusing the stupid, we installed it with this border at the bottom, so it read upside down. But the customers were stupider than that; they still asked if this was really a post office. So for this stupid question I programmed myself with a stupid answer: "Sure. Hayden and I are in opposition and this is our opposition post office. If you don't like the mail you been getting, you can get your mail from us. If this goes well, next year we're going to open an opposition town meeting." They'd go away shaking their heads. What other answer you going to give to such a dumb question?

But now Hayden knew his costs; rent would be sixty dollars a month and, though nobody said so, payable when I got it. Hayden did me the honor of treating me like a native, as great an honor as being entrusted with Aunt Amy and her cortege. It was over two years before I ever paid him a dime, then I put in a gas station (at the gasoline company's expense) and supplied gas to his trucks until he owed me a couple thousand in his turn. Our agreement was a hundred percent verbal, including any rent at all and the part where I had the right to buy the place sometime in the future at a price then to be agreed on. At intervals, on request, Hayden would move in another building for me, finally a total of five quickie army-surplus shacks from the defunct training base, and when asked, blacktopped the drives. The rent went up each time, but his old trucks were insatiable.

And since I have interrupted my narrative again, might as well continue the interruption and tell how it came out. My wife, my father and my boss carpenter, a colorful Newfoundlander, began to get on me about building what had begun to look like a successful business on somebody else's property, not a word on paper. My dad offered to pay for the place, but we couldn't get Hayden to name a price. He was evasive, promised to name one real soon, but weeks went by and his evasiveness added to their anxiety and they added to mine. So we went shopping for another site. I knew no better than to think I needed waterfront, and lawyer Al Knight came up with some, at the head of Popponessett Bay where the water is only six inches deep at low tide and the mud is bottomless. A shallow pothole by now almost entirely silted up. I was confident that I would be able to dredge a basin in it with the propellor of *The Big Wheel*. To acquire it, we had to buy up all Congressman Gifford had died owning in the Town of Mashpee.

Mashpee has a picturesque history: almost all of it was Indian territory, with the land held in common in the Indian way, and when the Wampanoag tribe, in the 1870s, persuaded the state to break up the "district" (being state, not federal, it was not called a "reservation") and divide the tribal lands among tribe members, there was a long line of developers waiting to buy out the Indians with whiskey and trade goods. Near the head of the line stood Congressman Charlie Gifford, who for a while owned most of the town.

The games he played with all that almost worthless land, buying and selling, taking ten-dollar deposits and taking back mortgages which were never recorded, putting tracts in his wife's name and in the name of some corporations he formed and then dying with nobody knowing what he owned and under which entity. It all passed to his only daughter, Mrs. Florence Gifford Claussen, who had no idea what she owned in Mashpee, didn't need the money and was fretted by the descendants of unknown people all over the country, who were trying to find out where was the lot left by their grandparents and was it worth anything. Mrs. C. knew no more than they and was embarrassed to have to admit it every time another of them came along, so for its assessed value, incredibly little, she sold us a deed which included the words "Everything I own in the Town of Mashpee." The land amounted, as far as we have been able to find out, to somewhere around a hundred acres, most of it neither recorded nor taxed and looking exactly as it had when the Indians sold it. Gifford had maps made of it, ruled off into straightedge lots about twenty-five feet wide, made on tracings of the old commissioners' maps of the former Indian District. But I met the guy, by then very old, who drew the maps, and he told me he had charged scroungy old Gifford ten dollars for the work in about 1911.

He was a civil engineer and surveyor, but for that price he had never set foot on any of it, just ruled it up into paper lots and put numbers on the paper. No regard for contours or topography; some of the lots are kettle holes or parts of them, sides almost vertical, about fifty feet deep. Gifford seems to have gone around Washington with a pocketful of deeds which he peddled to anybody he met, to anybody who wanted a favor. That's how a congressman gets his kicks.

The adventures we had finding out more or less how much land we owned are a comic story, and what we found out about the way Gifford operated is even more comical, but nothing to do with this book. Betty went over to the courthouse and registry in Barnstable (the one that's a village), the county seat, and taught herself to be a hotshot title examiner. One thing she learned, and was able to prove, was that he had died owning twice as much as was recorded, which the town was glad to assess to us and begin collecting taxes on. And she became enraptured with the old deeds, all in longhand, dealing with vague bounds, some of which extended from an oak tree to a haystack. But Gifford was not quite stupid, and he had kept the waterfront in larger lots (some of those back from the water were only twenty feet wide), and title to that much of his estate was clear and clearly ours.

Here I chose a site for the new boatyard, and we started clearing and putting in a road, and Johnny made a new friend, Othal Curtis, who owned the bulldozer. He and Johnny loved each other; Curtis taught him and let him run the machine to practice. Still, to this moment, John Peck can wield a bulldozer as delicately as a scalpel. Unbelievable. But my papa did not have that kind of money, and I still had none at all, so we shelved the project. Meanwhile, that land, all shore and wooded upland, went right on increasing in value until it became too obviously valuable as home sites to waste by building boats on.

The Wampanoags just at this moment took us all to court, asserting that their tribe still owned the whole town, that the state action closing the district without consent of Congress had all along been illegal and that we and all others who took title through Gifford and his contemporaries had never owned any of it. This was a drama with no possible happy ending, no way somebody acting in good faith would not get hurt. It went all the way to the U.S. Supreme Court, which decided in favor of the whites. Since money had never been important to me, I was not quite silently in favor of making a deal with the tribe, my selfish purpose being to prevent all this beauty from being violated to build summer and retirement homes for nasty people. But the court forestalled me; I ended up on the losing side again, but not noisily enough to earn much enmity among the white interlopers of Mashpee, among whom I had never had many friends or customers anyway. Except the Indians, who were and remain the gentlest, most polite, most honest (and at the same time least reliable) people I have ever known. Winning and losing in court had nothing to do with their gentle good nature and kindness, before and after.

Betty and I carried on with the siege of Hayden. She was endlessly patient, waiting him out. He dropped by for coffee most Sunday mornings, bringing a nasty little dog he had. We talked in long sentences with long words, wore him down. He had meant it when he said we could buy him out; he just couldn't bear to part with any land, and this made him reluctant to think about what he would take for a bit of it. We had a powerful ally in the Internal Revenue Service. It and Hayden could never agree on a figure for his income tax for this year and for many years past. It wanted him to keep books its way; he had a first-class accountant on his payroll, but both he and IRS agreed that nothing could be "finalized" until you had a figure for inventory. Hayden couldn't even find his inventory, never mind count it. The antiques were easy; just shut your eyes and name a figure, but the used planks, boards and timbers and hardware were worth nothing until somebody wanted them. Though they were the main stock in trade, they had no wholesale value at all. Things have sure changed; in those days it paid Hayden to keep two men employed full-time pulling old nails out of old planks and hammering them straight, sorting them into old kegs. That's how cheap labor was right up into the 1960s and how great the demand for used building materials. Hayden's income tax went unsettled year after year. IRS was reluctant to close him; he employed like twenty men, maybe half of them illiterate in English, many of them alcoholic, and neither Uncle Sam nor Massachusetts wanted them on relief forever or to end up owning that unfindable, uncountable inventory, piles of old boards hidden in the undergrowth for acres behind Treasure Highland. They let it run on year after year, but they were getting sick of it. Poor Hayden was in a cash bind. So finally he said so-and-so dollars, and we bought the property with help from a mortgage from the bank and a second mortgage from Hayden, which we set about paying off in gasoline. Pecks' Boats now belonged to Pecks.

Bob Hayden was the second of the four friends with whom I was for years on a "last-name basis." He always called me just "Peck" and I always addressed him as "Hayden." And I was his tenant for like twenty years, and in all that time, whether he owed me two thousand real dollars or I owed him three thousand, neither of us ever asked the other for money.

We did business in an older way, in which cash was less important. And I am outrageously proud of being accepted into this club of old-time Cape Codders who did business this way among themselves. It included most of the boatbuilders and repairers, all of whom gave me credit and advice and lent me tools. Men like Chet Crosby and his cousin and competitor Manley Crosby, Rupe Nichols, Floyd Van Duser, Barry Kingman, Hume MacDougall, Forbes MacGregor, Spaulding Dunbar, all the old-time boatyards. It seems I may be the last of them, and it is almost a duty to write it down before it is altogether forgotten. If a customer wanted his boat blue, I would go over to either Crosby yard and buy a quart of blue paint. Charge it. They gave me a trade discount as well as waiting until the customer paid me. Toward the end, when the Boat Dealers Association renamed itself the Marine Trades Association and began filling up with quick-buck discounters, people indistinguishable from car salesmen, I gave that group my parting speech: "My competitors put me in business and I'd like to see the next man get the same break I got."

Hayden was always picturesque, right up to the time when cigarettes killed him. The Federated Church was filled for his funeral, as was the adjoining meeting room. Lines of former employees, many of them barely literate, waiting to say something in his praise. In my turn I spoke of the eccentric words. No talked, trying to acknowledge all th remote, of his subject to get a straight answer out of him. wonder it was so hard

Right below the Lilacs on the shore, actually in the water, was an oyster house, neatly shingled, wherein resided Jim Bells. I believe he and his family had a proper house out on School

Street, but Jim himself was most of the time on the shore. He was another character, incomparably picturesque. One would have thought he dressed to promote some image the way I do, I with my salty white beard, but not so. He was a simple man. He was dark; some of his ancestors were Cape Verdean Portuguese, but at least as many were Wampanoag. He was handsome; wore a black moustache which extended drooping out both sides of his face. Always wore high rubber boots, turned down low and floppy. Wore a slouch hat and a knife in a black leather sheath of Indian workmanship. He looked like a boy's idea of a pirate, but he was gentle and loved children, with whom he was endlessly patient. Taught them to row and scull, took them out in his motor launch *Billy*, a handsome double-ender "with a four-cylinder Gray into it," taught them to knot and splice. He had a beautiful varnished rowing skiff which rumor had it he had once rowed to Nantucket. Just one more of the attractions this place had for children.

So what became of him? One summer we came back and he was gone. It was said that he froze to death, drunk in that oyster house. The house stood empty for years, but it's gone long since. Just the memory of a grand old man in the minds of a few of the kids he befriended. My friend Marcia Toby Martin has written a little monograph about what he meant

Beyond the road, the shore curves back eastward much more sharply that the road, forming what is called on the chart childhood as Codman's Point, at least to the sailing kids. The club had a racing buoy, a red and white spar off the end of it which they called the Codman Buoy. It was an important buoy because the prevail-

Marcia, younger than I, is gone too. We all memoir.

ing wind in summer is "always" southwest when it isn't northeast, and the prevailing racecourse is therefore almost always "Codman—Taussig three times around" when it isn't "Taussig—Codman three times around." This takes the race back and forth past the Loop Beach and by some of the most pretentious homes, in and out of the harbor entrance where everybody can keep an eye on the kids and watch the sport.

The point was called Codman's because of its owner, Mr. Codman, the well-known Bostonian who is remembered for, among other peculiarities, being one of the world's most re-nowned "smoke-eaters," a firefighting nut of the most intense kind. A rich and distinguished citizen, he led every move-ment to improve the organization, equipment, training and pay of the Boston fire department. They gave him a special badge which got him inside all fire lines, and he ended his life as a professional with the official job of fire commissioner of the city. If his hobby extended to the Cotuit fire department, I never found out about it; he was an old man when I came here as a small child, and I never met him. Maybe he influ-enced us; Cotuit had the first motor-driven fire engine on Cape Cod, an American LaFrance chemical engine on a 1914 Model T chassis. This ancient little engine is here still, in run-ning condition, marvelously restored. I had a clumsy hand in its restoration when I was deputy chief of Cotuit and presi-dent of the Firemen's Association. I am a bit of a smoke-eater myself.

Relevant to my smoke-eating, I was out by myself one fall day in *The Big Wheel* pulling up moorings, using the salvage pump to wash the mud off them, and I got my hand jammed between a vee-belt and its pulley. It was not seriously injured, but it bled all over everything and made an awful mess. I got the boat tied up and myself home to Betty, who was bandaging me up, when we got a rescue alarm. Cyril Jones, who lived by himself in a small but handsome summer house at the foot of a lane leading shoreward between the Lilacs and Codmans', had evidently had a stroke the night before, but the maid had not found him until she went to see, at lunchtime, why he had not come down to breakfast. She found him on the floor and called us. I responded in time to drive the ambulance, and we loaded poor Cyril into it, he showing signs of life but not much more, and then we found blood on the ambulance bedding and discovered that my hand was still bleeding. I got somebody else to drive to the hospital, and I went home. Never thought of going to the hospital myself; why should I, when I had Betty waiting with the bandages at home, better than the whole Mayo Clinic?

But what consternation I thus caused in the Cape Cod Hospital! They went over poor Cyril for injuries and could find none, and they looked again. Nothing. Not a break in the skin. Our men had started up the ambulance and come home, and it was hours before they figured out that the blood was from the driver, not the patient. Some days life in Cotuit is just one farce after another. Cyril got better to the point where he could be driven around in his car, but he never regained the power of coherent speech. He occasionally used to be driven to my shop, where he would sit in the car and regale me with long discourses consisting of the only word he could pronounce: "Eggseggseggseggs." I related to him the comic tale of the blood on the sheets, in case he might understand more than he could say, but I'll never know if he understood any of it. He gave no sign.

Cyril had a sailboat, a little sloop with a modern Marconi rig of the class known as a "Lawley Fifteen," which he kept in his garage in winter and had me come and launch and rig every spring. These boats have a permanent lead ballast keel with a slot down the middle through which the centerboard, cut out of light sheet steel, pivots up and down. His neighbor Les Bendslev, who lived just across Ocean View, had another Lawley just like her, and hauling the heavy little things back and forth to water was a twice-a-year project. I had no trailer, just that light wooden skid which I dragged with rope behind the old Buick. It went forward as well as any trailer and was a lot easier to load, but there was no way to back it up. The Buick would not move on the beach even when not towing anything, so the last few yards to water had to be accomplished with planks and rollers, and those Lawleys with that shallow lead keel underneath were the most awkward loads we ever moved. I always launched them right near where they lived, down an unpaved lane, long and crooked, which led from beside The Lilacs down to a broad beach with shallow water at the edge where that marsh drains. First thing I acquired as soon as we had any money for decent equipment was a four-wheel-drive truck.

But that little lane down to the shore is there still and still barely passable, and many people swim at the foot of it and many keep their dinghies on the beach at its foot, but nobody will admit owning any of it. The town will not acknowledge knowing anything about it; I suppose if it was a town way people would expect the town to maintain it, and if any of its abutters claimed it they would have to pay taxes on it and kick the public off or be liable if anybody fell and hurt himself. So it just sits there, belonging to nobody, used by many, just as a lot of places used to be when I was a little kid. It is so narrow you can't even turn a car around at the bottom. Drop off into swamp on one side, steep hillside up toward Jones' house on the other. Have to back all the way out, around the sharp curves, trying to avoid the patches of soft sand. So, unless you are carrying something heavy, you don't drive down; you walk.

One more thing, though, about that rig I used instead of a trailer: explaining it is easy, but revealing what I called it and why is so complicated I don't know how to go about it. I called it my "helicopter" because, I would explain, it won't fly. This I made up to tease Patsy Platt, a lovely young lady I used to date who raced a skiff, lived across the water on Oyster Harbors, and whose father was an aeronautical engineer specializing in rotating wings. He had a contract to build helicopters for the Army Air Corps. He had a factory on the grounds of the Baldwin Locomotive Works, which was next door to the steel foundry where I worked before I joined the Coast Guard, and I could watch their experiments from our shop window. They kept their machine chained down, and it flew fine as far as I could see, right to the end of its tether. But only backwards. The Platt-Lepage helicopter never went into production, mainly because, Mr. Platt maintained, the government wouldn't give him a free enough hand to design what he wanted to. I was nerving myself up to propose to his daughter when I got a look at Betty. So all that survives of this relationship was the name of my helicopter, which formed part of the life of a whole generation of Cotuit kids until the Registry of Motor Vehicles made me take it off the road.

Codman's house is still standing, but there are now two or three others standing with it on the point. His is the big green one with the white chimneys, now occupied by a man named Sobin who owns the long beach both sides of the point and is perpetually at war with the whole neighborhood, defending his privacy on all of it. But there is history of another kind: between the smoke-eating Mr. Codman and the fire-eating Mr. Sobin, that house belonged to Mr. and Mrs. Sidney Kirkman, renowned for a nationally advertised product they manufactured: Kirkman's Soap. In its day, it was as well known as Ivory, and many thought it cleaned better. Kirkman's Pearl Borax was one product my cleanness-obsessed mother relied on. The Kirkmans were childless and seemed rather naive in the way they sought village popularity. When they first came here, Mr. Kirkman had a big motor yacht which was painted a sort of apple green, his yachting color, to which I promptly gave the name "USS *Pea Soup.*"

He had Crosby build him a pea-soup-colored Wianno Senior racing knockabout, the *Go Getta*, and, with a hotshot professional from Osterville, sailed in the races. When he grew too old to participate in Senior racing, which is a strenuous sport, he had Crosby build him an exact replica of one of these sloops scaled up to about twice lifesize and at last painted white instead of green and also named *Go Getta*.

The Kirkmans sought also to adopt the village in the manner of Cousin Lawrence. They gave generously to the library and to the cemetery, added to the cemetery some adjacent land whose titles had been muddied by the splashings of Congressman Gifford. In their efforts to make themselves Lord and Lady Bountiful to the village, they were dealing with independent (solely for the sake of independence) Yankee villagers who had been brought up to "loathe a Lord." They paid for expensive new curtains for the library and imagined this gave them final say in their color and how they were hung. The library board, a faction of very fierce ladies, undertook to disabuse them of this error. There seems to have been a scene so bitter that the Kirkmans went home and rewrote their wills, disinheriting the library and leaving everything to the Town of Barnstable, under trusteeship of the selectmen, income from the estate to be used forever for the benefit of "that portion of the Cotuit Cemetery to which the Kirkmans had previously contributed." A will so sure to start fights that one suspects it to have been an act of vengeance. The income, even before inflation, amounted to over a million dollars a year. Cash. My take on this at the time was that the dead were the only people in Cotuit who had ever been polite to the Kirkmans. Then they both died immediately, so it all went indeed to the cemetery.

At once arose throughout the village and throughout the town what I named the "Parlement of Ghouls," digging up legal ways to have the strict terms of the will set aside for the benefit of this or that worthy organization in which the individual ghoul had an interest. Even the selectmen, upon whom fell the impossible task of force-feeding all that money down the throat of the cemetery year after year forever, joined in seeking relief through the courts. Meanwhile, the Cotuit faction that was into sports managed to absorb tremendous quantities by hiring hotshot college-age ballplayers to work summers in the cemetery as a bottomless way to subsidize the local "amateur" ball team. In those days, Cotuit was unbeatable in evening baseball and during the day was plagued with wild, conceited and lecherous young men. And still the unspent surplus grew, and the rumors with it. Pirate ways always return as soon as there is rumor of booty. The pirate way to dispose of loot you can't spend and want to hang on to is to bury it; the cemetery board is said to have had its athletes dig a huge ditch in which they buried truckloads of enriched, imported topsoil. Allegations like that polarized the village, drove everybody not pre-convinced of the primary importance of baseball into the

Parlement of Ghouls. They petitioned the probate court (Bierce was the first to call it the "Crow-bait Court") to allow the will to be altered to conform with practical reality and with what it was prayed to construe as the Kirkmans' true intentions. I was on the library board by then, and by then I had joined the ghouls, had become a little ashamed of the antics of my neighbors in the presence of an estate. The crow-bait heard our prayer. Cemetery still gets first whack at the income, but what it can't find a legitimate way to spend now goes to other causes shown to have been dear to the Kirkmans: the Cotuit Library, other cemeteries in the town, other libraries.

The selectmen also got themselves down off a limb where they had climbed by retaining from sale Sidney's collection of valuable old books, more precisely of valuable bindings. He had many Victorian classics, which always come in long sets, expensively rebound in leather and gilt, fit to grace the office walls of an illiterate broker. Also his truly valuable collection of ship models, authentic in the best way; his models were crude because they were all carved right aboard the ships, by working seamen. And now we used some of his money to build a room onto the library to house them. Everybody got to swim in the Kirkman cesspool and came out smelling like a rose.

One anecdote I cannot bear to leave out: Right in the middle of all the fracas, Rhoda's husband died, and she caused to be erected on a prominent spot in the subject cemetery, fronting square on Putnam Avenue for all the world to admire, a bleddy-great tombstone bearing in large letters only one word: his name, COCKS. The Kirkman comic opera is now complete.

Except for one detail for me to gripe about: Once I was no longer on it, the library board, with its wealth, chose to throw away its card catalog and substitute computers. Which had the effect, in this now geriatric community, of making the entire collection inaccessible to anybody who cannot drive a computer or talk computese. We have already, to help us communicate, a language which is the glory of all who speak it, from Shakespeare to Foster Nickerson, and with one stroke of the computer we have rendered it obsolete. Shame!

Sure, the library is staffed with obliging ladies, but some of us can't bear to ask directions. I have been known to drive my car hundreds of miles in the wrong direction rather than "ask somebody." Not the librarian's fault, but some men are just like that, as psychiatry is finding out. It is all tied up with one's anxiety about one's manhood. Women don't suffer from this. It is one reason my wife won't drive anywhere with me. So I can never again use the library, and I resent it. I stubbornly refuse to replace our language with grunts and snorts like "www dot com org." The only recognizable part of this is "org," as in orgy. An orgy in garbage, like a dog in rotten meat. My grandfather was a city librarian, one of the few to deal with Carnegie face-to-face. My aunt Harriet was a college librarian. In protesting this "progress," I speak for generations of library people. I am, by my own choice, forever barred from "Web sites," can never order a tape of a public TV show. Org! Such hard-assed old men are deservedly left behind, but this village is now largely populated by just such old people. It is distressing that progress need be this wasteful of trained and valuable old minds. Everything is now aimed at developing the minds of the children; having failed year after year to teach them to read English, we are making tremendous strides in teaching them computese. Encouraging them to learn gibberish, and we are proud they do it so well. For centuries we have gotten by in school with nothing better than English; now all of a sudden, a child who must attend a school without computers is thought to be forever handicapped dot com!

VIII
NOT ALL CROOKS
ARE IN CONGRESS

T HERE IS, ALAS, no turning back. Continue south and west along the shore. Beyond Bluff Point the beach curves back, and Ocean View Avenue comes once again almost in view of the ocean, separated only by the width of the large estates. First of these was, in my childhood, named "Evergreen," the estate of R. M. Rolloson. Who he was or how he got so rich I never knew; he was a step ahead of any other local millionaire in having a truly pretentious yacht, at first *Bald Eagle*, white, gold and mahogany, a schooner of what looked to me then of enormous size. So big that she carried, when marine engines were ponderously heavy, an engine-driven launch which, when she was at her mooring off Rolloson's pier, was secured to her by a boat boom amidships. From this launch you climbed aboard (if you were so lucky—I never was) up an accommodation ladder (that means a folding flight of steps with a handrail) supported by a tackle from a davit. This incredible vessel was succeeded in a year or two by a black and gold schooner, *Janelburn*, no smaller and lacking none of the big yachty features, and even handsomer, looking longer and lower. But I have learned in the yacht business that a black boat looks inherently longer and lower than a white one. The schooner was rigged very like a grand-banker, but nobody could mistake her for a commercial ship with all that varnish.

Mrs. R. brought with her to the marriage a son or two, and she bore Rolloson one or two more. I never knew for sure how many boys there were in this family—four, I think—but I learned their reputation all over town just from hanging out at the grocery store or Gibbs' Sandwich Shop or Loring's Garage. The youngest of them was like ten years older than I; they all had cars, and I won't vouch for it, but I think they were all Packards, open ones. They ran with a crowd of similar spoiled young men, including two Shreves from my end of town, and they were all in constant trouble with the law, though I never heard of any criminal behavior. "Not mean, just wild."

They had a camp, back in the woods, reported to be better furnished than most homes, where they took bootleg liquor and wayward girls. I saw them in action just one time: they bought and in a single afternoon destroyed a priceless antique: a pre-1920 Peerless with what must have been the world's first V-8 engine. It was a convertible with two doors and a back seat, altogether a look ahead at what everybody was building and everybody was coveting right through the 1990s, a museum piece even in the 1920s when this happened. I was hanging around Loring's Garage, a place where something was always happening, always in slow motion, eating as usual from the store of apples in my shirt front, when they rolled in down the short drive behind the Cotuit Grocery—the build-ing's there yet, today some sort of arty establishment—tow-ing the Peerless behind one of the Packards. They had found the car jacked up in somebody's barn and had, perhaps, bought it. They borrowed one of Henry Loring's service batteries, filled its tank with Socony at his gas pump and towed it around the maze of dirt lanes back there until they got it running. It ran well, considering it had been sitting in a barn for years. Bunny Burns, the only Rolloson I knew by name, was driving, and he ran it into a brushpile. In his efforts to rock it back and forth so it would back out, it caught fire. I remember his very words: "The damn thing's on fire or something." It burned up right there. The Cotuit fire department arrived in the tinny Dodge fire engine with the pump out front, too late to save it. They saved the woods. Mr. Seabury Childs, who constituted the local fire chief and police force all in one, spoke severely to the miscreants, but they hadn't done anything for which they could be arrested, and while they were polite to Seabury, they knew it as well as he. The hulk remained there for years; I used to walk back there and look at it every summer or two until it disintegrated. Not there anymore; indeed, the area is now cut up into house lots. These rich young men were part of the Cotuit of my childhood.

Beyond Evergreen came the Hotel Pines, property of Mr. Calvin D. Crawford, said to have been acquired by him through marriage. Like everybody I write about, Crawford was a character, writ large right across the page. His family hotel, with the guests, mostly but not all elderly, all over the grounds, all over the beach, all over the porch, all over the three-story wood main building, was typical of summer hotels of that day. The aim was to supply everything a guest could want so that no member of a visiting family need ever stray off the hotel grounds and spend money anywhere else.

On anything except alcohol. Though it was never openly advertised as a "temperance hotel," guests who drank were not sought. Crawford was so opposed to "strong drink" that it amounted to a crumbling of the barricades when, after repeal, he allowed "setups" to be served to guests in their rooms. Never in any of his public rooms. He came down thus loudly on the conservative side of any issue, particularly those in any way affecting his business. He was a founder and supporter of WOE, of Cotuit for the rich and the social and nothing for anybody else.

To satisfy the wants of his guests, Crawford provided all sorts of clean summer amusements, many of which the village kids, winter and summer, also found amusing. He had a swimming raft with a saltwater pump at the top of a ladder to lubricate the slide, and one sport we all enjoyed was swimming off this raft after dark, making enough noise so Crawford would row out and chase us off. The most amusing feature for us was the waitresses he provided for his guests, college girls whom he kept imprisoned under a matron in a fortress-dormitory he had. Such girls were more refined, more appealing to his guests than working-class women and, if you are in the business of providing food and lodging, cheaper to supply. In those days, if you hired such help you were supposed to make a show of providing for their virtue. You didn't have to mean it, you just had to offer it. Any girl who got involved in scandal was summarily dismissed; short of that, it worked about the same as such regimes usually work, that is, about as well as no regime at all. I grew up in a college town, and I know about such chaperonage. The girls could indeed maintain their virtue if they wanted it all that maintained; Crawford just gave them a refuge, a level playing field, as we would say today. Get back to the dorm and you're home free.

Also interesting (I was about to write "even more interest-ing," but who'd buy that after the waitresses?) was the hotel's old Butler catboat *Challenge*, which took out parties of hotel guests in her enormous cockpit on fine days. She was big for a nonworking catboat, twenty-four or twenty-five feet long and about half that wide and, as originally built, way overcan-vassed like all of them. Their design principle was that you spread all the canvas you could ever need in the lightest airs, all in one piece, and then tied in a reef or two or three for ordi-nary weather. This was the catboat answer to the schooner, with her sail in at least five smaller pieces which could be handled one at a time, or to the full-rigged ship with at least fifteen. The catboat's huge sail could be handled without going aloft. Just be sure you reefed soon enough, usually before you cast off your mooring. *Challenge's* main boom extended like twelve feet abaft her stern; you reefed the outboard end of it while standing way out on the rudder, almost impossible in rough water.

Crawford's way of maintaining a boat was minimal; he was a tight, scroungy old bastard, but he did know boats and what you could get away with. When the lower part of that giant sail—the part that was exposed, when furled, to rain and to solar radiation (called sunlight in those days)—began to rot away, he cut it off down to the first reef line, then the second, finally sailing with triple-reef canvas as his full sail. In spite of the cut-down rig, *Challenge* would regularly outsail the high, modern racing yachts in open class whenever the Mosquitoes thought up an anniversary and held another "Tin Cup Re-gatta." As also did Ed Ropes' smaller Butler catboat *Monomoy*.

Old Crawford got particularly snotty about public access to the water, opposing all suggestions for acquisition of any-more land for public beaches or landings, but he hung on fiercely to those we already had. His principle and his interest coincided in a tiny strip of public beach, no wider than the lane that led down to it. He guarded this tiny bit jealously while opposing any attempt to enlarge or improve it. Many knew, but not many dared say, that this bit of public access, near but not adjacent to the Pines, was where his black kitchen help swam. Naturally, his guests must not see them, and naturally, he was not going to provide such a place at his own expense. But it would hurt his business for Cotuit to have a fine public beach almost next door. Might attract riff-raff, noisy people, bringing food, lunch papers, cigarette butts.

So he was less devious than usual when the residue of the Kirkman estate was left to the town—not to the nonexistent village—for benefit of the cemetery. This estate included the house and more than a mile of perfect beach on both sides of Bluff Point, walking distance of the village center. A movement began to take shape, led by Ken Turner the plumber, Crawford's longtime critic and opponent in local politics, to persuade the selectmen to hang on to this beach, or part of it, for public use. Crawford was aghast at any such idea, got up and said so, spoke in Freedom Hall, right in the face of Turner and everybody else. He said, "I shall beat you if I can." I was there and heard him. The effrontery of the man. As though the very idea of there being a place where, as Turner expressed it, "our children can put their feet in the same water" as the rich summer visitors came straight from Satan. Or as though it were a sort of trivial game which Crawford played in deadly earnest. He knew instinctively all the techniques that CREEP later thought up to reelect President Nixon; he demeaned Turner's character shamelessly, harping on the cruel assertion that Turner had once spent time in a mental institution. To be fair, Turner himself was not above such ad hominem attacks. The dispute became mean, dirty, nasty until the more squeamish people dropped out.

But in the end, Crawford won by finding a buyer rich enough to close at once. Before the rest of us knew what was happening, before we even knew what we wanted to have happen, the entire property was sold to a man from Chicago, a buddy of another Ocean View millionaire, the equally rich and scroungy Pemberton Whitcomb. The selectmen were not about to oppose the will of such a powerful and vindictive man as C. D. Crawford. As I mentioned before, they were already out on a limb when they withheld from sale Kirkman's collection of ship models and book bindings and Crawford was unscrupulous in his pursuit of his ideal virtue, which consisted of perfect Christian hypocrisy.

Owning one of the world's great public beaches would make Cotuit just another cheap resort, no longer unique and exclusive. I have to remember that there was a time when I thought that myself. An opponent all that self-righteous is frightening, and our selectmen had certainly hung fire in following the strict terms of the Kirkman wills. And Crawford in his wrath had no scruples; he called attention in every public debate to Turner's psychological problems. Don't mess with C. D. Crawford, certainly not for a village that doesn't yet know its own mind, may just as likely go the other way.

Thus Cotuit lost one of the world's great sheltered beaches, which it had, for a moment, actually owned. The cemetery got enough money to plant shrubbery to hide Cocks' tombstone, the library got enough to build the Kirkman Room to house the old gent's collection of bookbindings and ship models and enough more to install computers in place of English, and we are all better off. Aren't we? Time passed, most of the Rolloson boys grew up and moved away or died and when

Evergreen came on the market, Crawford had scrimped and saved and built up his credit and scrounged enough to buy it. It was adjacent to the Pines and became part of his hotel, and the residential zoning he had fought so hard for seemed not to apply to him. He put in additional amenities for his guests, like square dancing as a spectator sport. He knew about the dances I put on for the yacht club children, and he hired me to do the same, once a week, for his guests. The guests came as spectators, not as participants. Those kids generated far too much steam for elderly people, who were always pro forma invited to dance but never did. I brought eight or sixteen kids with me, called them "the experts" and had them do their thing, vigorous and barefoot, on Rolloson's expensive grass, now Crawford's. He paid me my regular fee for putting on a square dance, paid the kids in sundaes and sodas at the hotel fountain, which the kids accepted graciously, glancing over the glasses at each other and at me. They were at the age of experimenting with cans of beer, but they enjoyed the ice cream and Crawford's naivete. We all knew that his naivete went the same way: toward his britches pockets.

One more anecdote connected with Evergreen when it was part of the Pines: Susie Rothschild, my favorite sailing student and square dancer, if I must choose among all that beauty, married Ned Peirson, one of the best of the boys who had worked summers in my shop. For her daughter's grand wedding reception, my good friend Florence Rothschild hired Evergreen and had Crawford cater the party. Only affair I ever knew him to be associated with where there were drinks. What was I saying about his britches pockets? Susie, Ned and I had a secret: they left the reception not in the limo (that was only a blind) but in my committee boat, in *The Big Wheel of Cotuit*, via the back door while everybody was holding rice beside the front, down the lawn to the pier and awa'. Old boat was just rebuilt, with an imitation tugboat house and a genuine used diesel engine. The escape came off beautifully until we were out of sight behind Samson's Island. Then my new engine quit. Seized right up. We got towed in, and the newlyweds caught their flight to Florida for the honeymoon I had arranged for them—along with Dr. Higgins' son Reid and his wife, Joan, to bring back Bill Southworth's motor yacht, which I had left in Fort Lauderdale after Southworth died.

My boat, engine and all, was tied up most of the summer. My competitor, Chet Crosby, with the generosity typical of my competitors plus some more of his own, lent me a tiny inboard launch so I could fill my yacht club commitment. Life went on.

Beyond the hotel, behind a high, ivy-covered garden wall, was Rosemead, the estate of Miss Mabel Riley, another Edwardian spinster right out of Edith Wharton. She never moved in society, never went out to parties, but she loved people and flowers and children. She was a soft touch for any solicitor for the church, the Boy Scouts, the library, and she had secret causes not generally known. Every five years or so, she bought Foster Nickerson a new, gasoline-powered invalid's car and paid Dave Leland the smith to refit it to Foster's peculiar needs, handicaps and abilities. When Betty and I moved here with our children from the sophisticated environment of married students in Cambridge, Betty busied herself founding the Cotuit Cooperative Nursery School. She ignored the conservative, "good enough for father" attitude of the villagers toward anything new. She called on Miss Riley. Betty charms everybody without even being aware of it, or how she does it. Not only did she work it on me our first date, she still works it on me whenever she chooses. (That's how come we have any children at all; wasn't my idea. I was then and remain a Malthusian, but I've got no guts.) What she wanted of Miss Riley was not even money, which must have been a shock to the old lady; she wanted Rosemead as a stop on her fund-raising house and garden tour which would raise money for picture books and tiny furniture and educational toys to put in the school basement, which she had already charmed out of the school authorities. And above all, funds to pay a "qualified" teacher.

Miss Riley was enthusiastic. "My house is nothing," she said. But her garden, hidden behind those high walls, was a low-key showplace. She and Betty hit it off so well that she was invited back for tea, and to bring her children. Betty wanted her boys to love flowers as much as she did, never mind their coarse, macho father the boatbuilder. They were walking down the garden path toward the beach—there was a high wall on this side of the garden, too—Johnny leading Miss Riley by the hand the way little kids do when they are at ease with you. Suddenly he began to run, almost pulling her off her frail, arthritic balance. "There goes my daddy," he shouted. I was going by in *The Big Wheel* following a skiff race. With me were the usual four or five kids, for riding the committee boat had become one of the unpredictably popular activities among the young teens. My Coast Guard license allowed me to carry up to six passengers, and besides the Race Committee member, when there was one, that left me room for five. These were among the girls I had taught to sail, to dance, some of the experts from the Pines, and some, maybe all, of them were going through crushes on me. I enjoyed this but was careful never to lay a hand on one. Today, not unusually, I had five student bikini-fillers. Fortunately, they all had parents who could afford bikinis worthy of them.

Miss Riley's take on this vision, as Betty told me later, was, "Isn't it nice of Mr. Peck to give those children rides on his boat?" Can you believe such innocence in a grown-up lady in 1950-something?

Beyond Miss Riley's was the lane leading down to Crawford's black beach, just one car wide, and then the two separate estates of the Whitcomb brothers, Carter and Pemberton, sons of the same millionaire (railroad equipment, I was told) who grew up in the same house and lived side by side on the two separate estates into which they had cut the family place. They didn't speak to each other. They didn't speak to much of anybody else, either, outside their separate tight social sets (Pem was a crony of Shyzee and Ed Ropes), so it was not much noticed. Pem had a shy, charming wife; Carter was, until late life, a bachelor. Pem liked boats and his lawn; Carter liked baseball and flowers—he liked flowers so much he had another estate, back from the shore among the cranberries, where he grew things like azaleas by the acre. Except for these things, they were equally tight and scroungy.

I had a sort of speaking relationship with Pem, from whom I rented that cranberry building to store boats in. He always hoped to chisel things out of me for his crappy old outboard-powered quahog scow. He took his serious boating elsewhere; *Spitfire* was a one-of-a-kind motor launch for fishing, from Crosby Yacht, designed and built to his order. I hate to think of Pem chiseling Cap'n Manley Crosby, who was used to customers paying his price without argument.

Whitcombs' properties were at the harbor mouth, exposed

to southerly winds, and in 1954 came Hurricane Carol and smashed up the area. We lost maybe a dozen skiffs, and the entire fleet suffered some damage. Damaged Carter's beach house and destroyed Pem's, left *Spitfire* a heap of broken oak frames and short pieces of broken mahogany planking half buried on the beach. Pem made a deal with Hayden to haul away the remains of the building and with me to get rid of the wreck of the boat in exchange for the salvage. What I wanted out of it was the Hercules gas engine to replace the junk Chevy I had in my boat. My boat was way up the bluff waiting for Hayden to get around to relaunching her, but with the engine completely ruined. So I went with Hayden's crew down onto Pem's beach. To get there from the foot of that lane I keep talking about, the one to Crawford's Jim Crow beach, we had to cross Carter's beach, and Del Perry, Pem's gardener, told us as we took down the fence how lucky we were just to get permission.

It was by now late in the season, and the summer flocks were closing up and going home. Hayden's crew (whom I have told about before), those wild young drinkers of various hues under the leadership of Joe Robello, who had never learned to talk below a shout—I called him Silent Joe—were all there when along comes Bluetooth Carol Rollinson, no longer sporting the blue tooth but displaying her maturing "figure that kills" and her wide-eyed look of total innocence. Carol was one of the most striking of my dance troupe. A beginning bikini-wearer, she loved to ride the committee boat. She swayed all the way down the beach from the loop to give me a good-bye kiss in front of them all. She felt sorry for me; my motorboat had gone ashore and destroyed her engine, full of sand and silt, in the breakers. Carol walked the length of the beach, aware of all the eyes, to bestow this mark of favor on me. All hands, even Silent Joe, were struck dumb. Then she walked back, presenting another view of herself clear over the horizon. Never tell me that a hurricane isn't good for something!

Of Carter Whitcomb there was a story told in the village of an unhappy love for a local girl. Eventually he married, late in life, a lovely lady. She had real class, like Jackie Kennedy or my wife Betty. Everybody was eager to be friends with Carter because of her, and he came a little way out of the shell, made up for the ball team some of the lost Kirkman money. So Cotuit was able to keep leading the league by hiring professionals.

But fate was preparing something special for each of the Whitcomb brothers. Carter's lovely wife died most horribly in her car. He didn't exactly go back to being a rich recluse, but the spark seemed to go out of him. He continued to support the team, the Kettleers, but without so much enthusiasm. Once he gave Betty and me a tour of his second estate, in Santuit, where he grew those extraordinary flowers, and when he was satisfied that Betty was likely to make his azaleas bloom, he gave her some plants. But he never accepted our invitation to come and see them bloom.

Fate had something even more horrible for Pem: burned him up. I got the call on my new fire department two-way radio in the middle of the night: "We have a report of a building fire at 185 Ocean View Avenue, the Whitcomb residence." I caught the third engine out, and when we wheeled up in front, there was plenty of smoke showing but no flames. Radio came on again, voice of Chief Spike Dottridge (Seabury's grandson): "Get some ladders 'round back. We got people in here." I grabbed the lightweight aluminum extension ladder off Engine 3 and ran back there, where were the chief and his deputy, Steve Hamlin the builder. Steve had a ladder against the house at a crazy angle and was up on it beside a second-story window. I put my ladder up alongside his, also at a crazy angle. All around the house, right against it, grew an arborvitae hedge maybe four feet high and so thick and wiry you couldn't push through it, nor foot a ladder in it. Your ladder couldn't penetrate the hedge; if you tried, you ended with a ladder beginning four feet off the ground and too wobbly to climb. I had to foot my ladder, as Steve had done, way out from the building so it met the wall at about forty-five degrees. Then when you climbed it you had to lay your chest against it to even reach the wall, and in that position you could do no work, lift no weight. And when I got it up, it was just in the way; there was one ladder there already. The whole night was taking on a nightmare quality. Nothing worked; nothing was substantial. I got my ladder out of the way and tried to figure out how I could help. I was aware all of a sudden that Bea Whitcomb was with us on the ground. She must have jumped or fallen into that hedge. It was the finest safety net you could devise; they both should have done so before we even arrived. By this time, flame was showing, lots of it. The couple had evidently shared a room, or occupied adjoining rooms, directly over the living room fireplace, where a log they had left burning had rolled out and set the hearth rug on fire. Just then Pem slipped from Steve's grasp, and he too fell into the hedge. But too late; the flesh of his hand came off like a glove when Steve held it. Horror!

Our EMTs brought the stretchers and loaded the Whitcombs into the ambulance and away to the hospital. For the firemen, the nightmare continued. I heard the chief on the radio calling in a second alarm; indeed, it went to so many alarms I lost count, and none of the best training and none of the best equipment seemed to make any difference. It was an old house and had been added onto inside and out, over and over, but never properly. Nothing was ever ripped out, just boarded over, walled in. In places we encountered three partitions, one behind another, dry wood with space for air in between. You could feel the wall, not burning but hot. There would be another wall burning behind it. All the plaster was on metal mesh lath, hard to pull down. The chief's nephew, Captain Benny Dottridge, led a party of firemen up the stairs fighting fire, but Benny pulled them all out when he heard flames roaring behind the ceiling above their heads. Some of the younger firemen, at my suggestion, and with difficulty and danger, got ladders onto the roof and cut a hole in it, standard practice to let the heat and smoke out so we could fight the fire from below, and they found another roof out of reach under there. We called in an aerial ladder to get above the roof and had to use chainsaws to cut a gap in an even more massive hedge to get it onto the grounds, and then the mud was so soft we couldn't get it in reach of where we wanted it. Lucky not to lose the truck as well.

We had plenty of trained, brave men, plenty of modern apparatus, plenty of water, plenty of skilled advice and help and the place burned to the ground right under us. It was humiliating for the department and for me. I had thought of myself as a good fireman, had taken a course in fire engineering at Penn State, had been a port-security firefighter in the Coast Guard all through the war, had attended fire school at the Philadelphia Navy Yard, but this simple residence fire defeated us all. It would have been no different had I been in charge, or even old Codman himself. We would have lost the building just the same, as well as the people. It might have been designed to burn, beginning with those impenetrable hedges and then all those built-in hidden recesses full of dry wood.

Talk went round the firehouse that the smoke detector had been found still in its store box in a closet, but I didn't see it, and I don't think there was as much as a closet left intact to find it in. Pem Whitcomb, from hospital, ordered the place rebuilt just as it was. He stayed in that bed all summer, never left it. Bea never lived in the rebuilt house either. Maybe that horrible night drove her crazy, medically improbable, or perhaps she was coming down with Alzheimer's already. She lived with her sister and attendants in the sister's house just around the corner for the rest of her life. And the Whitcomb houses still sit there side by side. Somebody lives in them, but the Whitcombs are gone.

Next place beyond Whitcombs', in my childhood and young manhood, was Baileys'. Bigger house than the two Whitcombs together, bigger acreage than the Pines and Evergreen combined. It was too big and included too many houses, each with its outbuildings on a fair-size lot, and each with its tax bill, to survive into this generation. Summer houses they were, in the manner of 1920 and earlier, like Cousin Lawrence's, with water pipes shallowly buried, meant to be drained every winter.

The big house where Mr. and Mrs. Bailey lived was showy, something like an antebellum house on a southern plantation, though it looked out not over cotton fields but, from its high bluff, over the harbor entrance and Nantucket Sound. It was painted white in those days and had a row of two-story pillars around one end holding up the roof over the porch, where the pillars could be seen both from the road and from the water. Altogether incongruous, as out of place as Mark Howe's chalet or Wadsworth's hacienda. I have to remind myself of such misplaced places when I get irritated over the monstrosities newcomers are building. "Nothing new beneath the sun," my mother used to say about all sorts of things. I was inside the place only once or twice, but I remember it as a formal mansion, designed to impress. Mr. Bailey was a dignified, quiet man with a little moustache; Mrs. B. was flamboyant, said to be Italian. I never heard her speak; never got that close. Only one anecdote will I repeat, said by Vincent, her youngest son, just my age, describing his mother learning to smoke. It would seem she took up this vice late in life. "She lights the cigarette and then she begins to drool and she drools and drools all over the cigarette until finally she puts it out." Vincent had a gift for description.

Baileys had inherited the whole place, and the whole fortune, from a childless old gentleman named Sears, a textile baron whose business affairs Mr. B. managed after the old boy retired and whose health, in his declining years, Mrs. B. attended to. People seemed impressed by the fact that his wealth came from a firm named "Wellington Sears." Some summers they rented out the grand house and moved into the house next in opulence, but wherever, always they lived in Mrs. Bailey's baroque continental style.

They had four handsome sons, great natural sailors, powers in the Mosquitoes, who also showed precocious talent for making me appreciate my unimportance. They owned two skiffs as well as a Wianno Knockabout. One of the skiffs, *Comet*, was Butler's last and fastest; Vincent could make her perform incredible tricks. The other one, *Aloha*, was a "standard," built by Bigelow of Monument Beach over on the Buzzards Bay side. Any of the four brothers could make her win as effortlessly as *Comet*.

Baileys had not one but two piers, one to go with the great house, the other for all their other houses, whether occupied by family or tenants. They were fancier, more elaborate wharves than any other private ones in the village, three planks wide and with a handrail on both sides and a tee on the end, and for several seasons in the early thirties the Mosquitoes met and started races off one of them. The kids in skiffs were everybody's kids, and everybody with waterfront sort of took turns hosting them when their own kids were skiff age. But Mr. and Mrs. Bailey soon came up with a better idea. Just across the narrow harbor entrance was Samson's Island, and Sears had left them that too. It was just a pile of bare sand with spartina grass and dunes in the middle where seabirds nested, and here they granted to the yacht club permission to erect its pier, thus got them off the Bailey place. Samson's had once been a separate island, when the harbor entrance channel ran between it and Dead Neck, but that channel had filled in, and entrance for all vessels was now west of the island rather than east; the sea had cut through a marsh and made a new, narrower and more devious route, relatively shallow, and the island was now the west end of the bay-mouth bar called Dead Neck. The old harbor entrance was now cut off completely at the sea side, leaving a blind and shallow bay which old-timers called "the old harbor" and young people called Cupid's Cove in honor of erotic uses they made of it. The tide rushed in and out around Samson's like a waterfall and had piled sand in a long, curving tail which geologists call a tombolo and had cut the channel beside it so deep you could dive right off dry beach into deep water.

So they moved the kids here to get them off the Bailey place. The yacht club kids were allowed to erect their own pier just where the deep water is closest, so the pier need not be very long. Most of the labor was supplied by the bigger kids, and hard labor it was in the swift current. I was not old enough to be much help, but I used to race from that pier, the end of

Photo by Dorothy I. Crossley

A Cotuit skiff race about 1968. Number 39, in foreground, is one of eighteen of these boats built at Pecks' Boats.

which was one end of the starting line, and in these races I distinguished myself by losing the Junior Series (fifteen and younger) to Edith Mattison, who was sailing an antique boat, who was two years younger than I and a girl at that!

One advantage of having our club in this private location was our own beach. The channel was so deep you could dive right off dry land and you always came up fifty yards or so down current. Today the whole notion of turning a bunch of kids loose to swim unsupervised in such a place would be considered impermissibly dangerous, but we did it year after year and nobody gave it a thought. A disadvantage of the location was that you had to sign on your crew in advance, bring him (her) with you; there was no way to pick up a crew at the start, for nobody could get there without a boat. I liked to defer this decision until I got a close look at the weather, decide how much ballast I would want. I was thus handicapped by my discomfort with numbers; number of mph it was blowing told me absolutely nothing. You couldn't pick up a crew on Samson's Island; nobody lived there but Atlantic terns, and the most you could get out of one of them was a face full of bird shit. The Bramley brothers had a little Boston bulldog named Jimmy who sailed with them and who always took off into the grass to relieve himself and always came back with a tern chick in his jaws and a jaunty, self-satisfied air.

After a few years of this arrangement, the Baileys had a still better idea: they gave the whole barren island to the Audubon Society, thus freeing themselves of its tax bills and their horizon of all those kids, passing on to others the pleasant task of kicking people off. Atlantic terns were just now discovered to be endangered, but the only change those of us most intimately associated with them could observe was an evolved improvement in their aim.

But, on the subject of Samson's Island, it achieved a transient notoriety twenty or thirty years later. President Kennedy and the adorable Jackie used to come there on Sundays in the family motor yacht *Marlin*, seeking loneliness like everybody else, but with better reason. Of course they brought the crowd with them; a small cutter of Coast Guards, two speedboats full of Massachusetts state cops, the Barnstable police boat, miscellaneous stoical men in business suits who had to be Secret Service and who were dressed that way to conceal their sidearms, any number of motorboats carrying press photographers. The Kennedys didn't come ashore; the president sat in the after cockpit in a therapeutic chair of some kind and rested his sore back. They usually came here in mid-afternoon when the Mosquitoes had their race. Cotuit Harbor was big enough to tolerate both activities at once, and nobody interfered with the kids in their sailboats. But of course, where a skiff race went, I was with them in *The Big Wheel of Cotuit*. President Kennedy acknowledged my passing by waving his hand minimally, but Jackie ran to the rail and always gave me a big wave. I loved her, and I still do.

Another thing Jackie liked to do was waterski, behind one of those fast police boats. Waterskiing is prohibited in Cotuit Harbor, and I, the harbormaster, was chewed out by some WOE members for allowing it. I mean, what did they think I could possibly do about this activity of the First Lady and the cops? They would have liked to have the law on Jackie because her husband was a Democrat, but expecting me to arrest her was just one more of their absurdities.

I had ways of my own to get public attention, but arresting Jackie Kennedy was not one of them. Like, one Sunday, the *Marlin* came to Cotuit a little earlier than usual and tied up to Bailey's pier. The big Bailey house was rented that summer to Katherine and Phil Graham, publishers of the *Washington Post*, people of such power that the president himself went to call on them. Because they were early, the race hadn't started yet, and it was to start off the Sinclaire pier, next one up the beach and real close. I was anchored for the occasion right off the end of this pier and was enjoying the prominence. Said to my passengers, "Watch all these cops jump when I start the race." For one of my toys was a ten-gauge cannon with black powder shells, a starting gun. Made a prodigious boom and a cloud of black smoke. And indeed, all the cops jumped until they all saw it was only Peck, playing the fool as usual. After Dallas, this prank seems less amusing, but it happened in

Cotuit and is part of the picture. But speaking of bangs, this memory always put me in mind of another bang, in Dallas, and the TV film of Jackie scrambling to the assistance of that Secret Service man about to be thrown from the back of the car. Talk about gallant! To act so bravely and so quickly at such a time. I loved Jackie more than ever!

There are no Baileys left in Cotuit. The boys married and went their separate ways, met with good fortune or ill—had sons some gifted, some retarded—beautiful daughters who married well or beautiful daughters who lost their minds. But all beautiful regardless. *Comet* was destroyed in the 1944 hurricane. After the parents died, the estate was, of course, broken up. None of them had the cash to pay the tax on an inheritance this size. The oldest of the sons, Charles Bailey, called Buddy, bought his house, fixed it up and hung on in Cotuit for years, raised his children here summers and went on winning races in *Aloha* until she became a basket of leaks, then traded her in for one of my new ones. Once again I felt honored and vindicated that such a talented and scientific sailor should choose anything I had built and win races in her. Indeed, for its fiftieth birthday in 1956, the Mosquito club held a Tin Cup Regatta, and not only did Buddy win the skiff division, but his little brother Vincent came for a visit, borrowed another of my new boats and got second. My cup of conceit ranneth over.

Now Buddy and his family are gone too, some of the houses have been torn down, replaced by more pretentious ones, more houses have been built, closer together. The great house still stands, no longer white, and west of it right on the shore, between the great house and Loop Beach, stands a new house built vertically up the side of the bluff to fit onto a tiny lot all the amenities a rich family can't do without. Even a swimming pool, within a hundred or so yards of the shore! Like in Miami. It was built by a big-time contractor, and he may still own it for all I know. Incongruous, but it is the future. In spite of my sneering, in spite of WOE's ranting they will all be building high-rises because there won't be any ground left. All filled up with people seeking loneliness. Latest word is that between these two crowded houses, somebody has fitted in a third.

IX
LOCAL UNDERSIDE POLITICS

COTUIT ENTRANCE channel makes a sharp left here (outbound, that is) and runs straight southward into Nantucket Sound, right through all those shifting sands, narrow but straight. And not very deep; about four feet if I must waste one of my scarce numbers. I remember when it was dredged; I was a little kid, and I am astonished how it has maintained itself ever since. Over sixty years. Maybe the army did something to it during the war when I wasn't watching. They had an amphibious training base then, way up the Narrows above Almys' (a difficult place to achieve and to hang on to; the army is powerful, but it isn't a Lowell!).

This base was called "Camp Canduit." I'm not sure how official the title was; it was on street signs to help you find it. I wasn't here much during the war, but I always contrived, ever since that first long boat and train trip, to get a few days here every summer. I would get leave, and Betty and I would pile into the old Ford, then Packard, finally Buick and come down, driving all night so as not to waste time on the road when we could be on the water. Time in bed was low on the list, like third priority. "She says" (as *The Joy of Sex* would put it) that I brought an alarm clock here on our honeymoon lest we miss any sailing time. I went off watch at midnight, and Philadelphia to Cotuit took exactly eight and a quarter hours. If we hurried we could be in time for the Saturday morning skiff race.

I was saying about the amphibious army: When we were sailing around—formal racing was more or less suspended during the years of hostilities—the troops would go by in their landing craft, and the welcome they would give us—I wore my undress white uniform, as required—was enthusiastic. We knew, of course, that it was mostly for her, not for me, but it made me feel proud. Betty was a sight to be proud of in her bathing suit or her sailing clothes.

The base was a large undeveloped tract at the head of the Narrows and around the point into North Bay, property of Theron Appolonio, another character. More conservative than ex-president Hoover, more anti-newcomer than WOE. An anecdote: Theron sought me out years later, when I was harbormaster, and burst all over me with indignation. "Do you know who those people were?"

I didn't know what the silly man was talking about. "What people?"

Seems a family or something, in a boat, had camped for the night on Samson's Island. He was aghast at this trespass and that I, the nearest he could come to an official in charge, didn't even know about it. He lectured me about how it was a bird sanctuary, on and on. I, along with the Bentinck-Smith boys, the Cobb boys, the Bailey boys, had camped out there when we were kids. When I had heard enough of this, for about half an hour, I said, "Yes. They gave it to the birds to keep people like you and me off." A recurrent pattern with me is to speak intemperately when angry and regret it forever after, but of this explosion I was and remain proud, even though it was unkind to the poor fool.

I don't know what the army paid Appolonio for the duration-long base site. They were incapable of not paying handsomely, unless the man let them have it for nothing as his patriotic duty. One thing known throughout the village, which is enough to cast doubt on it, was that the army undertook to restore it precisely to its pristine state when the war was over. That they certainly did. Not a trace to be found of massive buildings, wharves, ramps.

One more tale of Appolonio, but before I can tell, it I must introduce a couple more flamboyant characters. First of them, and I see his squat, sinister form before me as I write, and hear his tough, grating voice: Charlie Savery, ex-bootlegger, civil engineer, land surveyor, politician for all the wrong reasons, showily corrupt. Contemplating this man, I almost wish I had taken a course in psychology; he is a classic case study. Charlie grew up among bootleggers and their underworld connections, and from the movies or somewhere, he got the notion that a gangster was a desirable thing to be. He looked a little like the gangster star Edward G. Robinson, and he cultivated the resemblance, made an image with slouch hats, never seen without a cigar in the corner of his mouth, drove the image Packard. He was connected with local politics, always in ways ostentatiously corrupt and with shady real estate deals, buying up land and reselling it to quick-buck developers, opposing restrictive zoning. The worse his neighbors thought of him, the happier he was. This last attribute particularly appealed to me. Charlie was anathema to WOE, delighted in twisting WOE's tail. How those respectable hypocrites hated him, and how he loved their hatred.

I am a bit of an iconoclast, and I loved that man, envied his apparent imperviousness to public loathing, a quality I can never attain. He didn't give a fart what they thought of him, whoever they were. Hate went with the character he cultivated.

The second character in this pisspot drama was young Ned Ackerman, a grandson of the Wellmans. I don't know who the Wellmans were, how long they had been in Cotuit or anything else about them. Not sure I ever laid eyes on either of the older Wellmans, but they owned the biggest estate of several on the shore between Little River and the Narrows, or, to put it another way, between Mary Barton and Martha Wadsworth. A big Victorian house. They had two daughters, both very marriageable because very rich, and one of them married Ned Ackerman's father, which is all I know of him. They had three children, Ned, Jill and Tod, and all three worked in my growing boat dealership at one time when I thought to run a branch marina. Of Ned, the oldest, my son John, who followed me into the business, once said, "He can't receive because he's always in transmit." A Johnny Peck metaphor if ever there was one. Old Wellman seems to have had at least one hobby which must have soaked up a lot of his money: classic European sports cars. Even in his day they must have been out-of-sight expensive, but by Ned's time they had appreciated like a hundred to one. Franklin Childs, Ned's uncle by marriage, used to drive around in the four-seat open Lancia, but he hardly ever took the Bugatti two-seat roadster on the road; it made so much noise he kept getting tickets. That vintage Bugatti would sell for like a million today.

Well, that is the sort of fortune Ned Ackerman and his siblings came into at just the time when Charlie Savery made one of his flashy secret deals and bought out Theron Appolonio's estranged brother Tony's undivided half interest in all that waterfront property at the head of the Narrows. Nothing was said to Theron until the deal was a fait accompli, and then Charlie went to Theron and, the way Charlie told it to me, said to him in his grating, gangster voice, "Do you want to buy me out, or do I buy you out?"

That has to be about the cruelest act I ever heard of, Charlie Savery of all people, but this story must be read like one of Chaucer's fabliaux—no sympathy for the cuckold—and Theron was not only a fool but a nasty fool. But Ned was a friend of his—Theron let him do a large part of the talking, I fancy—and Ned came up with the money so Theron could buy Charlie out. Theron, an old man already, left it all to Ned in his will, and the value of all that waterfront land, so recently worthless, went right up out of sight. Ned sold it to developers and what he did with the money is another whole novel, but it didn't happen in Cotuit.

I have no idea what Charlie charged Theron and Ned for his half interest but it cannot have been anything like what Charlie could have made if he had bought them out and developed the place on his own. Charlie's secret was that he aspired to crookedness for its own sake, not for profit, and loved to "shove it up" those who took him at face value and despised him for his corruption. One of the things he did which nobody remembers is he saved Sandy Neck. Sandy Neck is an enormous sand spit, covered with big beautiful dunes, property of the Town of Barnstable, on the other side of the Cape. North side, where the winter storms hit it right on. A little of it washes away every winter, and along in the sixties it was eroding faster than it was replenished, and there was fear of its washing away altogether. Charlie came up with the idea—not original with him; he never clamed it was—of getting everybody to leave, in January, his used Christmas tree on the beach. He got some publicity, spread the word and so many trees were brought and precisely placed under Charlie's direction that they formed an enormous collision mat and did, indeed, stop the erosion in its tracks.

Charlie was a good engineer, and he had the largest surveying operation on this part of the Cape, two or three transit crews working all summer and winter. He did some work for people near our Mashpee property, among them a young man, the snotty son of a prosperous banker, who bought at a tax sale a couple of lots in another part of town but with numbers similar to a couple of bayfront lots we owned, and knew we owned, near our non-boatyard. The silly kid found the right numbers on the wrong map and had Charlie send a crew in to find the lots, define them with cement bounds. Charlie had to have known, even had I not pointed it out to him, that these were our lots, but he waited until the survey was completed, the lots found precisely and the bounds set, the fee in his pocket, and then he came to me and said, just the way Edward G. Robinson would have said it, "Well, guess you got a couple of your lots surveyed."

Charlie made a lot of money, that's for sure, but his crookedness was to him a sign of success rather than a way to profit. As I said before, our deed from the daughter of Congressman Gifford included wording like "everything I own in the town of Mashpee." So Charlie came to me one time and said, "There's a landlocked piece, about thirty-five acres, south of Quinaquissett, registered to 'owners unknown,' and I think it belongs to you."

So it did, as Betty, once directed to it, soon found out. And Charlie could have maneuvered things, tax takings and tax sales, and acquired it himself. That's what everybody would have expected him to do, and the fact that he did no such thing I have always regarded as a sign of esteem, like being granted credit by the Crockers and by Hayden. Proof we are "in." Solid. This parcel was burned over, and we got off it a couple winters' firewood, seasoned on the stump by fire. Got the whole crew from the boatyard working there most of the winter cutting charred scrub oak, ignoring charred scrub pine. We have since sold this parcel to big developers for a lot of money, along with some more of the Gifford land, and pretentious houses now stand on it overlooking a golf course. I am grateful to Charlie but even more grateful for the insight he gave me into an unusual personality.

And, as I often say, to sail by Loop Beach is a weird experience, for as far as you can see either side of the crowded beach and crowded parking lot it is all gorgeous beach, pristine beach without a soul allowed on it except its owners. Who can't be bothered except to kick trespassers off. Thus absurdly they preserve an illusion of loneliness.

But, talking of Loop Beach, not on the shore, but across Ocean View from where that new vertical house now stands, there stands an old, much enlarged house formerly the home of a Captain Nickerson who was dead long before I was born. Chat Churbuck, for whom I worked, was a descendant of his as well as of the other captain, Thomas Chatfield. This house was once one of the Bailey properties, where they lived when they had a tenant in the great house, and as they began retrenching, they sold this house to the William Walker Sinclaires, who occupied it every summer and way into most winters in the days when I was teaching sailing and square dancing. The Sinclaire property included several hundred yards of beach, and here they built their pier, a modern one with real piles, pumped down or hammered down clear to hardpan, built to stand ice and even hurricanes This pier was for years the almost permanent home of the Cotuit Mosquito Yacht Club. Never mind generous; the Sinclaires were bountiful.

There was a perpetual party going on at Sinclaires', "fun for all ages." Their two pretty daughters and their big, handsome son entered into all the kids' activities of this kid-oriented place. Older people also hung out there, where the drinks were free and without stint and the conversation bright but never brilliant. Mrs. Sinclaire, Mary Katherine, dominated all the entertainment. She was a big woman, like two hundred pounds, always laughing with a laugh that shook all Cotuit high ground. Of course, such an endless wide-open house attracted a wide range of freeloaders. Mr. Bill Sinclaire — Willy Walker, his wife called him — held much stock and a sort of undemanding executive job at Corning Glass. He was a dapper little man with a little blond mustache. He couldn't laugh as loud as his wife, but just as long and just as often. Sometimes she called him Esky, and his kids did too, after the cartoon logo of *Esquire* magazine, the *Playboy* of its day, and he and Esky had a lot in common besides appearance.

Corning Glass was a firm out of the nineteenth century, maybe the eighteenth, managed fascistically by an unsavory executive who was so powerful and dictatorial that none of his outmoded prejudices was ever challenged, even behind his back. When he cracked the corporate social whip, even the Sinclaires jumped. They once had to cancel a party they had planned, invitations had gone out, because their boss commanded all his corporate sycophants to a party of his own at his summer place in Marion. He would have nothing to do with Jews and as little as possible with WASPS he couldn't control. The Sinclaires weren't like that when they were out of sight of him. They once put on a formal party at the Wianno Club, long dress and black tie, for the debut of their oldest daughter, Tootie. Only time I knew she had another name, Mary Carol, and the only time I ever saw her with shoes on. Among the kids in the yacht club was one whose parents were Jewish and never bothered to hide it. The Wianno Club and all Wianno society were stuck in an earlier century and refused to admit Jews. Mary Katherine never blinked; she canceled the party. The club blinked; Tootie came out at the Wianno Club, and this boy was there. Reminds me of C. D. Crawford and his britches pockets.

A date sticks in my number-deficient memory: New Year's 1948 and another party at Sinclaires. Betty and I came and stayed with the Sinclaires, though we were then living with other married students in Cambridge, and we brought our first son, Bill, then five months old. We had a nonstop good time for three days. Even Bill had a good time; he was all worked up, was sick all over the pretty ladies from Mary Kath on down, and they all made out they loved it, all made a fuss over him, which he was already learning to enjoy. I with my prodigious memory enjoyed swapping dirty poems and limericks with Willy Walker and his cronies. Betty charmed everybody, as she always does. She was nursing the baby, which gave her even more bosom for the old goats to ogle and gave me just one more reason to be proud of her. Sinclaires gave this party every year, though they never spent the whole winter on the Cape. By 1950 we were living year-round in Cotuit, and Betty had her nursery school going. That year, or a year or two later, when school reopened after Christmas and the teacher asked all the little kids what they had done to celebrate, they all told of visits to grandparents who either fed them turkeys or were turkeys themselves. But Bill announced, "We went to Sinclaires and danced and had a drinkie."

I spoke of Bill Sinclaire's cronies. He had many, of course; after all, he kept open house with open bar, but one couple must be mentioned because of their children: Charlie Winding from Yorkstate, a VP of Marine Midland Bank, and his sweet wife. They had a son born without hearing. Consulted specialists who could not cure the child but were most assuring: they were highly unlikely to have another child with the same handicap, so they had a daughter, and she was deaf too. These were rich kids, and nobody could ever call them neglected. Parents gave them everything that love and medicine could offer. But Charlie Winding was apt to trade a bit on his children's handicap, accept special consideration and like that. Beyond that, both of them did their best to bring the kids up "normal," just like, and mixing with, normal children. And they were the greatest of great kids. I taught them both to sail, and they learned as fast and as keenly as all the others. I was the one who had to learn, mainly to reach out and nudge before instructing. They could both speak comprehensible, a little odd-sounding, English, but reluctantly.

I taught them to square dance too—rather, the other kids taught them and I got the credit. They somehow felt the beat, maybe right through the earth, and the steps and figures they memorized, helped by friendly pushes from the others. When I was starting out as a teacher, the statement "The only remarkable thing I ever did was to teach two deaf and dumb children to square dance" was a calculated part of my résumé. So, it was a damn lie.

Bill Sinclaire was proud of his Highland heritage, always wore the bright red Sinclaire plaid somewhere on his person. The Sinclaires of Corning and Cotuit (and Colorado) were the same family that owns (still) Caithness, the northernmost castle in Scotland, on a cliff overlooking the Arctic Ocean. For a while, Tootie's buxom and bonnie sister Hellie, who married well, actually resided there. Braw cauld it mun hae been. I once encountered Tootie and her husband living on their boat in Newport, Rhode Island, but I have not seen Hellie since she was a bride. I remember that she and her bridegroom put on comic disguises and stayed right here, did not go on any honeymoon, they were having so much fun at the reception. Just as well we have not met; an encounter with Hellie would be a disaster. I am told she is as outspokenly conservative as I am liberal. Bill Sinclaire the younger was engaged to a Cotuit girl named Kay who outshone the whole Cotuit firmament of beauty, but she died of cancer. He was altogether devastated, but I guess he must have gotten over her. One does. He is married and has kids of his own. He suffers from an ailment of the eyes which restricts his activities. A pity; like his father, he was a hotshot polo player, but they say he is deep in horses in the West. Tootie's husband, as nice a guy as anyone in these pages, also died painfully, I forget of what. As John D. MacDonald, a successful but under-recognized writer, put it, "they keep emptying out the world." Or, as I told Harry Crocker after the death of Dave Leland, "Everybody I love dies."

This long, laughing house party came to an abrupt end between one summer and the next. We awoke one year to find the house sold, the Sinclaires gone. They didn't go broke or anything so prosaic. I guess they sort of outlived the party. Maybe Cotuit had served its purpose. Both the daughters had found husbands and flown. All I was told was that Willy Walker got tired of supporting a never-ending, ever-growing list of freeloaders and up and sold Hospitality Hall. *Fin de siècle.*

X
WESTWARD HO!

O<small>N THE SHORE</small>, beyond what has long been called Loop Beach (or simply "the loop") because here Ocean View loops back on itself and rejoins Main Street, lies what was until recently the property of William G. Morse. With Morse the Harvard connection comes flooding back; he was employed there, in financing or purchasing or something. Published a book entitled *Pardon My Harvard Accent*. Morse was all his life a prominent mentor of the Mosquito Club. At various times, before Bailey's, the club sailed off his pier, an awkward one to build every spring because it must reach way out over a humongous shoal, one of a whole complex of shifting sands stretching eastward from Waquoit Bay almost to Hyannisport, continuously eroding and continually nourished by more sand eroding into Nantucket Sound from the high bluffs at Succonessett. These shoals completely block the entrance to Popponessett Bay with places only six inches deep at low tide, nourishing Dead Neck across Cotuit entrance, shoals reaching out a full mile into Nantucket Sound. Professor Kirtley

Mather, a great man, made it the basis for the section he called "the work of waves and currents" in his freshman geology course, the most rewarding course I (majoring in English) ever took in all my five years at Harvard.

A digression. Now back on course, one last thing about Morse: he was a nice guy, and the kids all loved and respected him, myself not least. He has left on me the impression of a retired officer in the Royal Army right out of Kipling. Maybe it's his writing style. Sometime in the forties or fifties he wrote a piece about the Cotuit Yacht Club, "A Program for Juniors," published in *Yachting*, with just the genial, condescending air of a Kipling retired colonel in the Indian army. He fitted the part: the short, gray hair, ramrod-stiff back, crisply athletic to the end and a twinkling eye. These are just impressions; actually he was tall, mostly bald, altogether genial. He used to race his skiff, the *Tyke*, before the hurricane and then his new one, the *Dipper*, on Sunday afternoons, sitting way outboard on his deck where his arse was visible, the port cheek of his pants showing a big red patch, the starboard cheek a big green one.

They both were here long before I was, so I don't know the relationship between Morse and William B. Dunning, his next-door neighbor southwest along the shore. Brothers-in-law I think, not sure. Maybe cousins. One thing is clear, though: from Morse westward the Harvard connection is back. Not Lowell relatives but scholars of distinction on their own. I don't know what chair W. B. Dunning filled, but his son Jim, who taught me to sail, became dean of the Harvard School of Dental Medicine, so far as I know the only school in the world so ambitious that to graduate as a dentist you first had to complete the whole four years at Harvard Med and then an additional year studying dentistry. You came out of that with a

DMD, and I have the impression that Jim was the one who invented and enforced this heavy program.

Dunning Senior lived in an old red house, long and low with a long roofed porch. Along with the Porter House, one of the simpler and finer of the old small houses, but this one had a beauty of line to which the Porter House never aspired. One of Jim's two sisters had a larger, less handsome place across Main Street. (Main Street, you see, continues southwestward past the Loop.) Jim built for himself and family the simplest house of all, up on the bluff west of his father's. Simplicity (part of their fundamentalist Christianity) was a big thing with the Dunnings.

They also had when I was a boy a handsome, black, clipper-bowed sloop yacht, *Hawk*, which looked to me like a Friend-ship sloop though Jim insisted, on some abstruse technicality, that it wasn't a true Friendship. She was likewise kept ostenta-tiously simple. She was gaff-rigged and not large but striking. Jim had also two pretty daughters and two pretty nieces, one of whom managed my office after Betty gave up trying to make sense of it. Julia Beebe was first among all the pretty girls who rode my committee boat, but in general most of the Dunning women revealed a strain of evangelical Christianity which put me off. Which probably helped save poor Julia from my rapa-cious clutches. She was distractingly buxom, and I used to harangue her about her tendency to overeat, put on flesh. Her cousin Cornelia, Jim's daughter, was at the same time the most beautiful and the most devout of them all. Lovely long blond hair. I wouldn't have thought of pursuing her, but she turned out to be a heroine, and I am forever indebted to her. She swam out in the height of a hurricane and cut my newest skiff loose from her mooring so she drifted in to the beach and I could haul her out of there. Her owners had gone home, and I had held the boat in the water for just one week so I could sail her in just one race myself; she was my responsibility. May her absurd God bless Cornelia every day.

Harvard appeared again in the next estate beyond Dunnings, the elaborate Victorian summer home of Professor Frank Taussig, the conservative economist of the laissez-faire school of the first Adam Smith. He wrote a book, indeed, he was one of those who wrote the book of "don't meddle with the market" economics, the theory—its proponents talk as though it were fact—that if government and society let business alone, everybody will get richer and richer. By turns ignoring and bewailing the obvious fact that the poor obstinately insist on getting poorer and poorer, thus spoiling the true system. The theory, which I call "coattail capitalism," asserts that if Steve Forbes gets richer, Joe Blow will get richer too just from being around. I read a little of Taussig when I made the mistake of signing up for a course in economics when I first went to Harvard. I was the most conservative of all my friends at that age, but I was out-of-sight left of Taussig. All the while scorning Roosevelt, the New Deal and all its works, I unconsciously bought the whole idea. In the fifty years since, I have gotten only more liberal.

Apart from his pernicious doctrines, Taussig was one of the more influential elders of the Mosquito Yacht Club. He was often called on to present the prizes at the close of the sailing season, and he harangued the children the way he must have harangued his classes, not without wit but at too great length for such a young audience. There, truthfully, is the only place I ever saw him; by the time I was racing skiffs, he was very old. One thing for which he should be remembered is that he bought for his children Butler's first truly world-beating skiff. Or perhaps his son Bill and his sisters were natural-born world beaters. It was all before my time, but the name of this boat, *Schwastika* (long pre-Hitler), dominates all the early records of skiff racing and appears over and over on all the permanent trophies that date back so far as the 1910s.

The old professor had just one son, whom I never knew, though I liked his grandson Bill, who was handsome and outstanding witty. But the old man had a houseful of daughters each more striking and talented than the last. I was too young to be aware whether any of them were also beautiful, but they were all, each in her own way, as overstated as any of the men I have been writing about. Mary Henderson I knew because her children were my age: two daughters, one of whom led her class at Harvard Law, and a son Gerry who still lives in Cotuit year-round and is still, at almost eighty, as good company as ever. He survived more than twenty years of marriage to Edith Mattison, which is about as challenging a life as you can have. I'll come to Edith when she comes round.

Helen Taussig, the professor's daughter, I knew because the world knows her. She taught medicine at Hopkins and collaborated in the discovery of the cure for a devastating heart ailment of infants known as "blue baby syndrome." She built an ultra-simple summer home right down on the beach way west of her father's estate, which she left to Johns Hopkins. The school sold this property for a lot of money, like millions, a waterfront lot in such a location, to a buyer who never lived in it. Tore it down and built on that fragile beach one of the most elaborate houses in Cotuit. Fate is always messing in unpredictable ways with people's plans; that site was, for years, one of the most threatened by erosion in all this part of Cape Cod. The sea has recently broken through and washed away a long barrier beach that Professor Mather used to tell his geology students about, which had formerly protected that bit of property and half a dozen others, but it piled all that sand in one lump, an island or peninsula, right in front of this one house, so it is now better protected than ever. Fate, however, is never finished. The whole thing, including that gorgeous new house, can wash away in a single winter. "A breath can make them, as a breath has made."

The Taussig Betty and I knew best was the professor's daughter Catherine, Mrs. Frank Opie, the screwiest of a great family of screwballs. Her kids have perpetuated the tradition; her son Frank, in particular, is best friends (since they were little boys) with Tom White, Ben's oldest son and no mean screwball himself. Both little boys were fascinated by snakes and kept a collection of them. On the front gate of the ornate house of the late professor they hung a sign REPTILE FARM. They charged admission. Soon they got more commercial; everything for business in the Taussig tradition. Next season the sign read

TAUSSIG

OPIE

HENDERSON

FISH FOR SALE

Frank had a sister, Helen, as nutty as he. As a little kid, she had ideas as radical as her brother and a wry, deadpan sense of humor. I think she came to me to learn to sail, though it doesn't seem like anything Cath would do. Anyway, she came, and I had a joke about money, based on the suggestion, "You could make a contribution to the Leonard W. Peck Foundation." So Helen took to bringing an old brick whenever she came, "for your foundation." She got screwier the older she got, as screwballs are apt to do. Got rid of her husband promptly and brought up their two kids without benefit of formal school. Taught them herself, and I haven't seen either of them since they were maybe third- or fourth-grade level, but I couldn't see then that they were learning from her anything of practical use in the world. Couple of entry-level screwballs but without any sign I could see of wit or humor. This isn't fair of me; I have seen too little of them to form a judgment fit to print, but it's instinctive with me and I let it stand.

Cath was a teacher with radical, Montessorian ideas and her own way of looking at and doing everything. No doubt that's where Helen gets it. Cath was not a particularly competitive racer but she could, like Jim Dunning, outdo us all in plain sailing. The sort who couldn't be bothered with an engine, and if she happened to be sailing a boat that had one, she just wouldn't be bothered starting it. Betty and I loved her dearly, but she was way left of me in politics. All but waterfront politics; there I was way left of her. I realize now that the difference is between those who own waterfront and those who don't. We had lots of differences besides those; she was opposed to my committee boat and particularly to being expected to help pay for it. There had been none in her day. But our worst dispute came when I, in my other hat, wanted to buoy a channel where one, in fact, existed and passed close in front of her sister Helen's house. It would bring more boats by her sister's beach. Mostly boats from outsiders in Mashpee. I will never be convinced, and she never asserted, that she was motivated by a desire to protect nature; she wanted to protect her sister's exclusive privacy. It seemed as though all her siblings and their children treated "Dr. Helen," the genius, as if she were a fool who needed protecting.

In spite of differences like these, we managed to remain good friends. When I was fifty years old, she took a hand in bringing me up! She heard I was planning a voyage down the Mississippi and was horrified to learn that I had never read Mark Twain on the subject. She ordered me to do so before I set sail. And, as I said at her funeral, she followed through. Quizzed me on it.

She was Aunt Cath to everybody. Betty's favorite Cath Opie story concerns a young couple, strangers to us, who came into our boat shop much bemused by a lady they had met on the beach. Just beyond Helen Taussig's is one of those one-lane-wide public landings, and there was this mysterious old lady busily shoving her sailboat off into impossibly shallow water and a lee shore. They offered to help; she offered to take them sailing, bundled them into the boat and continued to wade it out for what seemed miles, hoisted sails and took them on their first sail. There was, of course, no doubt in our minds who this mysterious lady was, and most impressive to us was that the boat was her son Frank's (and Tom White's) O'Day Mariner, nineteen feet with lead ballast and an iron centerboard, a heavy load for any one person to launch over a lee beach, and Aunt Cath was a tiny little lady anyhow. Long on nothing but determination. After she had a stroke and could no longer walk nor talk except "gobblegobblegobble" (not even "eggseggseggs") she had us to dinner, which she cooked from her wheelchair, still refusing all help. I was proud when her children asked me to lead off the Quaker-type memories at her funeral. And proud that my son mar-

ried her granddaughter, Frank's daughter. And proud that
my twin granddaughters show signs of ancestral brilliance as
well as of their other grandmother's beauty, qualities none of
which could have come from me.

Before I leave the family of Professor Taussig, I must return
to where I started: his house. Our crowd of young married
couples had great times there when our hosts were Edith and
Gerry Henderson. We played charades night after night, also
a sort of sexy version of hide and seek. I never could hide from
Edith; maybe didn't try hard enough. I discovered a new way
to get from the back door to the front of this three-story house
by going over the roof. In the dark. That's how much Victorian
ornamentation was nailed up on it. But memorable about
this house is that it shows the eternal stupidity of everybody.
Taussig moved it twice, back from the edge of the abyss as the
high sand bluff eroded. It would now be, if we are to believe
what we are told, a quarter mile out in Nantucket Sound if it
had not been moved. Frank Opie remembers the last move
landward, pulled by a rope from a capstan, turned by a horse
or mule driven round it, over planks and rollers. Moved over
a new foundation and jacked down onto it all without breaking
a dish. But now that the professor and his fortune are gone,
the house has been sold and the new owner, all unknowing,
has had all its Victorian finery restored and has had it moved
the other way, back again to the brink of the bluff.

> But wait, just wait
> We have not heard the last of fate.

One more tale of Taussig revealed by his grandson Gerry:
When our little local group of aging intellectuals gets together
to read poetry to each other, Gerry calls for the old professor's

favorite poem, "The Hippopotamus" by T. S. Eliot, in which, for those who don't know it, the poet compares the Hippo to the True Church, very much to the Hippo's advantage. I know this poem by heart, naturally. One of my favorites. And I produce it happily every time Gerry calls for it. One of the few things the old Prof and I ever agreed on.

XI
THE WEALTH
OF THE NATION

N OW AN ABRUPT change in the character of the neighbors. We are now out of Harvard dominance; next along
the shore and along Main Street come the three houses of
Frank H. Wesson and his sister, Miss Cynthia, both of them
more single-mindedly devoted to whatever they set out to do
than anybody I ever heard of. A family characteristic that follows the Wessons through generations. The Wessons came
here, I think, from Springfield, Massachusetts, the small-arms
town, where they made handguns. They made the world-
famous Smith and Wesson revolver, as loved by gun nuts as is
the Colt. Along with all my liberal ideas, I am anti-gun, but I
am as aware of the place of the handgun in the history of the
nation as anybody must be who has ever gone to the movies.
And, from what I saw in my prewar growing up and my tri-
fling military service, I understand some of the sexual adora-
tion men can develop for such a lovely, perfectly fitting piece
of machinery, the skin texture of machined metal, the precise
fit of the moving parts like a lovely body. It is a feeling and has

nothing to do with reason or words. There are as many Smith and Wesson nuts as there are Colt nuts.

What went on in the gun world at Springfield is not part of my bringing up; anyway, the Wessons sold (or maybe lost through losing controlling stock—I never heard) the company before I was aware of them, about the end of World War II, I think. Smith, whoever he was, had by then long been out of it, but sale of the company left Frank and Miss Cynthia, already loaded with cash, now overloaded with it. Frank had married a Miss Victoria Wilson from Wilson, Arkansas, a withering but stately southern village. I was there once when Frank Wesson, old Frank's grandson, took me on a tour of the countryside when I stopped in to visit on my way down the Mississippi. Young Frank and his mother lived on and operated the largest and most efficient farm I think there ever can be, outside the family village of Victoria, Arkansas. And here I am juggling, got three generations of Wessons in the air all at once, all with this common trait, this fierce drive and determination, and all programmed to marry people with the same trait.

Another trait they had in common, which was evident in the way they lived in Arkansas and in Cotuit: not only all they did, but all they had and owned and used, everything they manufactured or raised, must be the absolute world's best. I used to paint, launch and rig their skiff, and it was stored in what had once been their stable or their carriage house across Main Street from their houses, and such stabling you wouldn't believe. My family weren't poor people, but our children didn't have such accommodations as the Wessons' horses or, in another building, their carriages. By my time, they no longer kept horses or wagons, but the buildings were there, holding a few boats and a little gardening equipment. Big loose box stalls, running water to each; the horse just put his head in his private trough and pushed down a grill and let in water. Nothing ornate, but iron bars and gratings that were somehow classy, stall doors on smooth, noiseless hinges. Everything first class and spotless, but never showy.

Miss Cynthia gave her share of the proceeds from the sale of the gunworks to the employees, lock, stock and barrel (this cliché is a salvo from the firearm vocabulary). She was a rich lady many times over and didn't want more. Out of what she already had, she did secret charities in Cotuit and elsewhere. She made an even bigger thing of anonymity than did Miss Mabel Riley, but now, at least twenty years after her death and after her great-nephew Frank's death, who told me this in confidence, I hereby break down and reveal that it was Cynthia Wesson who, in secret, paid for all those dogwoods and other ornamental plantings that mask the unsightly macadam islands left when they straightened Putnam Avenue. She was always doing things like that, always in secret, and many world-class things she did have never been revealed. Those achievements of hers which are known are impressive enough: world-champion lady archer, world-champion grower and hybreeder of exotic orchids.

When my wife was compiling an oral history of Cotuit by taping interviews with old-timers, Cynthia showed her old photos of her part of the village as it was in her childhood, told her of what she used to see from her porch. Her porch overlooks a great expanse of water called on old charts "Cotuit Anchorage," where big schooners laden with coal from Norfolk, Baltimore and other ports where the coal railroads came down to the sea and bound for Boston, Portland and down east used to anchor to await a favorable wind, a sou'wester, before attempting to negotiate Pollack Rip Channel or Great Round Shoals Channel and get past Cape Cod. She had memories of over a hundred such vessels, three-, four-, even five-masters, all in view from her porch.

Next along the shore, Miss Cynthia had a larger house which she rented out most summers, often to relatives. Beyond that was the huge newer house of her brother Frank H. Wesson, a second- or third-generation gunmaker right out of Bernard Shaw and a strange paradox of flamboyance and anonymity. He had the Wesson tradition of perfection in all one did which showed in their farming, in their sailing and which made their revolvers so prized. If he indulged in secret charities as his sister did, he kept the secret well; I never heard of any. His lavishness went into the improvements of his estate, internal and external. He wasn't into boats and we didn't meet socially, so the only time I ever met him was when his fierce and beautiful daughter-in-law Matille hired me to put on a square-dance party for her son, Lee Wilson Wesson. The old gentleman presided as host, genial enough, but like all Wessons, he and Matille had their own ideas of how things should be done, and Cotuit's ideas didn't matter to them. They were paying for it, so it had to be the best.

The big Wesson house had a ballroom, and this was the only indoor dance I ever put on. The kids were so awestruck they even kept their shoes on. Frank and Matille had been told that to have a party for teenagers in Cotuit you had to have a square dance and to have a successful square dance you had to have Leonard Peck, nothing else would do. But then they found out that I didn't call the dances, only played records, so they hired a caller too, and an orchestra. This was the only time I ever worked with this guy; I think his name was Anderson, and he was good. He was Mr. Square Dance everywhere on Cape Cod except Cotuit, and we worked together harmoniously, though his dances were more conventionally sedate than my gang was used to. The kids enjoyed themselves, which was Matille's only specification when she ordered the party: "Nobody is to go away without having had a good time."

If I should have to categorize all Wessons, it seems this is the key to them: they have no patience with second best. Theirs had to be the best square dance ever. Not competitive exactly, just there could be nothing better. Everything any of them does has got to be the world's best. All the rice, all the cotton, all the soybeans they grow out in Arkansas is too good to eat or wear. Brings a premium price as registered seed. The old gentleman's grandson, for whom this party was given, was one of the quietest, least assertive of all the skiff-racing square dancers, but Lee Wilson Wesson had this same drive to excel. Later, as a young man, he had a larger racing sailboat custom built for a try at Olympic gold. He was too quiet and underplayed to suit his father, Frank Lee Wesson, so he was sent to military school and later served as an officer in the marines. He came out as gentle and easygoing as he went in. Everybody liked him; he was a thoroughly likable boy. He was commodore of the Mosquitoes one year. And handsome as well.

I have been going on about Lee Wilson Wesson, his grandfather and his great aunt Cynthia but nothing at all about the Wessons of my generation. Frank Lee Wesson, son of Frank H. and Victoria Wilson Wesson, husband of Matille, father of Lee Wilson and of the gorgeous Vicki and round, curly-headed Frank, was the most fiercely competitive of them all. He seems to have grown up on family property in Arkansas which came into the family along with his mother Victoria, and he had a loud Arkansas laugh and a coarse Arkansas sense of humor which were part of him, but only part. This macho image was so much a part of him that he took it for granted, not only in himself but as an essential part of every man. He told me that he had sent his gentle son to military school because the boy wasn't manly (by which he meant macho) enough. But along with it all, he was subtle, clever, even sensitive and, above all, diligent. He and Matille had no patience at all with indolence. How hard he worked was, to them, almost the sole measure of a man. Even sports, like boat racing, deserved the utmost effort, the expenditure of fortunes but, above all, sweat. Nothing slipshod or second rate ever. I loved the man, and I seem to have successfully fooled the whole family into a notion that my diligence met their standards. After all, I worked long days in the boatyard and then put on square dances four or five nights a week and, with Hayden's help and help from my father and a few others, I built the boatyard from nothing at all, and the whole must have shown signs they thought they recognized. At any rate, they chose to accept me and my whole family into their exclusive fellowship. And my inherently charming wife, who is in truth far more diligent than I, was in this, as in everything, a huge help to me. Betty was for years the supreme commander of the annual auction of the Cotuit Federated Church, and every one of those years, Matille contributed to this auction quantities of flowers from her vast gardens. These gave the proceedings a sweet and festive air and brought in a final burst of money the last day when they too were auctioned off.

Matille and Lee had a second son, Frank the Lord knows the how-manyeth, who never bothered to pretend any interest in sailing or any other society things. Frank's whole being seemed to exist to run the farm on all those acres surrounding the family village of Victoria, Arkansas. I spent the best part of a week in his company when I visited there on my way down the Mississippi, and one of the most important things he taught me was the true extent, the true meaning of the

Mississippi Delta. For all those acres which are submerged every spring, it means a brand-new, never-used layer of top-soil each year. The delta reaches all the way upstream almost to St. Louis. The Wessons don't rotate crops; they bring out the big Cats and plow up a new layer of topsoil every year on land that was for centuries underwater every spring. Their topsoil is everywhere over a hundred feet deep! Frank described it to me as "the wealth of the nation."

Another thing which no doubt helped this friendship along was the time in midwinter when I ran into Lee, Frank's father, in the Cotuit grocery store. He was in town by himself out of season on some sort of family business and with nothing to keep his restless body and mind busy. And that very evening, by the kind of luck of the unworthy which seems always following me, was the evening of the monthly meeting of the Boat Dealers' Association of which I was an officer, so I took Lee along as my guest. Of course he made a hit; he had an Arkansas drinking style which showed up like a skyrocket on Cape Cod; he was never burdened with shyness, and his presence reflected credit on me. The kind of customer I had! We had a speaker, Captain Norris Hoyt of Newport, a blue-water yachtsman of the bluest water, a professional speaker with a tray of slides of a horrendous heavy-weather transatlantic race. Thus I came to Lee's attention as more than just another kid half a generation younger than he and a far less competitive skiff racer, or as the owner of a small boat operation, not even on the water, convenient for hauling and painting his skiff. I now enjoyed the friendship and patronage of Lee Wesson and lived in fear of his idea of a joke.

Like one time I had a boat on the beach alongside the town wharf and was standing in water above my knees doing something to her bottom when Lee came up to the pier in his fast motorboat, going too fast, as usual. I was then harbor-master, and people expected me to restrain other people from going too fast, which in truth had nothing to do with the job. The harbormaster is supposed to control anchoring and dock-age, not speed. Anyhow, like I say, Lee came barreling in, throwing up an ungodly wash which soaked me up to my shirt pockets. I strode dripping down the wharf to read him out, and this is what he said: "Well! It couldn' a happened to a nicer gah. Know what? Ah ain' even sorry."

Lee lived as vigorously as Teddy Roosevelt. He had Inar Edwards, of Edwards boatyard just up the shore in Waquoit, build him this fast motorboat to Edwards' own design, ingen-iously stout and lightweight, the first really fast motorboat I ever saw with diesel power. Full of innovative ideas of Edwards' and of Wesson's. Lee Wesson, for example, dared openly to despise sport fishing in this place where it is almost as holy as golf. His boat was laid out to make fishing from her impossible; in place of the open cockpit all the way to the stern, she had living accommodations aft. Live-aboard cruising was not what Lee wanted to do; that cabin was a statement, pure defiance. And most characteristic, most defiant of all, was the Arkansas name he gave her: *Ginwhistle*. He had to explain it to me, but he did it cryptically: "Every farmer in the South, he gets his ass up to it." It meant the steam whistle on the cotton gin; in Arkansas, it regulates life. On Cape Cod, nobody knows what he is talking about, which is altogether satisfying. Typically, Lee Wilson once waterskied all the thirty miles to Nantucket behind *Ginwhistle*. And typically, never said a word about it.

The name was appropriate with an irony Frank Lee never got to appreciate. He died of a heart attack resulting from the exertions of fighting the fire that destroyed the Victoria cot-ton gin. Matille told us bitterly that the gin was "an ol' wreck

anyway," they were thinking of tearing it down. Matille Over-
ton Wesson! Talk about a character. She and her husband
must have agreed about everything, or they would have torn
each other apart, for neither was capable of conceding a point.
The irresistible force etcetera. The things they agreed on,
right or wrong, included dislike of hired help. Matille said,
"They don' know how to work an' they don' wanna learn."

I ran into her one day at the Cotuit Post Office and she said
to me, "Lennaard, Ah heah yore goin' down the rivah in yo'
boat. Yo' won' see a thing in that ol' rivah. But yo' an' Betty
come see us. Give us a call when yo' go by Osceola, y'heah?"
Writing the way they talk in rural Arkansas ain' easy, but I
can't recall Matille's words without Matille's voice. I could
not, in the few chances she gave me, explain to her a delicate
and private matter. Couldn't get it into her head that I was
making this voyage alone; Betty was not going to be with me.
Our marriage was going through a rough time; I was going
past fifty, had a young mistress and was sailing away by
myself. "May come back, may not. See other men. Make yourself a life without me." Matille wouldn't hear this. People she
associated with don't act this way.

Matille Wesson was like Amy Coolidge or Alice Ropes; an
invitation from her comes without the option to decline. So,
when my tugboat and I were coming down the Mississippi,
when we had reached the point, half a day above Memphis,
where the chart shows Osceola, Arkansas, I did indeed call
Matille. And anchored up a chute and went for a visit with
Matille and her younger son Frank, and Betty flew out and
joined us. I have written up this visit in some detail, but it is
no part of this informal and inexact history of Cotuit, so I
have omitted it from this book. If anyone imagines he wants
to read about it, it is available in a short pamphlet.

But I should explain that one argument I used to get Betty to join me for this visit was catfish. One of the new things she had taken up in my absence was the study of aquaculture; she had gotten herself made a deputy shellfish warden so that she could legally possess seed oysters, and on some of our waterfront she was experimenting with oyster propagation, trying to get the stubborn creatures to breed once again in our waters. And the Wessons were very much into aquaculture, for in reclaiming their Mississippi bottomland they had left deep pits where they had taken fill, and since nothing in their universe must ever be wasted, they had put the ponds to work, too, growing catfish for market. Frank showed us the whole operation, but Matille refused to cook anything so working class in her kitchen or serve it on her table. Frank had to take us out to a restaurant for us to taste any!

Just one more Wesson, and then I'm through: Victoria the younger, Vickie to lucky people like her friends, like me. Tall and willowy, graceful, looking very like her mother, but far less bound by southern notions of what is ladylike. My first memories of her were of a very young maiden screaming with an Arkansas voice in mock terror, fleeing from a crowd of pursuing little Yankee boys, running like a deer which she so much resembled, Vickie and her petite, black-haired friend Tucky, just as childish-beautiful though built on a smaller scale. The sight of the two of them growing up barefoot all over that part of Cotuit, learning to wear shoes not only on the feet but on the personality, was enough to make a man twenty-five years or so older rue the loss of his youth.

XII
LARGER THAN LIFE

S O FINALLY, AFTER a prolonged visit with the Wessons, Betty and I left in the boat; she rode with me down to Memphis, where I tied up the boat and flew home with her for a visit, maybe leading to a reconciliation. Nothing definite yet. Then back to the boat and continued down the river and around Florida, so up the coast and home. My second childhood was over (I am now well into my third), and I slowly discovered that I wanted nothing but to get back to Cotuit and Betty. Not surprising; the surprising part is that she consented, a little reluctantly, to have me back. I had left thinking of myself as Ulysses, Tennyson's version of him. I came home truly like him, to a house full of suitors.

And back in this book, after a hiatus similar to the one a little of which I have just recounted, I take up again our interrupted stroll south and west along the beach and along Main Street, pausing to look in on people who are interesting, which, in such a place, means eccentric. Before 1955, the classic Popponessett sand spit stood close offshore protecting miles of fine beach with high ground behind it, but before that, in the time of which Miss Cynthia Wesson kept photographs, there used to be an island just off the Wessons', where there was later shallow water and swift current in and out of Popponessett Bay. It must have been a more substantial island than Dead Neck or Samson's, for they tell of pasturing cows on it, and no cow ever was tough enough to live on beach grass. Assateague ponies can subsist on such a diet, but not dairy cows. This island was there in the memories of folks who were still alive when I was a child. In its place when I was racing skiffs was the Taussig buoy we used to race around, and just west of that the tip of that sand spit, entrance to the huge, almost landlocked Popponessett Bay, but you had to sail the best part of a mile behind the spit before the bay opened. The spit was joined to the mainland at its west end, in Mashpee, and was made of sand dropped in its transit eastward by the wave-caused current called littoral drift.*

So all the expensive summer homes west of Wessons had this barrier beach to protect them from storm damage. Some ground here was low, and people built their houses almost at sea level, like the Porter House but without high wooded land

---

*The waves roll in from Vineyard Sound, driven by the prevailing southwest wind, and roll out toward the southeast at precisely the same angle with the shore, in a way analogous to light reflecting from a mirror. They erode the shore where they strike it, bouncing off the high sand bluffs of Succonessett in Mashpee and taking sand from these cliffs with them in a current of water eastward. And when, for any reason, this current slows down, it can't carry so much, and it drops some of its sand right there. Across the mouth of broad, shallow Popponessett Bay it slows down this way and leaves this long bar of sand. Sand from it is blown by the west wind and piled up clear of the water, and there is this long bar continually washing away eastward with the wind and current and continually replenished from the west. At its east end sand is deposited, and the bar grows in this direction, eastward toward Cotuit, increasingly unstable the farther eastward,

to windward for protection. And then the barrier beach washed away in only one year, practically before our eyes, and left these houses almost in Nantucket Sound. It was popularly believed that Hurricane Carol, 1954, which hit Cotuit practically dead center, was what caused this sudden change; certainly it made a breach in the spit way up at the Mashpee end, and it is possible that if one had had on hand a bargeful of sand and rock and had dumped it in the breach within twenty-four hours, the future might have been different. But Professor Mather would tell you that causes of geologic change are far more complex, and the gradual building and sudden disappearance of this sandbar are all part of a recurring cycle. I am, myself, convinced that man played a part in it this time; he was taking steps, all ill-coordinated and many ineffective, to protect those bluffs at Succonessett, on which he was now building expensive homes and condos, from further erosion, building piecemeal groins and seawalls,[†] interrupting the flow of sand to replenish what was washed away downcurrent. For the spit was no way solid; made of sand in motion, some washing away and more taking its place, and now there was suddenly less to take its place.

away from its source. It builds until something occurs to change its pattern of replenishment. It had, by the 1950s, grown out past the bay mouth and continued to build eastward for nearly a mile, separated by a narrow channel from solid ground in Cotuit. The ebb and flow of the tides of Popponessett Bay kept a channel open behind the spit deep enough to sail shoal vessels like skiffs in and out at any tide and barely wide enough for a singularly agile vessel like a skiff to beat through even against the wind.

[†]A seawall (bulkhead) is particularly vulnerable. A wave breaks against it, just as it is supposed to do, the top of the wave splashes over, maybe as spray, and the top of the wall keeps it from running back over it into the sea. So, when the soil is pure sand, it sinks in behind the wall and seeps back to the ocean underneath. More waves follow and the ground is saturated, and all that water undermines the wall until it collapses

Anyway, there now ensued a flurry of demands for unrealistically expensive artifacts to protect the shore and those expensive homes in Cotuit, and a line of seawalls and many groins were built to keep the waves and the littoral drift from washing those homes away. When the people who sought this relief could not persuade some level of government to do it for them, and quickly, they did it for themselves, in good or less successful ways.

The people in these houses are almost as unstable as the shore itself. Except for a few, whom I will mention, many of them come and go faster than one can get to know them. The next house beyond Wesson's, last stop on Mr. Milton's milk route, was, until recently, the summer home of Alva Morrison, for years before his death a good customer of ours, father of Sally, a pretty lady a little older than I, a good skiff racer, and mother of Vicki Wesson's pal, the beautiful Tucky Kerlin. Old Alva once hired me and my first motorboat to transport him with his camera and blind to Samson's Island, where he wanted to observe a rare waterfowl which, evidently by mis-

into the hole washed under it. To remedy this, you must be right there to call for a truckload of rock and a load of transit-mix to pour from above into the gap behind the wall to fill the hole. Quickly.

Groins, which are for our purposes the same thing as jetties, are more stable, and they work on a different principle: they capture more sand rather than retain the old. They are long piles of rough rocks, each weighing several tons, extending out from the shore; each rock must be placed precisely, so they interlock, by a long-boom crawler crane working right on the beach. And if the rocks are heavy enough not to be tossed about by storm waves, they slow up the littoral drift so that it drops some of its burden of sand at each groin and so forces the drift offshore. Groins are expensive; require a skillful and experienced crane operator and a large and expensive machine exposed to sand erosion and salt corrosion. So marine construction remains one of the most take, was nesting there. A shearwater. The parent birds could hardly be missed, huge, shiny black with long, narrow wings like a B-24, bright yellow feet and bill as large as one from Abercrombie and Fitch. They flew just above the surface of the water with the lower part of the bill actually immersed, scooping up fish which were forced by the jet of water right down the bird's throat into its stomach. I watched them, fascinated, before Morrison got into the act, marveling at this efficient way of fishing. The old gent had me help him pack all this gear to a site a few feet from the nest, right on the ground among the beach grass, and then walk back to my boat and go away so the birds would think we had both left. Birds, he explained to me, can't count. (Like me, only worse.)

Worked fine; he got some marvelous pictures of the wrong birds. Turned out they were not shearwaters at all. He had misidentified them; they were great black skimmers, much less rare. Just as rare to me; I had never seen either species in my life, but not remarkable to ornithologists; just unusual to see them nesting on "these inner beaches." Unusual but not unheard of, so Morrison's learned article never got published.

Alva Morrison was a fine gentleman and one of the early fathers of the Mosquito Yacht Club. He had a hand in commis-

costly of all the works of man. And politicians are shy of being found doing such expensive favors for the very rich. The entire revenue of all layers of government would hardly suffice to protect all the shores of all the nation. Anyway, again as Professor Mather would have told us, nature works in cycles. In time, it will replace the sand spit in some form, but probably not until the present houses are gone, certainly their occupants. Long term, probably all of what we now call Cape Cod will be washed into one huge sandbar, mostly underwater, and may then, or meanwhile, be glaciated again. Short term, I see that nature is already taking care of the problem, for offshore, way out into Nantucket Sound, the water is so shallow that it is barely navigable even at high tide. Much of that Succonessett sand is still out there, just underwater, still helping protect the summer homes along the shore.

sioning the standard skiff design and, around 1926, bought two boats built to the new plans. One he kept for his own children, the other he didn't like because the keelson was outside the bottom planking. She was as fast as the other, but he sold her, and by my time she was the property of Barbie Hale. So much beauty all around me in my adolescence!

After Morrison's came a house which changed hands several times, always seemed to be occupied by someone who was into boats and became our customer, then the starkly simple cottage of Dr. Helen Taussig, already mentioned. These three houses face the open sound, but behind the three of them is a body of water called Oregon Pond, sometimes called Rushy Marsh Pond, a landlocked salt pond always remarkable for the quantity and variety of the bird life. There was a pair of swans raising a brood there every summer at a time when wild swans were exceedingly rare. Oregon Pond is separated from the salt water of Popponessett Inlet by a narrow isthmus over which still runs a narrow dirt driveway serving the three houses, over a plank bridge under which, some years, the tide ran in and out of the pond and which in other years spanned merely mud. And just where this drive comes out to Main Street, Main Street and its pavement end, and after a gate always left open and a "Private Property" sign, you come to a fork which once said Pine Ridge Road to the left and Vineyard Road to the right but is now Vineyard Road both ways. The road is a loop, circling round in the woods for about two miles and coming back to the same fork. Both ways it leads to the front gate of the grounds and summer home of Horatio Gates Lloyd. Both these roads carry on like unpaved extensions of Main Street. The one to the left, closer to the shore, leads past half a dozen waterfront homes, each now behind some sort of seawall, before achieving Lloyd's. Some of them, to my slowed-down point of view, seem to be changing hands almost continuously. That is true also of waterfront homes in Florida, where they are retirement homes, and to be able to afford one, it must already be on the skids. One of them belonged, before he died, to H. G. Lloyd's brother Richard. Another belonged, for a short while, to the admirable Ben White, who is still alive but has been all his life a restless resident, changing summer homes every few years. This one was rented, for a summer or two, to my friend Florence Rothschild, who had three beautiful daughters, pupils and disciples of mine, good skiff racers and enthusiastic square dancers. I have been more or less in love with all three of them for almost fifty years.

Before going into more detail about these threatened homes and the people who lived in them and then moved on, it is time for another passage of disclaimer, a further qualification of what I write. Like the statement of the limitations of my numbers, not for measuring but for coloring, this concerns these childhood memories of mine and the way they change as the child who remembers them ages. The little child of the beginning of this memoir remembers facts with a precision that is absolutely reliable: who lived where and to whom he was related. The child made no value judgments unless somebody was particularly benevolent or particularly mean. But as I get older, the memory grows less reliable; it remembers things wrong. You are being shown people and events through the eyes of a grown-up (and please note to my credit that I did not say an adult) rather than those of a child. The account becomes more subjective, and details of events less certain. I did not anticipate this change, but the character of the whole book has altered even as it flows through my fingers onto the paper.

To illustrate this change in attitude, I here bring into my story, deliberately out of place, a girl from another part of town to show how boorish socially prominent people can be when their parents have no manners to teach them. Concerns a girl so bustily voluptuous that all the boys her age followed drooling wherever she went. She was born knowing how to use this musk to get her way, and she was smart enough to marry early, before she was overtaken by the fate of big girls: premature obesity. One time she was coarse enough to brag to me that she was a virgin when she married. To me, who watched her in action, that proves (or would, if I had believed it) only that, worse than a whore, she was a world-class tease.

When I was struggling to make a living out of that infant boatyard, one of the things I had going for me was a dealership in Cousens and Pratt sails. I had formed a friendship which went beyond just business with Mr. Harold Cousens, and when everybody in skiffs wanted a sail like mine, mine was the only place you could get one, an exclusive which I defended vigilantly by paying all his bills immediately on receipt. So this broad, the daughter of one of the snottiest families in town, ordered a new sail for her skiff. Then she divorced her husband. I have nothing to say about right and wrong in this case, except that the guy had to have been a sucker to have married such a tramp in the first place, but he had no use himself for a sail to fit her boat. He wasn't a Cotuit boy and had no skiff nor any use for a skiff sail. She had the sail and she hoisted it for every race, flaunted it in my face and refused to pay for it. Said her husband had bought it for a present for her and it was his responsibility. Tough for me; one of the things that happen in business. Only my business here was based on a slightly less arm's-length relationship than that. Tough on me again. What I resent about this was what she and her alcoholic father then did: got me sitting down between them at a party at Florence Rothschild's, where I was a guest and could not make the retorts that occurred to me, and set out to convince me that they were right and that I had no business asking them for money. Legally they were right; Lester Solomon, a New York lawyer of the toughest, said they were. He got me a judgment against the ex-husband in the place where he lived, but it meant nothing; all he had to do was move. And law or no, it was shabby for people who traded as they did on their old family name to cheat a little business like mine.

Back walking along the shore from Morrison's to Lloyd's, I could put together a list of the people who lived along this shore in the seventy (very) odd years my memory covers, but lists are tiresome to write and tiresome to read. I could mention Forrest Campbell, an irascible widower. He married a young wife who afterward divorced him and married his son, by whom she had two children. Campbell the younger made a huge play (unsuccessful she tells me, and I believe her) for my wife. I could mention Robert Schwab, who, plainly under the influence of Rachel Carson's *The Silent Spring,* wrote an article about Oregon Pond which he called "Death of a Salt Pond," published in the *Atlantic.* Tells of the extinction by human pollution of all the wildlife around the pond. A tragedy, tragically told. All caused by people, what else? Break your heart. Only trouble is that Oregon Pond ain't dead at all. It and all its wildlife—swans, herons, ducks and geese—are still here, as alive as they ever were. Maybe his article saved it. But Schwab is long dead.

Schwab was an avid sailor, always out in an old blue catboat he had, which he sailed so unspectacularly that she seemed to be sailing herself without his help. Now I think of it, just like he saved the pond. Schwab and his sister Frannie lived in another odd house, solid poured concrete from cellar to attic. Frannie Schwab married, late in life, an erudite English gentleman, Robbie Hewick, and the two of them were, for a while, in business selling Latin American artifacts in a former gas station just outside, as the law requires, of Cotuit.

We shared a love for English poetry, and Robbie never showed a trace of jealousy over my ability to outquote him. They understood that this talent of mine was the result of a trick memory and not of any special effort or diligence. I didn't work at it. I can memorize a poem that I like with just one reading and one review. Indeed, I have shown gross indolence in not making of this gift anything beyond a way to entertain parties and seduce girls. Frannie and Robbie were singularly good to me, praised my writing, wrote to the editor and praised it when I was doing a weekly column in *Cape Cod News*, put me in touch with a New York agent who found me a publisher for the book I was then working on about my solo voyage by tugboat around the United States and Canada and what makes a happy and successful man of fifty act as crazy as I was acting. So I had everything a beginning writer could want: top agent, number-one publisher, but only half a manuscript. Ran out of steam about Chicago, never finished writing it. I was, as everybody warned me, trying to make it carry too much. All the professionals I knew warned me: Kurt Vonnegut, Harold Brodkey, everybody else. Could be a travel book, a sex book, a marriage book, but I was not adequate to sustain all three.

After her brother died, that silly concrete house was sold, and Frannie and Robbie tried to live in an old, really truly working barn which they had Hayden move to land beside Oregon Pond. They brought some beautiful artifacts to that barn, but it was, they found, impossible to keep warm in spite of some original ideas, like a fabric ceiling in the center over a floor-to-roof well where the hay had been raised into the loft. Finally they gave up and moved to a modern house nearer the center of the village, a house designed by Betty Peck and occupied by us until our children were grown up and out. Then Betty designed us a much grander one on the shore of Popponessett Bay where the boatyard wasn't. You see, and in case you care, Betty and I got back together again after my boat and I came home. She too had had a good change and vacation for that year, but it is not my place to tell it for her. Except to say that all her adventures only made me more proud of her. Penelope indeed.

Another family along this shore leading to Lloyds' was the Luquers, Grace and Lea, Boston society by background, preservationists by profession. Lea was head of the Society for the Preservation of New England Antiquities. They had two stalwart and very handsome sons, both of whom were employed for at least one summer at Pecks' Boats, and Gracie, their rarely tall and superbly beautiful daughter, the "showpiece" of my expert dancers at the Pines, the showpiece of everything she graced. I am admittedly susceptible, but Cotuit has more beautiful daughters than any place this side of Hollywood.

*   *   *

And going along this shore, we must call also on Sue Herman, one of the best-known liberals of her generation. It was explained to me that her presence here was the nucleus around which accumulated many liberals of the 1920s and 1930s. Pat Jackson was one of them; she it was who persuaded him to acquire a summer home here, to bring his young family into this Lowell's mouth. I used to discuss politics a little with Sue but found her too liberally naive to warrant much attention. She was heart and soul into the effort to unseat Eisenhower and elect Adlai Stevenson. Highly desirable, I agreed, but too wishful. Not the least possibility for someone with all her experience to get so worked up about. I told her so, and she seemed truly shocked by my opinion. Can you believe it?

Sue was not too liberal to produce one more beautiful daughter, Marybel (I don't know how she spells it), who is married (still) to Dr. Will Cochran, a pleasant, genial guy with a tremendous talent for saying things that get a rise out of me, make me furious, and then he laughs.

One more friend I had out this way: John T. Connor, a top-level executive of major worldwide corporations, including some that were implicated in corporate dirty work, though John T. seems never to have been involved in any of it. And personally, he is one of the nicest of the nice people I have been privileged to know. He has a beautiful wife who comes on so friendly it still startles me. They have three equally friendly children, for whom I built the last of my eighteen skiffs.

XIII
OF HEROIC SIZE

Now, at the risk of offending many good friends and good customers along this shore by leaving them out, I will skip to the Lloyds, Gates and his brother Richard, the gentlest gentlemen I have ever known in a life surrounded by gentility. The Lloyds made, as Emerson wrote, no noise. They had something like what the Fred Lowells had, a family so large and so loving that they had little need of the rest of the world. I would probably never have known them at all except that their children got into skiff racing, and when such people get into something, they do it thoroughly. Gates Lloyd's house was the last on the bluff before it subsides into salt marsh, the westernmost beside the channel behind that ephemeral sand spit, where it widens and the water shoals into Popponessett Bay. Dick Lloyd's house was two wharves east of it, and between them the brothers owned all the land between the bays (Cotuit and Popponessett) except for those lots they had already sold, now occupied by the people mentioned in the last chapter (most of them) as far back as the end of Main

Street. The Lloyds sponsor the Popponessett Race every year, and they sponsor it thoroughly, complete with a cookout lunch after the finish, on their lawn, for everybody involved and their guests. Gates and Dick have passed on, but their children and grandchildren continue the tradition. There was a Popponessett Race in 1999 complete with lunch.

Skiff races traditionally start, hardly ever on time, at ten in the morning, all but the Sunday afternoon races, and to the finish line off Lloyds' isn't that long a sail from the Loop; guests start arriving for lunch before lunchtime. So, when I was running the races, I used to lengthen them by sending the fleet up into the shallow bay and round some temporary mark I would set out for the occasion—once had them get out of their boats and wade through six inches of water over bottomless mud to tag the guardrail along the highway which runs across the head of the bay—so as to end up at Lloyds' at a proper lunchtime. Also it was a pleasure of mine, part of the teaching I was always doing, to get the kids to know more about our waters, to make of them all-round sailors like Jim Dunning or Cath Opie, more than just 'round-the-buoys racers.

Popponessett Bay is another glacial pothole, left by a melting block of buried ice, open at one end to the sea. This particular block had been broad but not thick, so where the ice melted it left a hole more shallow than some, and the ice melted sooner and the hole started filling up with silt sooner than places like Cotuit or Hyannis, so it is ghastly shallow from end to end, and who knows how deep in stinky mud. It is close to eutrophication, a condition Betty learned about when studying aquaculture, in which there is so much life rotting that all the oxygen in the water and in the mud is used up, the bottom turns acid and life can no longer exist. Meanwhile, it is almost as full of exotic waterfowl as Assateague

Refuge: ducks, geese, swans diving and stretching their necks down to feed off the bottom, cormorants, terns, ospreys, herons fishing, gulls stealing from everybody, altogether a place the kids should not be allowed to ignore. They'll appreciate it later, even more than Latin. One couple, at the stage of being more interested in the nature of each other than in sailing or in wildlife, swamped their skiff. Couldn't capsize; water isn't deep enough for a skiff on her side. They ended up standing in their boat in water above their ankles, boat full of water sitting on the bottom, both laughing like fools. I had, of course, to go to their assistance; that's what I was there for. Brought *The Big Wheel* alongside, circulating mud and quahogs through the propeller, *clank clank*, took them aboard still helpless with glee, and their boat, free of their weight, floated up so I could pump the water out of her with my big salvage pump. Forgive this digression in an account of the Lloyds; it is right in line with my main purpose, to show what life was like in this idyllic summer community.

But, on the subject of Popponessett Bay, it is the same body of water at the head of which my father bought me the land for my boatyard, and the shallowness is only one reason, the least of many, why I never built the boatyard there. When I was little, I explored every inch of it in *Ariel*, as well as East Bay and Centerville River to the east of us and Waquoit Bay to the west. These potholes are also shallow. Cotuit and Hyannis were relatively major ports, while none of these was much more than a small boat harbor and shellfishing ground. And Betty and I now live on the shore of Popponessett Bay. That guardrail I had the kids tag can be seen from our bedroom windows.

Back a couple miles down the bay to the Lloyds: they are not Harvard nor Boston society, not New York society, either, but Philadelphia. Main Line, the people there call it, which is the grandest and most exclusive of them all. But the Lloyds, H. Gates II and his children, show no snobbery at all. Every one of them looks you straight in the face and talks to you as though you were the most interesting person all day. The oldest boy, H. Gates III, called Terry, married a Cotuit summer girl in every way his match, only prettier: Perky Wadsworth, from the opposite end of the village, from the big house with the red roof, one of my square dancers, descended from and named for the Perkins family, great people from all one hears. I just missed knowing any of them except Perky and her brother and sisters and her marvelously friendly and outspoken mother, Martha Perkins Wadsworth, a great sailor along with everything else.

Perky had no need of sailing lessons from me, but she was full of spirit and a graceful dancer. She and I had a special thing, for she loved English poetry as much as I. I introduced her to "The Miller's Tale," and she showed me the technical skill of Kipling. We were for years intimate without touching. She and Terry suited each other perfectly and were an example to the world of how perfect a marriage can be when there is plenty of money. They had I don't know how many children. They had also a handsome fiberglass sloop, thirty-five feet, which she bought him for a birthday surprise and which they once allowed us, like we were doing them a favor, to sail for them as far as New York the year they took her south. And they signed on our son Bill as one of the crew to race with them from Annapolis to Newport on the way back. Always they acted grateful for the favors they did us.

Noble people are noble in adversity. Gates Lloyd suffered from a lingering illness. Terry and Perky gave parties from time to time in his huge house, and those of us who had known him always took the trouble, one or two at a time, to go over to his wheelchair and spend part of the evening talking to the old gentleman. He was just as gracious as ever, even when you could tell he wasn't sure who you were. He concentrated hard until he got it straightened out, always said something to show he knew you, referred to something in the past. His son Terry did a Winston Churchill: when he was in London he stepped out of a car on the wrong side and was run down. He was physically handicapped the rest of his life. But his rising to his feet when he had a visitor was always gallant. His rising to any occasion, even bereavement. Perky was most gallant of all; she died slowly and in pain of cancer but never failed in graciousness, even with a scarf round her head to hide the absence of that lovely black hair. It had been lovely still, even mixed with gray.

The other Lloyds, Terry's brother Wingate, his sisters Minnie and Prue, are also gentle and gracious, though I am losing the ability to tell all the children and grandchildren apart. The boys are all friendly and polite, the girls also and pretty as well. One of the things I have gotten out of the life I have chosen in Cotuit is the privilege of knowing such people. From the Lowells to the Wessons to the Lloyds. I am one lucky man.

So I have led my readers along the shore from the Narrows to Popponessett Bay, introducing all the summer people I knew in over seventy years here. Still to cover is the part of town that is not on the water, the property of people of less affluence, more year-round people, many more of my good friends. But fewer of my friends every year. They are dying off and their children can't make their living here, and their places are being taken, their houses bought up by newcomers, their woodlots and pastures bought up and built upon by retirees looking for a peaceful place to retire and destroying the peace in their quest. Fighting for space. My mother had a line handed down from her Irish ancestors: "Foitin' loike divils for conciliation and hatin' each ither for the love o' God."

From Lloyds' there are two ways back to Main Street, either side of the same loop of road. Either will bring you back to the same place—the beginning of pavement and of Main Street —and it is possible to take a left a couple places along the left barrel and reach places beside Popponessett Bay, like the one the kids called Beer Beach.

This place belonged to Buddy Bailey; it has now been developed into one more suburb. Or enter a maze of one-lane sand roads through recent-growth woods, scrub pine and scrub oak and thus bypass the marsh and Oregon Pond, bypass Wessons, and get deviously back to Cotuit, but the direct route is to stay on the pavement which, after a sharp bend, runs straight back, the way we have come, to the center, past Taussigs, past Dunnings on both sides of you. Every side street has now been paved, a questionable improvement. Now they're putting in curbstones, even more questionable. It is all built up since I came here, full of people who, as Amy Coolidge said as we drove past the Sandwich dump on our way back to Wellesley, "people who have no business here."

We have already met, stopped in with or at least waved to everybody in the first mile or two: Gerry Henderson, his and everybody's Aunt Cath, Frannie and Robbie Hewick; must wave emphatically to Jim Dunning's buxom niece Julia. We are approaching Mattison country. When I first knew them, the Mattisons lived in two comfortable, unpretentious houses side by side. Joseph Mattison the elder (I met him just once; he was out of the picture by the time I came along) married the daughter of Dr. Woodman, a distinguished gentleman who, along with Morse, Morrison and others of their age, first tried to bring under control the design of the Cotuit skiff. I never knew Woodman; he and his daughter, the first Mrs. Mattison, were dead when I came on the scene. She left three children, all with Mattison's loud, raucous voice and his readiness to take charge of any unsupervised situation and supervise hell out of it. That way of talking, so unlike the gentle, soft tones of New Englanders, disguised the inherent kindness and generosity of these Mattisons. Anna, the oldest of them, was foremost in yacht club politics all through her childhood and beyond. Eminently sensible in all the decisions she didn't hesitate to make. Back home in Summit, New Jersey, she ran for coroner, with the one-line slogan "Abolish Coroners."

Always lecturing in that voice, she taught me how to teach kids to square dance. She and I, but more than either of us the kids themselves, created that wild, loose, exuberant style of dancing which took hold here. She married Archie Murray, an insurance executive who specialized in the number side of the business rather than the merely human policyholders. He was huge, tall, stout, agreeable, but beside the dash and color of Anna, he was almost invisible.

Anna had a sister Ruth, quieter and prettier, too smart to compete with Anna on Anna's ground. Ruth was the best of all of us at any sort of intellectual parlor game, where her share of the Mattison competitiveness came out; had a huge store of miscellaneous lore of history, literature, theology, even science. She could even compete with me in quoting poetry. Once we were playing "the game," and I thought up the phrase "Balaam's ass" for Ruth to act out. None of her team could figure it out, for nobody present, though all Harvard graduates or equivalent, had ever heard of the animal. Ruth could not believe such ignorance. "Don't you remember?" said she, "he tied his ass to a tree and walked seven miles into town!"

Ruth Mattison devoted her life, successfully it is assumed, to keeping her explosive husband Will from flying apart from the swift, eddying current of his own ideas. They are still together, living in an old-folks depository. Joe, old Mattison's only son, is exactly my age, a sharp and competitive yacht racer in Wiannos and larger boats, a born winner, and he has a lifelong history of quiet acts of generosity. No cause so hopeless that Joe won't contribute if a friend asks him to. He lent me a thousand dollars (a lot of money then) when I opened my boatyard. That was all my working capital when I went into business. It is astonishing to me, with the prejudices I carry, that such a man should choose to become a stockbroker, but that is what Joe did. Successfully; once had his own seat "on change" and is still working at it. Joe Mattison was "all heart." When a guy I knew put me in touch with Bob Rich, a genius boatbuilder down Maine who built classic lobster boats, Joe gave me an order for one. A simple and lovely boat for Joe at a down-east price, a further step into serious marine business for me. And a broadening of my acquaintance in the trade, which did me much good for the rest of my life.

Mattison the elder's second wife was Philadelphia society, but unlike the understated Lloyds, Edith Mattison the elder was overstated, with a loud, brassy Philadelphia voice and Philadelphia money. She built the second house alongside the first, which had been Woodman's, and the two houses were known as "The Ship" and "The Helm." Mrs. Mattison was a "fierce lady" and had one fierce daughter, Edith, and a gentle one, Faith. Edith suffered all her life from competing with, trying to match, Anna, which she just about achieved in dominance, but she never had any idea of Anna's gentleness and affection. She crowded poor Faith right out of the picture, right out of the village. She was perhaps the best sailor among the Mattisons—they were all good—certainly the most competitive, the one to whom it mattered most. She married Gerry Henderson (grandson of Professor Taussig), and the fighting couple formed one of the pillars of the young married set of which Betty and I, also fighting a great deal of the time, formed another. She and Gerry had their own skiffs and they kept up their running battle on sea as on shore. Over the water you could hear more of it. Didn't mean anything; that's how the two related, but Edith was a born fighter, and Gerry was nothing of the kind. She could outreason, outargue and outshout him or anybody else. She bore him five children to prove that they found time to do something besides argue, and when they were mostly grown, she left him for a guy with a bigger boat.

Next house toward the center lived, when I was a boy, Roland Nickerson, who seems to have been racing skiffs before I or the Mosquito Club was born. He it was who won, in 1905, that bronze trophy that is now in my attic. He lived there on Main Street with no wife, but with his daughter Jeanette, my age and my friend, and owned a handsome twenty-three-foot motorboat, a double-ended ship's lifeboat fitted with a one-cylinder gas engine that was, I think, an afterthought. She was built strictly for rowing and looked sort of like a whaleboat. I afterward owned this boat—she made the rounds of Cotuit like a whore—and before me, she belonged to Bucky Botello, before him to Tom Fisher, and I later sold her to Bobby Madeiros. She became my first *Big Wheel of Cotuit*. She had, by that time, a six-cylinder engine lifted out of a thirties Chevy and coupled half-assed to a marine reverse gear which had been part of a truly marine engine, a Gray or a Kermath or such. Sure and consistent trouble until I replaced that gear with a modified Chevy automobile transmission which had to be scraped into gear each time I sought neutral or astern but worked reliably once I got Dave Leland to further modify it by welding the teeth back on and hardening them in his forge. The Chevy had more power than the little boat could ever use, even as I used it towing up to a dozen skiffs to Hyannis for their regatta.

It was Stan Nickerson who put me in the picture on Roly's past. Strange, these Nickersons acknowledged no relationship to each other. Cotuit is full of year-round Nickersons who never admit to being related. It is all part of what I see, from my lofty pedestal, as the inbreeding that went on on Cape Cod. I say—have never done anything, but say it—that I could draw you a map of Cape Cod in pre-automobile times based on family names. All Nickersons in Cotuit, all Crosbys in Osterville, all Giffords in Marstons Mills, all Lawrences in downtown Falmouth, all Chases in Harwich, on and on. Seems the old-timers did their courting near home. In Cotuit I know three large Nickerson families who will not admit being related to one another. It is a phenomenon not restricted to Nickersons, but some families in Cotuit show the same superficial signs of inbreeding as some of the Lowell relatives.

Not all of them; the village lost a great man when Stan Nickerson moved to the city to seek his fortune. He never came back except for brief visits. Imagine what a history he might write of a generation ahead of mine. That's one of the things that inspired me to write this. Not only write a history; Stan made history. He was the first and the only person to this day who ever sailed a racing skiff to Nantucket. (I better say here that I am aware that this was done also by Chat

Churbuck's deliberate cousin Tom Fisher, but Tom's boat was not a racing skiff, more like a commercial shellfisher, smaller sail, much heavier hull.) Stan's trip was a dangerous, many would say foolhardy, undertaking. The currents in the Sound are stronger and less predictable than anyplace this side of Fundy, the winds are stronger and there are unmarked places out of sight of land with only six inches of water. You have to know where you are every second. Stan had a gift for tale-telling, and his oral account of the voyage was breathtaking. An encounter with the island steam packet which thought to rescue him, and his difficulty, from boat to ship, convincing the ferry in sign language that he neither wanted nor needed rescuing. The tale is part of my childhood; it left me with a wish to sail my own skiff to Nantucket. I never did, but when I was a kid I used to lie about it, say I had.

Across Main Street, where Ocean View rejoins it, Ruth Mattison Ebling and her husband Will built a new house for themselves and their four children. They had endured, for an astonishing time, sharing The Ship with Anna and Archie and their kids. House wasn't big enough to begin with.

Except for this corner, everything on the east side of Main Street for a long block was former Bailey property, all recently purchased by Brownie Swartwood. I have known Charles Brown Swartwood since his aunt, Mary Katherine Sinclaire, sent him to me for sailing lessons, which he proved at once not to need. The Sinclaires were a boaty family, and he had been around their boats since babyhood—his cousin Bill's Wianno Knockabout as well as his skiff, his uncle Willy Walker's fast sport fisherman *Falcon*—and he knew a lot about them. I was supposed to teach Brownie to win skiff races. There was one just starting, a "Cove Race" sort of like the Little River races twenty years before, sponsored by the mothers and not sanctioned by the Mosquitoes and just for beginners. Anyway, I turned my skiff, by that time another old Butler world-beater with that Cousens sail, over to him and went ashore and watched him win his first skiff race. That was Brownie's first and last sailing lesson. He didn't need me; he was a quick learner, and it seems to me still that this intensity, this ability to concentrate, is a great gift. He shows little imagination, no sense of humor that I can relate to, but a concentration that is frightening. Today he is one of those who want to tie up skiff specifications in a tight mold, no room for improvement or progress. We are at opposite poles in this trivial dispute, but he will win. He cares so much more, he and his cohort, Chat's grandson David Churbuck. Brownie's concentration will never let him see how unimportant the whole argument is. I feel that even if specifications broad enough could be drawn, this is the worst possible time. Fiberglass is not the final boatbuilding material; it is just the first of a whole age of better ones. Who knows what material we will have in a year or two if we don't prohibit it now. Anyhow, trying to make rigid something that has been free for a hundred years can't work; attempts to do so are merely annoying. Brownie and his cohorts will win the argument, but it won't happen.

Now another digression, to which I have been led by writing more about skiffs. Along about 1938 (keep before you my problem with dates) I chartered my old *Ariel* for a week or two after Labor Day to Dick Smith, a young protégé of Aunt Lillie's, here studying the hotel business. This kid was at the age when nobody could tell him anything (that seems to be the time of life which our wise society sets aside for us to learn). He was employed at the Wianno Club, which sits right out on the bluff with nothing but open water in front of it for the thirty miles to Nantucket, and against my specific advice, he anchored *Ariel* there so the staff could see he had a boat too. Nobody else kept a boat there; nobody else was that stupid. And of course, it blew up a September gale and she broke loose, washed in to the beach and was pounded to pieces in the surf against the wooden bulkhead. I was devastated, got off from work and came down to see, showed my grief in ways that still embarrass me.

Young Smith was contrite, of course, wanted to replace my boat, and at this point it was fortunate I was on the scene. Good old Henry Robbins was trying to sell him some old clunker he had, but Joe Mattison persuaded the Shreve family to part with the Butler skiff they had sitting in their barn. None of the wild Shreve boys were interested in anything so slow as a skiff, even a fast one, and besides, it was for me. And thus I replaced a slow (except in a gale of wind) Crosby-built with a fast Butler. With *Shiner* my skiff-racing career took off, at age nineteen, and because it was so late starting, I moved to Cotuit after the war and completed my childhood.

These events, to me personally, were crucial. Betty, who married me early in the war (hell, give it a date; there are few enough of them to give) in June 1942, was able to persuade me to go to college at all and to make that wild application to Harvard—I was a high school dropout—mostly because of Harvard's connection and proximity to Cotuit. From then on, until I turned pro and retired from competition at about the age of thirty, a slice of my mind and my meager fortune were set aside to refine and beautify *Shiner* until she looked as unbeatable as she was. Betty wanted a baby; I was even then

Malthusian in my principles, but she put pressure on me until she got her baby. And I got a new nylon sail, cut special to my theories (with some input from Lee Wesson) by Harold Cousens, of one of the great old Boston houses. With this "cheater," *Shiner* and I won all the prizes the Mosquito Yacht Club awarded. Now I feel a little guilty using, as I did, my money and my trade connections to beat kids in a kids' sport, but by then it was no longer so much a kids' sport; there were like twenty adults racing along with me, most of them far richer than I. But indeed, the Cousens sail and her Butler shape and lightness made her almost unbeatable. Beating to windward, *Shiner* taught me things like don't bother trying to pass a boat ahead of us to windward and get involved in a luffing match; break through to leeward and then point up right across her bow. *Shiner* would do that over and over. I used to say to my sons when they grew old enough to race, "Just let her alone. Don't get in her way and she'll win the race for you." She really was a thoroughbred, like the best racehorses. Couldn't bear to have anybody in front of her. In 1951 or thereabouts I won every trophy offered for adults in skiffs and retired with my prizes, took to running the committee boat myself instead of hiring an operator, devoted myself seriously to running my business. Grew up?

Shiner's gone now. After all, she was built about 1923, and a lightweight wooden racing boat can't last forever. I might have saved her with drastic surgery; I knew how, but by then I was playing out myself, over seventy and so arthritic it hurt to bend over. And I confess that by then my interest had grown arthritic too. Nothing seemed that important. So I broke her up instead. I'm not proud of myself for this; after all, she gave me a belated childhood I would not otherwise have had.

*   *   *

On the left side of Main Street heading on northward were houses of people I never knew, since they were not active in skiffs or in boats of any kind. For such people, the ocean is to look at, and they crowd along the shore admiring its loneliness. Or as close as they can get, depending on how much money they have. But one of these people bought from me a new O'Day "Day Sailer," the future made manifest, almost my first sale as a dealer in factory-produced plastic boats. Other such sales followed; the Day Sailer is a more satisfactory boat than is a skiff for anyone who is not young, athletic and with lots of money or lots of time.

By now a plastic boat is less expensive to buy and to maintain. An open wooden boat like a skiff must be sanded and painted, every inch, inside and out, every year, and when you get all done, skiffs are not fit for anything except to race against each other. Not suitable to take your mother-in-law out sailing of an afternoon, and hardly fit for sex. I was George O'Day's first dealer when he was still importing state-of-the-art molded wooden boats from Britain, and when George got his hands on the capital to acquire a couple good designs and set up to manufacture fiberglass sailboats, I was first in line to retail them. Good old Mosquito Club helped me by admitting Day Sailers as another racing class, running races for them on weekends. We bought a new demo Day Sailer every year and turned it over to our son Bill to race, and he won all the races, so the boat sold at the end of a year for a premium. And next year Bill had another new one.

If I had had the capital, if I had been turned on to the idea, I might have become one of the world's largest boat dealers. And might have, as happened to George O'Day, lost my whole operation to bankers and corporations. It was never part of my nature to become a cutthroat competitor. I was rude to customers who hinted for a discount. So I stayed small-time. Cutthroats were always after my O'Day dealership; some of them got it away from me from time to time by buying more "units" than I could afford or hope to sell at list price, but they were doing it with borrowed money, which costs interest, and they lost the valuable dealership in a year or two and I got it back. The local bank loved me because my financing, unlike my politics, was so conservative. This is not the history of Pecks' Boats, later incorporated, just a one-line account of what I have learned from fifty years in business.

Also in this block of Main Street is a house formerly belonging to the Heppenstalls, nice people with a couple of nice kids, Jim and Judy. They both learned to sail and to square dance with me. Wonder where they are now? That house now belongs to John Murray, son of Anna Mattison Murray. To avoid confusion, I better say now that he is no relation to another John Murray, husband of Sylvanus' granddaughter. This later John Murray was the best part-time boat carpenter I ever saw, at least the equal of my son Bill. He worked for us summers and was the top employee, better than at least one lifetime professional I hired. He was our salvation the year (I even remember what year—1968) I was struggling to finish my ultimate tug—committee boat while tottering around on a broken ankle. John was one of the smartest kids I ever knew, too smart to be taken in by my appeals to stay in boat-building, even by the offer of a share. He was his father's son and chose to continue his education and become an accountant. Gross folly, I still say, but he has made a success of it.

XIV
AND LARGER STILL

Now, HEADING back north on Main Street and skipping a couple houses whose occupants I didn't know because they didn't sail, we come to that unremarkable-looking landmark house which for a generation housed the Odences, Marian, Meyer, Gates and Larry. Meyer was somewhat like me, you might say, the last floundering in a struggle to keep alive an already dead business. He was Boston's last surviving manufacturer of handmade cigars. He employed up to a dozen (I think) immigrant cigar makers from eastern Europe, as his father had done. But these, lacking the Odence drive, were impoverished. Meyer, like his father before him, kept the business going by exploiting and sweating these poor souls, all the while sure in his heart that they were better off with him than they would be on the streets. He asserted this argument without abandoning his contrary position that he was all business, incapable of any softness toward anybody, including wife and family. Hard as nails, but all the while with a heart overflowing with love which he would have felt ashamed to acknowledge.

Love for flowers was what you saw first; he couldn't hide it, so he flaunted it. His function in Charles Odence Company was to drive all over the country at top speed, selling his quality cigars to all the best hotels and the most exclusive clubs in all the big cities. My daddy, a cigar smoker all his life, admired Odence cigars. So "Pa" Odence was on the road most of the time, came home every week or so to sign the paychecks and to instruct the old lady who ran his office in his creative bookkeeping. He had a system: overbill and keep the confusion stirred up until the customer was glad to settle for credit in merchandise, thus assuring repeat orders. When he came home to Cotuit, always unannounced, the back seat of his Oldsmobile (once he tried a Cadillac, but he didn't like it; it was always being broken into and his samples stolen) piled high with loose blossoms, armfuls of which he would carry in and dump on the dining room table, then arrange, his big pudgy fingers moving fast and sure, into lovely ephemeral works of art.

My pretty, pert wife was his special friend. She just laughed — her laugh, in three notes, is one of her most beautiful qualities — when he went into one of his habitual rages, calculated to scare people, about his help, the traffic, his family, the government, until he laughed too, out of one twisted side of his face. She had a blank check on anything that grew in his garden, and she brought her little boys to visit him as fearlessly as to visit Miss Riley or anybody else.

Mrs. Marian Nathan Odence was a contrast to Meyer, as outspoken and nonstop talkative as he was dour, silent and surly. She was so obviously insecure that it drove her to embarrassing measures to get people to like her. She put on elaborate dinners, more than one a week on average, absurd heaps of delicious food. Everybody she knew was invited, the more prominent the better, with no thought whether they would get along with each other. She was very much into politics, strongly Democrat, but it had nothing to do with whom she seated at her table. Most prominent people around here were loud Republicans, but the food was the best. She was heartbreakingly sensitive, unreservedly sentimental, yet she put up with shameful rudeness from me because Betty was so patient and affectionate toward her. As was our little boy Bill; Marian loved him with all her immense heart. Bill, who as a child was always naming people in baby words he made up because they fit some description in his mind, called her "Dodence," and many people from those days still call her that long after her death. Her daughter-in-law, Larry's wife Sue, for one. Indeed, Marian took to calling herself Dodence, proud to have a Bill Peck name. Best characterization of her I ever heard was the words of Fr. John Smith (so he called himself, though he was a "Federated") at her funeral: "No one ever gave so much of herself. No one ever demanded so much for herself."

This unlikely couple had two likely sons (each one more likely than the other) who divided the characteristics, the personalities of their parents in ways more clear and precise than anything of the sort I have ever heard of. Gates, the younger, took his father's sharp and merciless business sense and combined it with his mother's nonstop wordiness. His opinions were strong and unequivocal, and he proclaimed them in whatever company. Until he was a full-grown man, he showed no diffidence at all, then you suddenly realized that his loud boorishness was as embarrassing to him as to his friends; it was something he couldn't help. He would burst upon you in the middle of a conversation you were having with somebody else, couldn't contain himself, couldn't wait to discuss with you something entirely different he had just thought of. As irrelevant and effusive as his mother, Gates never learned to sail well enough to avoid running into things, and this was evident also in the way he drove a car, forgetting the driving, gesturing with both hands. Just like Marian, of whom I used to say, "People are always driving sideways into the front of her car." But he took up fishing so intensely you came to realize that he truly loved each individual fish; catching them was the only way he could express it.

Gates went to Oberlin College. He here revealed another latent talent: music. Rather than an artist, he became a sort of impresario, brought to Cape Cod for the summer the Oberlin Gilbert and Sullivan Players (Goldberg and Solomon I called them, which amused Gates far more than the sorry pun deserved). This was before the Korean War, and they're still here. Repertory and hall and other conditions have altered over the years, but Gates turned out to be right; it was a good idea.

The army sent Gates to Korea as a buck private and he there did something unheard of: he liked it. He went back on his own after discharge, went into business there, showing again the promoter side of his mixed-up character. Imagine! He chose to return to Korea; only case of its kind I ever heard of. Most GIs came home from Korea hating the place with a passion. On a visit home he tried to talk me into supplying him with a sample of every piece of bronze yacht hardware (this was before stainless) in my stock. He was going to take them back to Korea, there to be undetectably hand-duplicated, low cost, out of the vast heap of spent brass cartridge cases and shell casings left by our troops. I didn't fall for it; that hardware was expensive, and no way was I going to give it away to Gates Odence. Now I realize there was a chance it might have worked, but nobody else seemed willing to trust Gates either, for it never happened. One of his brainstorms did work: he perfected a typewriter with a Korean keyboard which not only worked but was a key element in the swift revival of the South Korean economy, credited by some with starting the whole sudden economic recovery of East Asia. Eventually he returned to America, bringing his Korean wife. His huge heart failed and he died young; Kimmie and their daughters now run a Korean restaurant in Cambridge.

Gates' brother Larry has long been one of my dearest friends; Betty's friend too, loved by everybody in town. He still lives here, and he is uncomfortable being written up, even though I have nothing but good to say of him and of his whole family. But I can't leave him out; Cotuit would be incomplete. Like his mother, he involves himself deeply and personally with everybody he is fond of, and everything about them. Intensely involved with skiffs, skiff design, skiff history and skiff people.

The winter of 1950–51 was the only winter since the 1940s that my family and I did not spend in Cotuit. I was back at Harvard for a quickie master's degree in teaching, and we took an apartment in Cambridge. That year Larry was an undergraduate at MIT, and he and some kids his age and some couples our age all hung out in our apartment. Betty was just pregnant with our second child, which didn't slow her down any. Larry spent a lot of time with us, played with Bill, brought Hellie Sinclaire and other kids with Cotuit connections to visit. One of these was Larry's friend and classmate Sam Bidwell, grandson of old Judge Almy and the least snotty of the Almy family who owned the Cotuit side of the Narrows. Sam was a skiff racer of terrible competitiveness. His standard Bigelow boat just wasn't fast enough to keep up with my old boat, so he resorted to tactical maneuvering to keep ahead of me. Sudden changes of course, luffing matches. These tactics work only between boats more or less evenly matched. He never gave up trying but the effect of it all was just to delay me, sometimes long enough to keep me from being first. The annoyance made me grouchy, which was probably his whole idea. Almost as good to him as winning. I was sort of an icon among the kids his age, and Sam was always an iconoclast.

Sam knew more dirty songs, rhymes, one-liners than Boyd White. The horniest kid ever seen. His friends called him "Evil Sam." At an early age, he cut a broad swath among local girls, au pairs, Pines waitresses and such. I remember overhearing Dodence—you couldn't help overhearing her anywhere in town—screaming at her son concerning Sam and some friend, "All right. They can come down, but they're not to go out with those floozies!" Sam was bright enough for six. Tutored Larry, helped him get through MIT. He married a Pines waitress and died of leukemia in his twenties.

Larry was bright too, but not so bright as Sam or even Gates. Everybody loved him, but not for his wits. He was sort of cute, cuddly, without being fat. A skinny Teddy bear. He had a delightful talent for malapropisms, always using familiar words and clichés just a little bit wrong. Like Churchy, the turtle in "Pogo." Associated words not by their meanings but by their sounds. Never got angry when we all laughed, pretended not to know what was so funny. His shrewd father gave him the most guaranteed-for-success education you could ever dream of: bachelor's from MIT and MBA from the Wharton School at Penn. Add to these Larry's born talent at making everybody love him, and you come out with an ideal recipe for success in industry and a prosperous life. But what Larry was born excelling in was love, genuine affection, genuine interest in everybody he met. He is easy to talk to because he really and truly wants to hear what you have to say. Can't wait to hear.

This ultimate endearing quality Larry gets from his mother. But the last thing anybody would expect to get from her was sixty seconds of concentrated thought on any subject. She fooled us all; she wrote a book. It was published, at her own expense, and entitled *Pa* and was a brief account of her husband's life and personality. Pa and Marian can astonish us even long in their graves, and their descendants go right on surprising us all to this day.

At Odence's, Nickerson Lane intersects Main Street, and north of it a distance equal to about a city block comes in Shell Lane, so named because, like most of the streets in Cotuit and surrounding villages, it was paved with oyster shells right up to the 1930s. Shell pavement makes, in dry times, a fine white dust which settles quickly and leaves a beautiful bleached white surface, prettier than blacktop. To grow oysters, it is necessary to put many of the empty shells back in the water; seed oysters cling to them, and they will not survive without something solid to cling to. Like some girls I know. But there were enough shells left over (before it became against the pure food laws to open oysters by the bay) to pave every road and driveway on Cape Cod, and these white roads were, in those days, part of the unique beauty of the Cape. "White in the moon the long road lies / That leads me from my love," wrote Housman.

I rode over many of them on a bicycle I rented from Phil Brackett, and the surface, once the shells have been broken like pottery shards under the traffic of hooves and wheels, is more solid and firmer than sand. Very like unscreened gravel. And of course there were, until recently, vast reserves of shells all along the shore, left by centuries of Indians before white men were invented. Such roads take a lot of getting used to if you walk around barefoot.

These lanes led back into the woods and marshes which lie between Cotuit Bay and Popponessett Bay, and back there lived a population whom, with a very few exceptions, I hardly knew. One was Captain Shirley Nickerson, a famous yacht captain and a builder of small boats of local fame. He had a pretty daughter; Evil Sam was after her. Back here also lived Manuel Garcia, a gentle, dark Portuguese—Cape Verdean, that is—with strong, Old World ways. Manuel kept goats, right in the house with him. He kept also a full beard which resembled the goats in a couple ways. His daughter Mary Mattis and her husband Al lived next door. Mary kept house for Dodence. Many people came and went, back there in the woods; I was acquainted with only a few of them. Ruth Goodall, the electrician's daughter, and her husband Bobby Behlman lived there for a while. Housing back there was cheap, and the cheapest was very primitive indeed but accommodations varied with affluence. There was electricity but no town water. Ruthie was our favorite baby-sitter in her high school days. She still lives in Cotuit, still the same strong, handsome face and lithe body. Many of the local girls baby-sat for us one time and another, even one or two of the boys, but Ruthie was always the first one we called. Bill called her "Roots."

And next door to Odence's, across Nickerson Lane, lived another famous yachting pro, Joe Burlingame, one of the hottest of the hotshot skippers in the Wianno Yacht Club in the days when the pro was allowed to direct the trim and the tactics aboard these little sloops. He was not supposed to touch the helm, but anything else he did was legal. Joe's son

Richard was one of the two who ran my committee boat when I was racing myself (the other was Faith Mattison), and Joe's other son Lee worked in my boatyard for a while building skiffs. He was fun to work with, had a slow, sudden punch-line Yankee wit. This form of joking still survives down Maine; consists of saying the most appalling insults to somebody without ever showing a hint of a smile.

From Lee I got a lesson about how working people thought in an earlier age: he quit me abruptly because he was offered a better job with E. C. Hall Co., wholesale grocers, Brockton and Hyannis. Not for more pay; I don't think they offered him any more, but for security. Once you were hired by such a forever firm, you were secure for life. Good as being a teacher or working for the post office. This meant a whole lot to people before there was such a thing as unemployment insurance. So he quit, with two boats under construction, partly paid for. So I had to quit my secure job as a teacher to finish them. People seemed to put a greater value on security in days when it was scarce. The final irony is that Lee was soon unemployed after all, for E. C. Hall was within a year or two swallowed by a larger competitor that closed the Hyannis warehouse and let the help go. Lee never got the security he sought. And Pecks' Boats is there yet. Under Mr. John Peck it today supports eight families. After Hall's went under, Lee never asked me for his old job back. He could have had it; he was a good worker and amusing to talk to.

Now, standing in the middle of Main Street at the corner of Nickerson Lane, I am surprised how few of the people along the street I really know well enough to write anything about. At the end of this block are some old but unremarkable houses that went with the Whitcomb or the Riley estates. Bea Whitcomb's sister lived in one of them, and after the fire, her poor lost sister lived there with her and with her nurses. In some of the other houses lived gardeners and such on the Riley place. These were on Sea Street, just a short block to Ocean View, almost matching up with Nickerson Lane on one end and on the other with the nameless lane leading down to the little beach where old C. D. Crawford used to hide his black help.

Continuing north on Main Street, on your right you pass the house of Marston Boden and family, the present generation of a year-round family with whom the Pecks have had a long up-and-down relationship. Here, "for a breath," I abandon my geographical record of people and start again at the beginning, which takes me back to Porter House days. Many of my days then were solitary, by choice. I sought to avoid the company of my sister and various cousins. I went rowing by myself in *Auk* or sailing in *Ariel* around the bay or to faraway places like Popponessett. Sometimes I anchored and fished, for like all articulate anglers from Isaac Walton on down, fishing is regarded as an acceptable way to avoid company. I caught scup, an indigenous food fish, baby ones that lived inshore to be out of the way of predators and were despised by grown-up fishermen as too small and bony to be worth cleaning, though white and tasty meat. Mature scup are known all up and down the coast as porgies. I caught them by tens and twenties, but to catch even scup you need bait, and through years of selling tackle in my store and for a few years trying to sell bait there and taking out fishing parties, I have grown more and more astonished at what a fish will put in its mouth. As a Chinaman I knew in Pennsylvania said about something else, "Same thing dassy baby!"

Anyway, my source of bait at that age was the bottom of the bay by way of this same Marston Boden, then about high school age. He owned a pair of quahog tongs, and a fishing trip took a certain amount of forethought: walk up the footpath to the turnstyle, turn left on Main Street, half a block to Nickerson Road (that's Road, not Lane—different street), turn right and first house on the left was then the home of Clarence Boden, his wife Clara and their two sons, Victor and Marston. If Mars were home, he would lend me his tongs and I would row out and tong up half a dozen quahogs, wash off their matrix of black, stinky mud. Then I could go fishing. Anchor just inside Codman's Point where the current was swift and the water clear. Scup swam deep but they were clean, not a mud fish like flounder. I would lower the sail if I were in the sailboat, maybe top the boom, crack open a quahog against a cleat or an oarlock socket and cut the hard muscle into bits to put on my hook. I never learned, don't know to this day, how to open quahogs with my knife. Don't like them to eat, maybe because I'm squeamish about the stink of the mud. Oysters I can open like a pro and I love to eat them as fast as I can open them, faster if I could. But oysters live in another part of the bay, and they all belong to somebody and they don't make good bait anyhow—too soft. I fished with a tarred handline which comes on a little square wood frame, and I would lower the weighted line with the hook on the end till the line went slack because the sinker hit bottom, pull it back up a foot and wait. If the wait was tiresomely long I'd find another place or go do something else.

If the fish were biting, I would fish for an hour or two, catch a dozen to twenty little scup, then go do something else, sail someplace or come in. Mother would cook scup only if I cleaned them, and if I did that, the smell and the gurry were so nasty I couldn't eat them afterward. Gave them away, usually to Mars Boden in payment for the loan of the tongs.

Probably he buried them, but he was always willing to lend me the tongs. One more thing about scup fishing: somebody showed me a picturesque way to carry home my catch strung on a twig. You peel the leaves off a slender branch about two feet long, all but the very tip where you leave the leaves undisturbed, thread the fish on by inserting the big end of the twig into the fish's gill and out its mouth, then do the same with the next fish, and so on until you have them all on there, overlapping like a big silver ice cream cone upside down. The leaves which you have so carefully left on keep the catch from slipping off the small end of the branch. You walk through the village displaying this pretty but slimy work of art.

And remembering his tongs when, sixty years later, I pass the house where Mars lived when grown up, reminds me of the row of tall, skinny poplars which stood, in my childhood, along the shore just south of the Porter House. Like weird characters from an El Greco painting, moaning in the wind like El Greco characters might do if El Greco had painted talking pictures.

> There, in the windless nighttime,
> The wanderer, wond'ring why,
> Halts in the grove to harken
> How soft the poplars sigh.
> > Housman (again)

I didn't miss them at the time or until now, when passing Mars' house puts me in mind of scup fishing, but those poplars were all killed by the salt wave of the hurricane of 1944. The poplars too were part of my fishing; their twigs were perfect to carry home my catch.

*   *   *

Bodens. I was writing about Bodens. Far as I know, the first of them to come to Cotuit was Clarence, father of Vic and Mars. He came here to teach school (back in the times before school buses, when Cotuit had its own high school and every kid in the village went to school here). Clarence married Clara Nickerson, sister of the ingenious Victor the plumber, who patented an expensive device called the Victor Wellpoint, well known and prized wherever the soil is sandy and the water underground. Places like Cape Cod and New Jersey and thousands more. You put it on the end of a pipe and drove it, with a hammering machine, deep into the ground, down within the water table, which was often found by a dowser, a person half witch, in whom many still believe, and the Victor sifted out the sand from the water you then pumped up the pipe. It was top quality; hand-machined and silver-soldered of bronze and monel.

You could buy an ordinary well point from the hardware store or from the Sears, Roebuck catalog, but a Victor was special, to last for generations. When your well silted up, you pulled it out of the ground and drove it into a new well. To do which you needed a well puller, a patented monopoly of another Nickerson (refer to the place where I say I don't know who was related to whom), which gripped the pipe and pulled the whole thing up, maybe a hundred feet. You could buy a Sears, Roebuck well point for sixty-nine dollars when a Victor cost three hundred, and Victor's grandson Merton handmade them all his working life. The Nickerson plumbing business went on under Freeman, Clara Boden's brother, no way as clever as his father, and under Freeman's three sons, not clever at all, and is finally, just now, defunct.

Clara Nickerson Boden had made, in childhood, a few voyages in her father's ship and, years later, wrote a couple of charming books about them. Maybe you can read them today, if they aren't lost in the library's computer. Her husband Clarence was the most gifted amateur machinist, cabinetmaker and all-round craftsman I ever knew. "Amateur" is the key word here; as a professional, he would have been a bust because he spent so much time fussing and cleaning his shop and tools. Had a shop in an old corrugated iron building, formerly part of Nickerson Plumbing, now crammed with Clarence's small wood- and metalworking machines, each mounted on the cast-iron base of a defunct Singer sewing machine, a foundation for tools which Clarence fancied. He was a fussbudget, but his work was meticulous.

Clara and Clarence's two sons, if you have been paying attention, were half a generation older than I. They both died, before they were very old, of heart attacks. Maybe congenital, maybe just because these attacks are most common among big, hefty men. Vic's son Fred almost died that way too, younger. I did not know either of these brothers anything like as well as I knew Gates and Larry Odence, but well enough to differentiate between their personalities. Vic went to work for a world-scale manufacturing corporation, and the corporate mind showed in everything he did. He was, I guess, a second-level executive and maybe was assigned second-level dirty work. He inherited, maybe from all those generations of technician ancestors, a superb hand with machinery. Built a skiff for his son Fred, as meticulous as though it had been the work of Clarence himself, and very fast. He tried to set Fred up building skiffs at their winter home in New Jersey, for Fred, a thoroughly nice kid, did not look like executive material. Fred and Geoff Jackson, Gardner's youngest son, built a fine, workmanlike skiff for Geoff, but she never did spectacularly well in the racing. This threat of competition, with the resources Vic Boden might assemble, frightened me when I was going into skiff building, but all that came of it was some novel woodworking techniques Fred picked up from some large boatbuilders down his way and which he shared with me most generously. These helped me to improve the boats I built; my first ones were a little crude and far too heavy, as was the first one of Bodens' which Vic built to learn on. So by 1959, Bodens had built three skiffs and Pecks had built eighteen. All this activity took place in the later 1950s and then we had caught up with the hurricane and the market was saturated for a while. Even though a good skiff lasts fifty years, the market was bound to come back while people go on making people, but the Pecks are no longer building skiffs. John Peck runs the company now, and his eyes are clearer than mine; he could see that we weren't making any money focusing on skiffs. It's a matter of numbers; the market is too small, and to devote all your attention to so small a market makes you in the end the slave of a few customers. I said a matter of numbers, and I have no numbers except those I have learned to read on a ruler. Johnny has taken us out of the skiff business and he is making money as far as I can see. I still have no numbers, but I am as good as the next man at spending it.

I was talking about Vic Boden when I interrupted. He seemed to aspire to social acceptance among the summer crowd right here in his hometown, distinguished himself in WOE's work. He was a leader in opposing the plans of some seedy out-of-town politicians to take over that restaurant on a former estate next door to Freedom Hall and to make of it a flashy hotel/night club/marina. Vic was sort of liaison with lawyers and spoke for the Association of the Yacht Club, thus becoming the voice of the voiceless kids in their sailboats. The president of the Association, Mr. Bud Bailey, always referred wryly to Vic and his committee as "The Watch and Ward Society." The way they went after Harbor View Club showed how ruthless Vic Boden had become in what could be made to seem a worthy cause.

Vic was a big, handsome guy, well-spoken and sometimes a little pompous. With Association money, contributed "to promote the safety and welfare" of the kids in their skiffs, he helped pay the lawyers who won for WOE the final court battle. U.S. Supreme Court, no less. Harbor View was ordered by the court to demolish its new and expensive pier and turn away its boating customers, most of them of the fast motor-yacht persuasion. That bight is too shallow for sailing yachts, and they were, I am convinced, a real menace, just as WOE said, to little kids in little boats, but the whole idea of keeping land you don't own and water that belongs to everybody under control by having the law on your neighbors is of itself pernicious. I was still the town's deputy harbormaster for Cotuit and strove to maintain a posture of uncompromising neutrality, not hard between parties both of whom I despised. Wrote one letter, when the fracas was beginning, to the Corps of Engineers, whose permit is necessary before anyone can build a pier, opposing the wharf, saying, to quote myself, "it will inconvenience more mariners than it will accommodate" and stood aloof thereafter. My support was sought, naturally; I was a local resident with a vote in town meeting, which most of the contestants on both sides were not, an established local businessman with a little influence, as well as harbormaster, but I rejected the blandishments of the yacht club parents, to whom I was sort of indebted, scorned the hints of bribery and free dockage from the management of Harbor View. These guys were coarse political types. I stayed out of the whole mess best I could.

As I saw it, the parents were acting human in the worst way: confusing their selfish interest with moral principle. For philosophical basis I offer Bierce on a Moral Principle and a Material Interest who met on a narrow bridge. What the court decreed, beyond removal of the pier, I can't remember, but it was regarded as a "landmark victory" for local home rule. Harbor View couldn't break even without the pier and had spent too much capital fighting the case, and the whole operation shortly closed. A triumph for WOE and a triumph for Vic Boden at his most pompous. But I should say here that it was exactly as Meyer Odence predicted: there aren't enough rooms in that hotel to break even even if they are all rented all the time. The property has now reverted to a private summer estate. The house is too big and the grounds too small and too sloping for most modern tastes, but somebody has found the interest and the money to refurbish it thoroughly. Good for him.

Viewed another way, Cotuit remains a disgrace to the human race. All those miles of beautiful beach and nobody allowed on it. All private. People forbidden to walk or to come ashore or to reach their boats, a conspiracy all the way from King Charles to WOE to keep other people away.

Vic's brother Mars, of the quahog tongs, grew up just as big and handsome and well-spoken but gentler and less fierce. He was into scoutmastering and such activities with little boys, good at it. He had a beautiful wife and three incredibly lovely children, two of whom, while growing up, worked in my boatyard. Beverly kept my books in balance and kept me off balance all at once. Jolly and good-natured, always kidding, but uncatchable. Today we have a name for my behavior—"harassment"—but Bev just laughed. We had a running joke based on the *Playboy* pictures on my office walls. I would say to a customer or a salesman, loud enough to tip Bev off, "Have a look at the sexy calendar in the office. Miss Boden, tell the gentleman what day it is." Script had her respond with day, month and year, without looking up from her work. Bev had as much fun with this foolishness as I did; she knew she was sexy, just not yet sure exactly how she did it. She told about this when she got home, and her father thought it the funniest act he'd ever heard of. Mars was a salesman himself, a "manufacturers' representative" in automotive supplies, and these guys always come into your store with a joke, dirty, racial or both. I was always making jokes, and Bev took them home to have them explained. Mostly they were word games, puns, clean, lily white, from my teaching days, but she imagined every one of them had a dirty meaning. No doubt she wanted it to. Mars and I had fun with her naivete.

Bev's older brother Richard was a fierce competitor in skiffs and a most enthusiastic square dancer. He it was who invented the variation that, when the record calls for the man to go 'round the set, has him go all the way 'round the house while he's at it. Like Bev, he was a shade insecure with my sort of joke, based on words. He was never in my employ as his sister and younger brother were.

Bob was the youngest Boden and one of the best employees we ever had, good mechanic, good repairer and decorator of wooden boats, truck driver and boat operator, all-around handyman. Sometimes less than punctual when the whistle blew. I led him astray by my unthinking example. For I was getting ahead as the world sees it, in my very small way; had, with my wife's help negotiating with Hayden, finally bought the property where I had been doing business for nigh onto twenty years, brought home my new Mercedes. This was 1971; that Mercedes diesel cost me less than ten thousand dollars brand new. It was an understated sedan of conservative dark blue, but still it was the highest you could go in flaunting success. But I didn't buy it for that; bought it because it was the only diesel car on the market and I am a diesel nut. Love their noisiness at low speed (Betty said it sounded like a trolley car), love especially the smell of the exhaust.

And I put the boatyard on the market. At age fifty-three I was tired of the rat-seasonal race. And none of my sons were, at that time, interested in carrying it on. The whole industry was changing; nobody could any longer afford the maintenance of a wooden boat, and the early plastic ones were ugly, bulbous, of doubtful quality. The fine gentlemen who had been my competitors and friends, all of whose shops, tools and inventories were always at each other's disposal, were dying off or retiring. We agreed it was time to get out rather than survive by selling, to fools, junk built by knaves.

Bob Boden had always been treated as the unwanted child, and his father had shown him that he was a mistake from his conception. Mars had a joke: "I've got two sons: Richard and Wretched." He told this over and over, salesman fashion, often in front of the kid. Bob had always been getting into trouble, and the more trouble he got into, the more his father's disgust was reinforced and the more clumsy and trouble prone he became. From cases like his I get my conviction concerning abortion: The cruelest thing one can do is bring into the world an unwanted child. Compared to this, killing it in the womb is a kindness.

Meanwhile, Bev had acquired a husband as good as she deserved, a husky, handsome young man named John Rogers from Chicago, whom she met in college. He seemed to remember his college experience for more than drunkenness and sports, which is rare even among Harvard grads. He loved poetry as much as I but was no threat to my trick memory. So I liked him. John had a small inheritance, and he and Bev risked it on a down payment on Pecks' Boats, Bob to be president and to run it. John had his job in Chicago.

A deal was made, strictly arm's length; nothing like the deal I had with Hayden; none of my family trusted Bob an inch. I had a customer, a fine old gentleman, Sumner Babcock, whom another customer in the profession described as Dean of the Boston Bar, a dear friend to all of us, who was still racing his Day Sailer at eighty, who went every year until he was almost ninety skiing in the Alps and was a semiretired senior partner in one of Boston's two or three greatest firms. Sumner had his office spare no detail in drawing up a P & S agreement and deed and mortgage and who knows what, a portfolio of legal papers three inches thick, covering every conceivable snag, strict legal verbiage for what we had all along agreed to among ourselves. Bev's husband John et al. were represented by John's family's scrupulous Chicago firm, and everything was agreed to. We had the best legal representation in the world, and we paid for it; more thousands of dollars than I thought there were in the world, and I have a feeling that the Chicago lawyers didn't have time to read every word. Why should they? We had basic agreement before the paperwork even began, and nobody had need to pull any fast ones. Such a firm as B, D & G would never be associated with anything shady anyhow. Much of it was just boilerplate out of the computer.

Bev and John were unwise, as I would have been had I been allowed to make my own deal, in relying on Bobby. He had no idea of all the work, the long hours, the years of going without that the Pecks had put into building the business. He saw the Mercedes and at once came out with a Porsche and all kinds of expensive toys which, in the end, came out of

John's inheritance. Bev thought—she told me so early on—
that nobody had ever believed in Bob and that she and John
were going to believe and it would make a man of him. But he
had never had to get that boatyard through a winter, when
there is no work. He had no bank behind him, for the paperwork forbade him from mortgaging anything he got from us,
and once John's inheritance was spent, he couldn't pay any
help to maintain the plant. Nothing to do but sit around the
office and read *Playboy* and pretend to be busy. It drives you
crazy. A car drives in, which may contain a customer, and you
say to yourself, "Oh shit. What's *he* want?" But more likely a
salesman, and you can be nasty to him.

There was an apartment above the store, and Bob rented it
to a young man (not so young as he) who was a gun nut. Got
Bob turned on to guns. So Bob would fill in those winter days
loading his own shotgun shells (with expensive hobby tools
which John paid for) and other gun-related activities which I
scorn because they do not appeal to me. Bob kept a boister-
ous young dog and a fat cat, and coming into that place was
not like coming into a serious business. Not what yachtsmen
were looking for. I am thankful he scorned to keep the Peck
name for it. His checks were bouncing. When a mortgage
payment bounced twice, I moved to foreclose.

I got the boatyard back. I had had five year's paid vacation,
had enjoyed a rarely lovely young girlfriend, been across most of
eastern Canada by canal, been through the Great Lakes, down
the Mississippi, left my wife and come back—why she should
take me back, or even consider having me back, remains one
of the things about her that remain too good for me to understand. There was no question I wanted her back; I turned out
to be no swinger, and she arranged her activities while I was
away to make certain I wanted her.

There are a lot more details about going back into this business, but most of them are not part of the story of Cotuit in the old days and are better skipped. Except one detail: my wife Betty had, as one of the activities with which she amused herself while I was away, learned silk screening, on cloth. She now turned out a mass of tee shirts and other garments to stock our bare store. The boat dealers put on our winter boat show in the Cape Cod Mall, and Pecks' was there with nothing much to sell except Betty's nautical creations with our logo on them, pictures of skiffs, prams, Day Sailers, "all that good stuff."

Betty's resemblance to Homer's Penelope must strike more people than me, who left her and sailed away calling himself Ulysses. Our old friend Kurt Vonnegut wrote a play called *Penelope*, and when he put it on with the Cape's best amateur group, he would have nobody but Betty to play the part. She alone, he said, had the class for it. His Ulysses, played by me, was a strutting, vaunting buffoon.

Pecks' reopened its doors in March 1977, and everybody seemed relieved and glad to have us back. Including the local bank, which was glad to give us a mortgage, and all our suppliers, astonishingly glad to extend credit to us, even slow as we had always been paying our account. So our first year back in business was a good one. We paid our bills more or less on time, met our mortgage payments, and our customers seemed satisfied with us.

We got our O'Day dealership back, but not Sunfish; we got Laser sailboats and Johnson outboards. Our son John took over all engine work, so that problem department was a problem no longer, and Geoff took charge of sales and moved us toward the front of the most mod sort of high-speed sailboats. We were soon doing more business than ever.

Then that fall the place caught fire. Geoff was living in that

apartment upstairs with his sexy, half-dressed little room-
mate Candi (we had finally gotten rid of those gun-toting
Lynches), and one night they came home from a party to find
the place hot and full of smoke. They called the Osterville–
Marstons Mills fire department, and Candi came in to Cotuit
and got me up. Geoff's eyewitness account, as well as the path
of destruction, indicated that the fire had started in the main
electric panel down in the store. That was important for an
entirely different reason: people were seeking to blame everything on the Mashpee Wampanoag Indians, who were just
then on the warpath, seeking to prove that they retained title
to all their ancestral land in Mashpee, some of it, through
Congressman Gifford, now ours, including the land underneath our new home. People, white people, were going around
saying that the Indians had set fire to my boatyard. But thanks
to what Geoff told me and what any fireman could see, I was
in a position to squash this rumor. That fire was the result of a
power surge, not of Indian insurrection.

All I really wanted to say about the fire was that I found out
what friends I had in the village and in the "business community." Next morning I had Paul Botello, who had built our new
home, at work on the shell of the building when the insurance adjuster got there; measuring for the plywood to board
up the smashed plate glass. Then in came, on his regular
rounds, Malcolm Fraser, a paint and hardware jobber from
New Bedford. He had tears in his eyes and his checkbook in
his hand, wanting to know how he could help. Next day, Sue
Rothschild Peirson and Larry Odence marshaled all the kids
who had learned to sail or to dance with me, just as I had
organized them for hurricanes, to come and clean the ruin up.
That railroad building was still standing; the Osterville firemen know their business, but the floor was inches deep in

crumpled, half-dissolved gypsum board, all mixed with tiny items of marine gear, burned fabric and charred cans of paint off collapsed shelves. The kids cleared the whole place up, swept it out, hand sorted who knows how many cubic yards of debris and saved grosses and grosses of bronze woodscrews. Some of those screws sold for a quarter apiece, but the time, the labor of sorting them out and cleaning them, would never have answered if I had had to pay the help. Twenty or more teenage kids worked for four days steady. An incidental bene-fit: it seems whenever these kids work with me there is some-thing valuable learned, by them and also by me. What that fire taught us all is the immediate relevance of something we had all heard and known: light-colored clothes are cooler than dark. Now we all saw for ourselves that of all Betty's silk-screened garments, on display in a part of the store where the heat was intense though the flames never reached, the black and navy garments were charred cloth and ashes; the white and yellow and pale blue were only water stained.

We didn't have to pay Paul and his crew even to sweep the floor; fourth day they went right to work rebuilding. And one more lucky thing, typical of the way things have worked out for me all my life: one of the stupid things my local lawyer had had me do as part of foreclosing and getting a bank mortgage was to have a formal appraisal of the property drawn up by a formal appraiser, complete with binding, photographs, tables, statistics, comparisons, all that shit. I protested paying for such nonsense, but now it suddenly constituted evidence that the property had not been "underinsured." Without that, under the standard rip-off terms of fire insurance on busi-ness property, I would have been stuck with paying for a pro-portion of the loss. "Coinsurance" they call it. So the insurers ended up having to pay Paul's bill in full, which they hated.

XV
THERE WERE GIANTS
IN THOSE DAYS

S O   I   H A V E   T O L D a little of my growing up. Nothing singular about it except it is all singular to me, the only growing up I had. I have sought to bring back the village as it was
when I was a child so that those who love it, not the way I do
but the way they do, can recall it through my eyes. I seem to
emphasize how it has changed, and at my age, all change is
bad. To write all this, I had a plan which worked well enough:
start at the village center and work outward along the shore
northeastward and then southwestward to the end of town,
then start back along the street. Trouble with this was that as
well as showing through my eyes what the shore looked like
and what the people were like, it showed what I was like and
reflected my growing up and changing, and as I just got done
saying, all change is bad. Maybe I will convince myself that it
isn't the new people who are worse than the old, it is myself
that has gone bad.

The trip back northeast along Main Street has brought me
to the vicinity of people, now gone, who made the deepest

impession on me, and I have been saving at least two of them for a smash conclusion. But before we get to these, let us first consider Phyllis Dudley, an unusual real estate lady (aren't they all?) who was the third of those with whom I was on that "last-name basis." Dudley handled all our few land and property transactions, calling me up and exploding into the phone the one word "Peck." In spite of this way of opening a conversation, she was not pushy. Very laid-back. I think the task of handling our Mashpee property, which was anyhow more Betty's thing than mine, was embarrassing to conventional brokers. They could not adjust to the fact that, though it had cost all Betty's time for years and something like fifty thousand dollars in money, the titles were still tainted somehow because it had all passed through the hands of Congressman Gifford, and it was hard to believe in the validity of anything he had ever touched.

Then, just when we had our little initial subdivision measured off, roads and underground utilities in place and all the other nonsense you have to go through, and our new home built, out of the woods came the Wampanoags with their claim that they still owned all of Mashpee, that the purchases by Gifford and others since 1870 were in violation of federal law. But even before any of that, Helen MacLellan wouldn't offer anything at all in Mashpee except at a deflated price and with a personal warning that all Mashpee titles are doubtful. We liked Dudley a lot better, but she wasn't pushy enough to offer a new development.

She was, when we first knew her, a widow with three or four kids, and Betty knew her far better than I. Betty worked a lot with kids when ours were growing up. She cast them in plays which she put on in Freedom Hall and organized suchlike activities for the village kids who did not, in those days, mingle so much with the summer kids and their organized play. Dudley was sort of like Meyer Odence; she put on this gruff, hard-ass front and behind that she was a pussycat. Even affected a hoarse voice and unfeeling manner of speaking, like his. Always she was something of a misfit in Cotuit, and her kids were too, and the final acceptance came almost as much because they required the village to adjust to them as because they had learned to adjust to us. And of course, as with Barzun and Hayden, the explosive word "Peck" showed what it was meant to cover up: genuine regard and affection, which they all knew was reciprocated. I always said into the phone "Barzun," "Hayden," "Dudley."

And I can't leave out Ralph Baker, though to do justice to the Bakers would take a whole book. He was one of old New England's "born tinkerers," with an instinctive understanding of how machines work and why they don't work when they stop, the ability to fix anything or to invent and construct anything out of old parts and scrap metal. No different in this from many of his neighbors out at the north end of town and on north clear to Maine, except that Ralph's generosity and interest reached up and down to everybody he knew or had just met. He was a genius at diagnosing the ills of early outboard motors or kerosene-powered tractors. Once when I needed something, I parked at the end of his drive and walked in, passing on the way a two-pound hammer lying on the ground, then a bigger one, about eight pounds, and finally a sixteen-pound sledge. "What you been doing, Ralph? Fixing your watch?" We both laughed, but he knew what I meant; he was no better at putting his tools away than I was, or my similarly gifted son John.

For several years, Ralph worked as crew chief, surveying for Charlie Savery, but Charlie was not a good boss. He underpaid his help and was abusive. Then for years he was one of Chet Crosby's hotshot mechanics, doing all the unrelated things needed around a boatyard: customer work mixed with plant maintenance and improvement. One of his attributes was finding in stock or in the junkpile the part you needed without bothering to look up the part number. He knew. He did all my outboard work in his spare time, not as an employee but as a contractor. For a while he was in the army in Korea and came back with military vehicles added to his vast store of mechanical information. And with more also added to his prejudices. Unlike Gates Odence, he did not come back loving the place and the people. An Asian was to him a "gook" until the day he died. But around home he built up a larger and larger store of friends, all of whom were indebted to him.

And then he went into business for himself and threw it all away, operating the New Seabury Marina. I had tried operating that before he did, as a branch of Pecks' Boats, and had given it up and it had given me up. A hard-case bunch of customers who had been snowed by the salesmen when they bought lots in this pretentious development and then began to discover the amenities which they thought went with the deed were actually extra. So they came expecting to be ripped off and thought they were, even when we tried to treat them honestly. Ralph went into business with a partner, an experienced marina operator, greedy and with a nasty disposition, who had failed to make a success of running Hyannis Marina and approached his customers at New Seabury as hard-ass as they, charged for everything, like use of his launching ramp. Not only to the customers; even to other dealers. It didn't take Al McCauley a year to alienate all Ralph's friends in the trade, friends Ralph had been all his life making. We were all just waiting for the opportunity to give Ralph the same hand he had always given us, and suddenly, when it was least appropriate, he took this arm's-length attitude.

Ralph is dead now, and we miss him. Anecdotes about him will reach from now to forever. He and William Gifford once installed a used GMC engine in my old Chevy truck and they came up to Boston with William's dump truck to tow me home when it broke down. They had to wait till Ralph got off work at Crosby's, because William had lost his license, so he had to have a licensed driver with him. That V-8 Ford of William's was the world's only hot-rod dump truck, by no means Ford's biggest, but with Ford's biggest engine, souped up with Mallory coils and all sorts of racing stuff. When William towed me, it felt like being the tail of a kite; my loaded truck hardly touched ground at all. When we rolled into the yard, William had just one question: "Did I keep the chain tight?"

This anecdote, when one knows all of it, gives a lot of insight into the way Ralph worked. They had brought with them a tough little kid named Russell Landers, from a truly Tobacco Road family, apparently befriending the kid, keeping him out of trouble. But really, the one Ralph was interested in helping was his friend William. By making him share the responsibility for Russell, he was making William himself grow up, quit hard drinking, get his license back, straighten out. Subtlest thing I ever saw done, and this by a man who called all black people niggers, all Orientals gooks, all men by such categorical insulting terms wops, spics, on and on. Ralph's psychology worked; William did indeed straighten out, grow up, become a family man, still responsible for his retarded brother. He never lost his taste for speed. He's dead now, like Ralph, both by my diagnosis victims of the over-loaded heart which seems to kill off big, active men.

One more anecdote about him: William Gifford used to win bets that he could take the engine out of a Ford V-8 and set it on his workbench. While it was running!

Through Ralph to William, through William to Thatch, we proceed through the tinkering end of the town, almost. Thatch Gifford, William's father, some sort of cousin to the late congressman, lived right on the fringe of Tobacco Road, where Russell's father, Bill Landers, lived just on the other side of it. Both of these two, when sober, were better-than-average mechanics whom financial and temperamental instability kept down among the junkyard tinkerers. And both of them were seldom sober anyhow. Thatch, back before I knew him, was evidently big, strong, handsome, a terror to all the girls of his generation. His wife (by the time I knew her, completely beaten down and silent) was of good family, Elizabeth Fuller from Centerville. They had four children: William I have been telling about; Maynard, who was retarded, mentally about seven; two daughters. Their mother had burned herself right up protecting them from their father's environment and morals. Poor Elizabeth was killed in a car accident while riding with Maynard and he came home without her, sat down to the supper she had been keeping warm for them and never thought to tell his family their mother was dead. A sad and sordid story; why do I tell it? I want to tell both sides of this idyllic village; I stood, perhaps uniquely, with a foot in each camp.

Thatch had an old, strange-looking motorboat, with a funny tumble-home stern, like an inverted fantail, and he had a wooden raft with a gasoline-driven pump on it. One of the things he could do well and quickly was put down piers a shade more substantial than the swayed-down kind. People came to me for all sorts of offbeat jobs, and once Mr. Charles Almy, head of the family after the old judge died, engaged me to put down for him such a pier. So, having never built such a thing in my life, I subcontracted with Thatch to do the work with his sons and his equipment. And Thatch specified the materials and where to get them. Major component was to be locust trees, up to about a foot in diameter and like twenty feet long, which I could buy from Ernest Hoxie of Sandwich. Buy them on the stump and Hoxie would then fell and trim them for me. So I took my truck and my checkbook to Sandwich and we got the timbers. Locust, of course, because it never— almost literally never—rots. Thatch didn't offer to buy the timber himself, I guess because he had no credit nor cash. Probably still owed Hoxie for the last load. So it came the day to put up the pier; Thatch and his boat and raft met me at the landing. Is it necessary to explain that, from Sandwich on the other side of the Cape, bringing the wood to Cotuit by water would take two days and by truck only an hour? But it had to be transshipped. There is no road access to the pier site.

Thatch's raft was pretty well loaded with planks and the pump and tools; I had expected to dump the logs in the water and let Thatch tow them up the Narrows behind the raft, but we found, or maybe Thatch knew it all along, that green locust won't float. Sank right to the bottom. We brought it to the site by bringing the raft back and loading it on. Those logs are some heavy! We got the job done, and we all made a dollar or two, and I had been warned not to pay Thatch until all was completed; his thirst for whiskey was high, but his tolerance was low. If that crew had gotten drunk first, they would never have finished, or somebody would have gotten killed. I think that pier is still standing after like forty years, two hurricanes, ice from the hard winters we used to get, when oystermen used to pull their dredges with Model Ts or small tractors on top of the ice.

One more anecdote: I had a customer from Cambridge, the tightest, most opinionated old tennis-shoe lady ever to cross the canal, who came looking for a house lot someone in her family had purchased from Charlie Gifford years before. This was not land in Mashpee, nothing to do with our property, but the congressman operated in the same two-bit way everywhere. She actually found the lot, but the only access to it was over some of the congressman's paper roads made, in fact, of thorny underbrush. Undaunted, she moved right in, pitched a tent, where she lived along with a pleasant, apologetic Italian carpenter who was to build her house. What they did in that tent was too weird to even speculate about, but next thing the unreal lady wanted was a well. I told her about the Victor wellpoint, but her ideas were not that high; she got one from Sears, Roebuck, then asked me who could she get to drive the well. I was familiar, by now, with the scope of her ideas, so I sent her right to Thatch and to Bill Landers. Last I heard, they were down in the pit they had dug, too drunk to climb out, had lost that well point in the sand. I should have advised her not to show any money until they had finished the job. After all, somebody had warned me; the fault is mine. I have never heard anything of Mrs. Hartman since, and I don't mind that at all. I have always thought of myself as a free spirit, but that woman was waaaay out there, beyond my sight.

But, more prosaically, I had been doing business with Thatch for years. One of the things he owned was a gravel pit yielding a superior product. Old-time lore that one gravel pit is better than another, but the old-timers knew it well. Gravel from this pit, when you got your loader down under it and scooped out the bankside, was a perfect mixture of sand, clay and gravel to make year-round roads, regardless of frost, rain or anything else. All the ground around Pecks' Boats was given a layer of it, spread by Curtis' bulldozer driven by Johnny Peck, so we could wheel trucks and trailers over it all year. We even had the little drive at our first home, in Cotuit, hardened with it and Betty told me that one of the scariest experiences of her life was seeing William's eyes as he looked her up and down. They're all gone now, Thatch, Ralph, William, Bill Landers, and who's to remember them if I don't? But they too are part of this village which WOE would preserve while making trades like theirs illegal. Without the likes of them, Cotuit could not have existed.

The corner where Putnam Avenue goes off from Main Street is a sharp right angle, made to seem more sharp by a house built, as they used to be built in New Bedford and Nantucket, right up to the street line on both streets. No room to put even a sidewalk. This house belonged to a character, remembered only as a presence in my earliest childhood, named Captain Phinney and, after his death, by his spinster daughter Hattie. I'll get back to this most important of houses after one or two more digressions. In my earliest days, a bus I never got to ride left Providence before dawn, came along the barely improved highways of those days, by way of Fall River and New Bedford and so across the canal drawbridge, and down the Cape all the way to Provincetown. Took a whole day, and it stopped for lunch at the Cotuit Inn down in the center. This hostelry, condos today, was not, like the Pines or the Santuit House, an all-purpose resort but more a commercial hotel catering to drummers and transients. Restaurant but no amusement facilities, no shuffleboard nor tennis court, not even a bit of beach. No bar; bars were illegal, of course. Maybe a poolroom, I don't know about that. Today there would be, in fact there is, a motel outside of town, but motels weren't invented until the thirties. Anyway, a quarter mile northeast up Main Street was that sharp intersection of two narrow roads with Hattie Phinney's house right up against it and right in the middle of the intersection, in everybody's way, a white porcelain lighthouse with an amber flasher. And that ACF bus, as enormous as anything on the road today, had to make a right turn there. Driver must have been a wizard not ever to have touched either the flasher or the house.

I'll get back to that house; saving it for last. Across Putnam Avenue (in those days the first block of it before the next sharp turn at Ropes' was called Maple Avenue) was a good-size old house, another property of Charlie Gifford until Sophie bought it from him and began to repair and modernize. It is Sophie Holdstein we are now meeting, a tiny, hyperactive lady. She had to have three-inch extenders welded onto the clutch and brake pedals of her Chevy so her feet could reach them, and the gas pedal relocated. But she had energy for a giant. Sophie came from somewhere in Britain, I think London, and she had a snappy way of talking, flaunting her British pronunciation every chance she got. She cherished this way of talking, still does today—she can't be much under a hundred—like a transplanted southern belle. Wally, her husband, with her help, was in the sporting goods business, wholesale, and it seems to have been, still is, one of the largest of its kind in the New York area, where they lived in winter. But Sophie was the dynamic one.

They had two daughters: Jill, the older, was chunky and serious. She took sailing lessons from me and became pretty good at it but never took fire. My word for Jill's sailing could apply to everything she did: competent. Sophie bought her,

of course, a new skiff which Jill, in the first sign of assertive-
ness I ever saw her display, painted bright "shocking" pink
with black trim. Like lingerie. Damndest looking thing Cotuit
had ever seen. She told me when the boat was delivered from
Bigelows', white as all his new ones were, that she was going
to do that, and one irrelevant characteristic was the New
York way she pronounced "shocking" so that you could hear
the final "g." "ShockinG pink." It was so ludicrous I think she
was doing it on purpose, but Jill's wittiness never showed a
smile. Sort of like a down Maine character.

Her little sister Margot was about as opposite as you can
get. Wiry, petite, elfin face. Took ballet and got real good at it
till she began to put on weight. All her movements, her gestures were dance figures, but she put enough of her unique
self into them all so they were more than just school figures.
She got her way with everybody by posing her little self in
childish yet knowing ways, maybe vaulting up into someone's
lap as a finale. I watched her work it on Sophie, who planned to
have Jill take sailing lessons from me but imagined Margot
could get by with the less expensive Mr. Sam Bumpus. She
improvised a whole ballet, ending up not in Sophie's lap but
in mine. She got her way, even got her own new skiff—from
Churbucks', not Bigelow's, one of the eight first built to Ned
Mairs' new plans. She never did much with it; too volatile
and abrupt. Jill was always a better sailor.

The Holdsteins still own that house, which had, when the
children were children, a big, bare playroom with all sorts of
games and music and kid things, where all the yacht club kids
and their guests and everybody else from Betty and me on
down hung out. The floor was painted bright red, and everybody in Jill and Margot's generation got to autograph it in
white paint. Even me. That floor has still not been painted

out, last time I looked. And the family still comes here summers, but seldom all at the same time. Wally is gone, but Sophie still is brought down every summer and still has ladies in to tea and sits on the porch and watches the traffic on that corner. Jill's husband, Ken, is a nice guy, though as sharp a businessman as you will find in New York. Jill and Ken have four boys, but none of them have made Cotuit as much a focus of their lives as did the previous generation. Too much family here, maybe. Happens often.

During their growing up, Sophie's daughters got everything Sophie could supply or buy, caviar to scoldings. She put on not one but two square dances every season, had the big lawn rebuilt and then had the kids tear it up again. Mrs. Arthur Burgess, down toward the Loop, was the only lady who could match this costly devotion year after year.

I could take you with me again (if I could get you to stay with me so long) northward out Main Street. There is only one more stop of real importance, and then the last one back here at the corner of Main and Putnam. Out Main Street there was, until the 1960s, an uncommon version of what was in former days a common establishment: village blacksmith shop. Combined, in this case, with machine shop, welding establishment, steam-boiler and steam-engine facility and repository of down-east lore. It was all (except for the occasional volunteer or occasional helper) operated by one man: Dave Leland, who came here from Maine. He was engineer on a steam tug which broke down just off Cotuit on a snowy night. I have presented in this book a number of eccentrics, but Uncle Dave was the only true eccentric, in that his eccentricities were none of them for show. Just for himself.

I have made two attempts to get him on paper, once for that column in the *Cape Cod News* and again when the Historical Society asked me to do a piece about him after his death. I am still trying to get him right; the facts of his life and anecdotes about working with him have not been enough; there is an aura, an essence about Dave Leland that still escapes, that, like the man himself, will not submit to dissection and analysis. So here I try again. Both those earlier attempts refer to him as a giant, and this one does too. He was a giant first of all in size, tall and massive and powerful. One of the things he did in the regular course of his work was operate a sawmill single-handed. All the jobs he did were likely to involve manipulating something heavy, like bulldozer treads or spuds from steam dredges, into place under his machines, under his gigantic hydraulic press or the power hammer by his forge. I never saw him shoe a horse — horses were almost gone by my time — but he could shoe a steam digger or a diesel tractor. But it was careless of me to say "all the jobs he did" involved "something heavy," for the first time I went to his shop seeking his services I found him welding up the carburetor of a 1930s outboard motor. Cast aluminum, no bigger than a pocket watch. Somebody had tried to unscrew the brass core plug from the side of it, and the whole casting had shattered like pottery. Dave was rebuilding it with aluminum rod and his acetylene torch, in fact, building a whole new carburetor bowl out of weld metal. I stood and watched, not daring to speak or distract him by letting him know I was there; the job was too delicate, and he might twitch a muscle and spoil it. He was standing, directing the flame and dipping the rod in a can of white powder and back to the job again, and sweating profusely in his black wool tee shirt. Finally he pushed up the green goggles, shut off the gas and said, still concentrating, "That's the best aluminum flux I ever saw." The carburetor was shiny, silvery new and there was not a bead visible on it; nobody could tell with the naked eye that it wasn't a casting. What Dave had accomplished was typical: an original, one-of-a-kind work of art so perfect you couldn't tell it wasn't an ordinary, cheap pot-metal casting.

That was how he made his living: fabricating things somebody needed for his livelihood, things not readily available on Cape Cod or too expensive. Every marginal, one-man business for miles around depended on him. I couldn't have kept my chopped-off automobile engines driving my motorboats without him. Carmel, the landscaper, couldn't have mowed grass on schedule if Dave hadn't been there to keep his antique mowers turning. All Miss Riley's bounty couldn't have kept Foster Nickerson mobile to deliver mail and messages without Dave's touch.

I can't remember Carmel at all; he survives for me only as somebody Dave was always talking about. Dave evidently loved the man, loved the funny half-Portuguese English he talked. Carmel was droll and seems to have played up this part of his character. Dave used to quote him. He would bring in a broken gadget. Dave would look at it, put on his little Ben Franklin glasses and look again, and say, "Carmel, you been friggin' with this."

Carmel would look him right in the eye and say, "If she go, no frig. Don't go, *dennn frig*!" That always made Dave laugh loud and long when he retold it.

He had a clear (to him) system of priorities: What a man needed in his work was fixed first. Who could pay was way down the list. My wife left with him a silver candlestick she prized, to have the broken-off top section soldered back on, and though she was a special friend and one of the people he most admired, she was still waiting when he died. Meanwhile, he had specially adapted two of Foster Nickerson's gas-powered wheelchairs, gifts of Miss Riley every five years or so, to Foster's special muscular-control limitations, so he could start and steer, accelerate or brake. Foster's only source of income was a verbal contract with the local post office to deliver all the special-delivery mail, and he ran errands for people who weren't on the telephone. Not only was there in his day no government care for a cripple, but Foster was as fiercely independent as Dave himself. People around town asserted that Foster had a secret income from writing numbers in the Mafia lottery, but I never saw evidence of any such thing, though he and I were fairly close and Betty and he even closer. So I don't believe a word of it.

Another eccentricity of Dave's was that many of the original creations he fabricated to replace obsolete parts required that he first fabricate a tool to adapt his machines for the particular job. Often the tool took longer to create than the part, but Dave never charged for the tool. He stuck it up on a shelf, where he alone would remember years later he had put it, to be used when next this job came round. So he ended up charging for maybe one hour's work out of three, getting all the while richer in one-of-a-kind tools.

Dave's most noticeable eccentricity was that he slept all day, opened the shop in the evening and worked all night. Said he did this so he wouldn't be bothered with people talking to him, and I guess that was true but too brief to explain much. Dave was too naturally polite to shut anybody off, and he loved talking as much as any of them, so from another point of view, it was rigorous self-discipline. Of course, having spent so much of his young manhood standing watches in the engine room, day work and night work were not all that different to him. Incomprehensible to landsmen.

Another eccentricity: he always dressed the part, that is, the part of steam engineer. The uniform consisted of a fine-knitted black wool tee shirt, and nobody had made such garments for years except an old lady Dave knew in Sandwich, who would turn them out for Dave on special order. Hat and trousers were irrelevant; sometimes he wore overalls, but the shirt was essential.

So many tales to tell. The importance of steam to his whole life. He came from the Maine coast "above" Damariscotta, where, in his boyhood, every farmboy who didn't grow up knowing how to build a boat grew up knowing how to harness the power of living water and live steam. Dave loved both these technologies. He had the first, for a long time the only, steam "digger" on Cape Cod. Built it himself. It had two steam engines. The road engine that moved it about was originally in a Stanley steam car, and it was, of course, geared way down to move, at barely perceptible speed, the ponderous device over the road and around the job. The "hoisting engine" turned the winches which pulled the cables to drag or lift the scoop or the clamshell or the dipper or whatever earthmoving device suited the job. But that hoisting engine, now. Dave built that himself. Literally. Cast the iron block of valves and cylinders in sand behind his shop, machined the pistons out of cast-iron pipe, sawed the piston rings out of the same pipe, tempered them in his forge, worked out the valve action (at this point, it gets beyond my understanding), fabricated the crankshaft and eccentrics. He welded the vehicle frame together out of old truck frame members, mounted the engines and winches. He put a corrugated steel roof over it. Retubed an old upright boiler. I believe working pressure was fifty to eighty pounds, but if you don't know enough to look skeptically at these figures, you have been wasting your time reading all this.

There is a village legend goes with Dave and the digger: they were proceeding at top speed—close to five mph—up the state highway out of town when the cops pulled him over. No license plate. No registration. They hauled him into court, where Dave confounded everybody by citing an ancient law that a steam-powered machine (under certain circumstances which applied here) operated by a federally licensed steam engineer is permitted to proceed over any highway. Dave came out of court triumphant, nearest to gloating he ever got. That wise-ass young cop had irritated him. What he was doing on the road (State Highway 28, then fairly new) that time was heading for the bluffs at Wianno to pull stumps of trees which the 1938 hurricane had broken off, capriciously, twenty feet aboveground. A steam engine is ideal for that work because, as Dave explained, it exerts full power at lowest speed; you don't have to rev it up and then clutch it in. Just open a couple valves and it just sits there pulling until something gives. To pull harder you just stoke up the fire. You can go have a cup of coffee. I don't think Dave would have taken a nap; he was too conscientious and the digger was his own creation, but the machine would just sit there for half an hour, no discernible motion, just little wisps of smoke from the stack, wisps of steam from the valves, nothing visible to show it was pulling at all until the stump would give up, come out of the ground, lie over and creep toward the machine, and then Dave had better be there to clutch the winch out or the stump would end up wound round the drum. But the silent power of a steam windlass is the best metaphor there ever could be of the way Dave worked: slow, no discernible movement and the job getting done with no fuss.

Even when steam power was obsolete, almost forgotten, even after the railroad had gone diesel, there were still low-pressure steam boilers out of sight all around us. They heated schools and public buildings, they heated water for laundries and in Dave's late days, and my early ones, even many of the better old residences that had heat at all used very low pressure steam. We lived in such a house one winter, one built and plumbed for his own use by Victor Nickerson, the well-point man. It was quick and cozy heat, just noisy when you turned up the thermostat and the radiators expanded.

Point is that the weak point, the one needing most attention in any steam installation, is the boiler. It is made of iron or steel and it heats water, and heat and water cause steel to rust—the more heat, the faster it rusts—so the tubes inside, through which the heat is transferred to turn the water to steam, need frequent replacement, and Dave was the last man around here to work at retubing boilers. The shell of the boiler, made of heavy steel boiler plate or, better still, of cast iron, and designed to transfer as little heat as possible to the atmosphere, often insulated with wood "lagging," would last for decades, but the thin tubes inside were never good for more than so many years. They passed through the open space inside the boiler, which would be full of fire and the tubes themselves full of water, or in some cases the fire was forced through the tubes immersed in water, and each tube poked through the crown sheets at the end (man, look at me throw the technical vocabulary around) and was expanded with a rotary device with rollers so it fit tight. It didn't need to fit quite watertight at first; a little corrosion would soon seal the joint, though it had to be tighter for higher pressure, but to guide the new tubes through (after the old ones had been cut off with acetylene) you had to have a man inside there, and he had to be small enough to go through the manhole, which Dave emphatically was not. So he hired a helper for such occasions, an alcoholic little man named Roy Holmes. Any boiler job began with locating Roy and drying him out.

There is a story about Roy too, so I suppose here is the place to tell it. "Don't be shy," as Betty used to say to Dodence. Roy was never anything more than a pint-size drunken qua-hogger, drunkenly talkative, until the selectmen gave him a temporary appointment as shellfish warden, charged with the duty of preventing other quahoggers from exceeding the limit of the day's catch or fishing in closed (usually because polluted) areas. This appointment had an unexpected effect: Roy suddenly had something to take himself seriously about. He sobered up, completely, off duty as well as on. He wore his absurd badge right out on the front of his overalls. He was sometimes seen directing traffic, which his badge did not empower him to do. The shellfish of the Town of Barnstable were never so well warded, before or since. Then it all ended; his appointment could never be permanent because he was too old, and the state, to protect its pension fund for public employees, excluded from permanent employment anybody above a certain age. Roy's reform ended with his appointment. He became once again a garrulous drunk.

But Roy understood what to do inside a boiler, perhaps because of his diminutive size or maybe it was part of general knowledge when he was a kid. Anyway, when Roy was sober, that's one place he might be. He knew the work. Dave was constantly complaining that Roy had no strength in his hands, but this Mutt and Jeff team retubed every last boiler on Cape Cod one time or another.

I started out saying that Dave came here off a tug that broke down off this part of the Cape. He and the cook rowed ashore in the tug's lifeboat, landed in a snowstorm at the deserted bluff now known as Wianno, walked to town, bused

to New Bedford, got whatever widget Dave needed to get his
ship running—he must have told me the name of it; he never
omitted the least detail, but I have forgotten. Must have been
a rare item, because steam vessels in the steam days always
carried vast stores of parts and of what was needed to fabricate parts and had a pretty good machine shop down there
alongside the engine and an engineer like Dave to make use
of it. But Dave liked the place, even in those pre-WOE days,
married a pretty local girl and went, a little at a time, into
business here. He picked up used heavy machine tools here
and there as he could afford them, but like a lot of us, he had
no capital in money, so he was often away running the engine
on some steamboat, and the first Mrs. Leland was not the
sort of girl one should leave behind. Dave and I got pretty
close, one of the things I am most proud of, and he told me
about it those long nights while the lathe turned and the old
Chevy engine halfway up in the rafters rumbled away.

"I'd go out the back door and he'd come in the front and I
was a-keepin' the both of 'em. I was a-keepin' the both of 'em!"

It seems, though I don't have the details in his words, that
Dave finally kicked the both of 'em out one door or the other,
got divorced all legal and married his second wife, whom I
knew, Mrs. Mary Cabral Leland, an old-fashioned, indeed,
archaic country girl with a will of iron and the best cook in
the whole village.

Nighttime was the key to Dave's friendship. Even when you
caught him awake by day, he was sleepy and lethargic. One
vivid scene I recall over and over, for it happened nightly, was
the ghost story of Dave coming to work. He had a running
feud with the electric company, and when the shop was running it made its own electricity, so the big old barn that housed
the shop was pitch-dark when he undid the padlock and went

in. The power to run the whole place (except the hydraulic press and the sawmills—they had their own engines) was an old four-cylinder Chevy (the last four-cylinder Chevrolet was built in 1928) on a platform level with Dave's head. He had put it there and he knew where to find it. He reached into the darkness just inside the door and fooled with things, turning on the gas and giving it choke, and a slow, reluctant grinding came out of the electric starter and presently the engine began to run, but all was still in total darkness. Dave reached above his head and felt a long wooden handle, polished and shiny from his hand when at last you got a look at it, which clutched in the overhead belt drive. The engine lugged down and then ensued a muffled squeaking all over the shop as the shafts under the roof began to turn and the flat leather belting squeaked on the pulleys and the power began to spread. When it got up to speed, he engaged another clutch somewhere, which engaged a belt from overhead which turned an AC generator and the lights at last came up, a little at a time until they were as bright as greasy, bare bulbs can get. The whole thing was spooky, unnameable sounds accompanied by the eerily slow and uncertain dawning of light. Sunrise in slow motion with sound effects. Stage lights coming up by rheostat. Altogether ghostly.

Then we could go to work. Helping Dave was a privilege, you learned so much basic stuff, what drives what, the properties of metal and how heat and certain chemicals alter them, how this or that cutting tool carves this or that shape. The whole shop, in case I haven't made it clear, was driven by those noisy, slow-turning shafts up among the rafters, which had pulleys which, when you clutched them in, pulled belts turning this or that machine. Two big lathes, a milling machine, a slotter, a planer, the blower for the forge, and beside it a fearsome *bangbangbang* power hammer, that generator, drill presses, the huge, slow-turning tool grinder. All powered by that old Chevy engine up on the platform. Whenever Dave clutched one in, which he did the same way you clutch in your car, easy, a little at a time, you could hear the belts squeal, the engine labor, lug down and then, once the inertia of the mass set in motion was overcome, speed up again.

At least once a week Dave had to come out before dark and climb his bulk up there to grease every bearing and fitting on all that shafting. Lubrication was critical to everything Dave did; it took for him the place of religion. He loved to teach, but the only time he sounded the least bit pedagogical was when reiterating the need for oil, more oil. He even kept the cutting tool in the lathe lubricated. On the lathe, close to the tool holder, was Dave's tobacco can—a square, blue Edgworth can—of bacon fat, "goose grease" he called it, from Mary's kitchen. Sticking out of the can was the handle of a little old paintbrush with the bristles all bent over, with which Dave would apply the grease to the tool and to the work. There it would crackle and hiss and smoke and smell, not like bacon or goose but like Dave's shop.

Also on the premises were not one but two sawmills. One was a conventional mill for ripping trees into boards and planks. The log was secured on a carriage which moved back and forth on a track sort of like a light railway. The circular blade was whirled by a Case tractor engine. It was about eight feet in diameter, and its teeth were set in the rim in such a way that they could be twisted out for sharpening. The log on its carriage was carried back and forth past the blade, the log adjusted in and out for whatever thickness plank was wanted. An awesome machine which made an awesome noise, but no way different from an ordinary commercial sawmill except that Dave's was smaller than some. The important difference was that in a commercial operation there would be three to half a dozen hands, each doing just one job. Dave did them all, which took special coordination, getting each move in the right moment. Miss the timing of just one of them and you are dead.

The other sawmill was so different you might say it was the opposite of the first; it was to crosscut, across the grain of the wood rather than rip with the grain. It was made of a Model T chassis with a circular blade on the rear end of the driveshaft where, in a car, the differential gears would go. It had a carriage pivoted underneath; you put a small tree, cleared of side limbs, on the carriage and tilted it back and forth across the path of the blade and it sawed off a length. This contraption was permanently parked over Dave's cellar door, and each log fell right into the cellar bin as soon as it was cut off the tree. Dave could advance the log a preset length and have the blade starting into another before the first one landed. When Dave was running this contraption (nobody else would dare come near it) the screech of the blade, the unmuffled engine and the thudding of the falling logs sounded like a war movie. Right under Mary's kitchen window, but I never heard her complain about it. They cooked, heated the house, everything else with wood fuel. Coal cost money and was only for use in the forge and to make steam, but wood fuel was to them like free. A man worked on his own place, and who was he expected to charge for it? Also, through a hole high in the shop wall, a shaft came out of the shop and turned a "pump jack," a crank to convert the rotation of the shaft back to reciprocating movement to pump the well, which brought up well water and discharged it into a pipe which fed a storage tank in the attic of the house. Dave didn't need to earn much; they spent practically nothing.

One more machine deserves special mention, chiefly because of its weird engine. Dave's hydraulic press, originally designed to press solid rubber tires on their iron rims onto wooden wheels for the heaviest kind of trucks and drays, had a round, slotted plate on top of a ram about two feet in diameter which rose out of a cylinder in a pit under the press, as driven by hydraulic fluid (a special oil) under pressure from a pump powered by a missing-link engine, the link between steam power and gasoline power. It was one big cylinder mounted horizontally, controlled by a governor which worked on the ignition, cut off the magneto current unless power was called for, more accurately unless the engine slowed down either from load or from inertia, when it cut back in and fired. It made a freaky sound: *bang bang whoosh whoosh whoosh bang bang bang whoosh bang*, the bangs more frequent when under load. Everything was open to the weather; you could watch the piston rod and the connecting rod move back and forth, the crankshaft turn the two flywheels, one on each end, around one of which ran a flat belt which turned the pump which pumped the fluid. Looked at from the point of view of pure physics, it went from reciprocating motion to rotary motion to linear motion and back with each bang.

I spent a lot of time at Dave's shop, and we became special friends. So good he even let me open up and run the shop for my own personal work when he was asleep or away on a job. Nothing fancy; I used his forge to melt lead for the centerboards of the skiffs I built or repaired. Dave had a ladle for melting lead or babbitt metal that was made of a truck's differential cover with a long pipe handle, so Dave Leland size that I couldn't even lift it if it was more than half full. And I drilled all sorts of things that needed holes bigger than half inch.

Only other man I know who enjoyed this privilege was Cap'n Bill Nickerson, whom I've mentioned before, an alcoholic fisherman and rumrunner who had inherited the design for a "well puller," a device to pull the pipe of a well back out of the ground so that one could save a valuable Victor well point for use in a new well. Every couple years Bill would run out of his stock of well pullers and have to turn to and make more to fill orders, and at such times he would dry out enough to run the shop and produce them. I soon got into the way of avoiding the machine shop when this was going on; Bill had a raspy and unpleasant voice and he talked all the time, altogether friendly and all bullshit.

I had learned to arc-weld before the war, before I joined the Coast Guard, and welding was a major part of Dave's work. He had a big welding machine with a Continental engine which he carried from job to job, mounted temporarily on the body of his big, antique Chevy truck. That truck, sky blue with red wheels, was the most all-purpose vehicle anybody ever adapted. It had winches, hoists, fairleads made of bent pipe, all over it. He could hoist that big old welding machine off it and back on, could go into the woods and snake out logs, haul boats out of the water. Dave treated his load-handling equipment as though it were all different ways of aiming and augmenting his personal strength.

One day Dave was sitting in that truck, parked downstreet in Cotuit center, when Hellie Sinclaire walked by, all her buxom self, dressed as briefly as usual, low-cut blouse and high-cut shorts. She said hi to me and Dave, naturally, asked, "Who's that?"

I told him all that would mean anything to him, whose daughter she was. He thought about it a moment and said, "Quite a woman. Reminds me of a story I heard: Man had to go out to dinner and when he got home his wife asked what it was like. He said, 'What d'you want to know?'

"She asked, 'Wha'd the women have on?'

"'Well,' said he, 'they didn't have anything on above the table. And underneath the table I didn't dare to look.'"

That arc-welding, now. I needed Dave's skill for something broken on my committee boat, which had to run for tomorrow morning's race, and Dave could machine it as soon as he got a new face welded onto these crawler treads for Turner and Breivogel. So I took over the welding. Nothing finicky about it; just cover the whole surface more or less evenly. Not like a welding job I once saw Dave do; he welded new teeth on a stripped gear out of a car transmission, and they meshed silently when he put the gearcase back together. The welder was noisy and we didn't talk much, but usually with Dave, the talk was constant. I learned all about the friends from Dave's down-Maine boyhood. Uncle Josh Webber had a water-powered sawmill up above Damariscotta. On and on.

I studied theology with Dave, the only religious doctrine I ever paid attention to. Like everything Dave encountered, he studied the problem and worked it out. His whole mind-set was built upon cause and effect. Like Aristotle's. He had observed how much healthier and faster-growing oak trees were near scrap iron, so when he first opened the shop in Cotuit, he planted on either side of the big wagon door an oak seedling. Now they were grown to respectable size, and on one side of the door was a pile of old iron. And sure enough — he showed it to me — the one by the scrap heap was twice the height, twice the girth of the other. His approach to God was just like that: he looked up at the stars, he knew a lot about how they moved and how one planet pulled on another and all were interdependent, and he said to me, "By Godfrey, Len, somebody figured it all out." He rejected my atheist notion that their balance could be random. It was too carefully organized, too complicated. Creation, to him, was proof of a Creator. And still I believe what he taught me; I am as convinced as he of there being a Creator. That implies no evidence of a concerned, caring, loving Creator who answers prayers. Not even of an interested Creator. He did exactly what Dave would have done: devised a self-governing system, set it going and then let it run by itself. While He went and did something else. To me, the daily behavior we are allowed to get away with is sure proof He doesn't intervene.

There was some of Dave in everyone in the village, in every country mind everywhere. The ability to make do, to make new use of a worn-out gadget or garment. If you can't eat it, the pigs can and then you can eat them. If it isn't safe to ride in, it can be made to cut wood. In touring about the waterways of the country and of Canada, I am endlessly amazed, endlessly admiring, of the unexpected uses people find for parts of old automobiles. In Lake Huron there are odd fishing boats which make a winch drum out of a pair of wheels with tires on them around which the miles-long gill nets are wound. This winch is powered by an old car engine, as is the boat herself, and steered by old auto steering linkage. It is inherent, far older than autos. I knew a farm boy in Pennsylvania who made an express wagon out of four old cart wheels four or five feet high. No thought of brakes. Going on top of this rig down some of the abrupt hills of Chester County was a good way to grow old prematurely. Or never grow old at all.

Dave had, as I said, a running dispute with the electric company. After all, Dave knew as much as man can about the generation and distribution of power, and the electric company's prices he considered what today we call a rip-off. His wish was to be independent, to be shut of them since they were too big to fight. He wanted his shop to be, like Uncle Josh's sawmill, powered by falling water. His shop was out toward the north end of Main Street, and no water falls there except rain, but he was preparing to move to a site he owned in Marstons Mills, next nonexistent village to the eastward, where once was a fulling mill. The mill is long gone, its dam and pond are now a town park where kids are brought to feed the ducks, geese, even swans, and where older kids come by themselves in spring to net the herring headed upstream to spawn. The dam has been restored using yards of incongruous concrete, and the more recent Route 28 crosses the stream just below it. And below the highway, Dave had the larger and less visible part of his project mostly in place. Eventually he would move all his machines into a building he planned atop all these flumes and waterways.

First of all, of course, was another dam to pond up the water. That was already done, and he had a water-driven turbine and generator, and on Fourth of July he turned the water on and the power on and lighted a string of bulbs. It was a slow-moving project; Dave worked on it whenever his customers let up on him, which was like never. He got no encouragement at home; Mary hated and feared the idea of moving away from her mother, who lived next door and with whom she spent most of her time. Dave assumed they would live at the new shop, stay on guard, when he moved his work there. He had valuable tools and materials, and Route 28 was a quick escape for thieves. He hung on to the dream and worked on it when he got the chance.

My little son Bill went there with me once to help. Bill was too little to be much help but big enough not to be very distracting. He asked questions, so I learned answers to a few of the elementary mysteries, to questions I was too shy, ashamed to show my ignorance, to ask. Bill and I supplied lunch: just one long loaf of salty rye bread, store sliced, and a pound of local cheese. Dave said, "These breads are good," and Bill picked it up and for years referred to them as "Davy Leland breads." After lunch he fell asleep in the cab of my truck, so I took him home for his nap and went back to the job. Incidentally, Bill's presence then gives me, the historian, a rare luxury: a precise date. He was born September 1947, so that makes these events summer 1951.

Dave was pouring cement. He had his own mixer, and some supply company had delivered to the site a huge pile of bagged Portland cement, and Dave had an even bigger pile of clean "sharp" sand. The mixer, like most of Dave's tools, was both old and huge. It had a one-cylinder gas engine to turn the drum. Dave had wooden forms in place, and we shoveled aggregate into the mixer and wheelbarrowed it to the location when Dave reversed the rotation and the mix came out.

The job was never finished; Dave never built his new shop or moved out of his old one, but he followed his dream as though it were the holy grail. It certainly partook of the grail's mystery; he had a bewildering maze of concrete water passages buried in the ground there, much locust lumber, and I still have the feeling that even if the earth were rolled back to reveal whence and whither they all led, it would still be a mystery to me.

But Dave never moved his shop; never completed the underground waterways. Mary's objection to moving out there, leaving her old home next to her mother's house, was formidable. To Dave's friends she was never much in evidence, but she wielded power. She took constant and meticulous care of the old lady, who was evidently a power herself, or

had been. There is, from what little I have seen of Mediterranean families, Italian and Hispanic, Portuguese like these
Cabrals, a scarily powerful matriarchy not very deep beneath
the macho life of the men. Mary took far better care of her
mother than her husband would permit her to take of him.
One thinks of this as a Mediterranean characteristic, but one
doesn't have to think very long to realize that there is nothing
racial nor regional about it. It is equally fierce among the
Irish, famous among Jews and Betty's Welsh mother was as
fierce as any of them. All, I guess, part of what is called "the
human condition."

Mary's cooking assured her of employment in the kitchen
of her choice among all the classy summer homes. A funny
thing happened to me one time when Betty and the boys were
out of town visiting relatives: I was bidden to dinner at the
home of Betty and Bernie Goodwin, a television executive in
the early days. When we sat down in the dining room, who
should appear bringing in the dishes but my good friend
Mary Leland. The way we handled this is a good memory: I
said, "Hi, Mary," and she said, "Hi, Leonard," and from then
on dinner went on as though we were strangers.

You see, Mary was next door with her mother or out working
for most of the day, and Dave chose to work all night, so they
didn't need to see more of each other than they could stand. I
wondered, and I still wonder, how much Dave's choice of
night work was thus motivated. Anyway, it's for sure he got no
encouragement at home toward the move that would make
him free, independent of the electric company. And other
brutal circumstances began to squeeze him too, even harder than
his personal "energy crunch." For Dave and Mary had a son
and a daughter, both of them as genial and oversize as he, tall
and broad and powerful. You can imagine that a girl that size

would start out severely handicapped in the sexual competition. Makes no difference how generously she was endowed with Leland geniality or diligence or competence; in things that boys seek in girls, she was heavily overendowed. With Dave Senior and Junior, size was noticeable but not shocking. Just part of the oversize personality. But the hugeness of all the Lelands must have been what, in my boyhood, was called "glandular," but what today is called "genetic." See how much wiser we have become?

Dave Junior was big too, getting right up there toward three hundred pounds. But people are more ready to accept such immensity in a man than in a woman. Young Dave's inheritance also included his father's huge good nature. He was into machinery as much as his father was, but he had no time for slow steam engines or slow, weight-moving equipment of any kind. He was into sports cars and hot rods, even ones he couldn't fit his body into. He loved to tune up stock cars until they were faster than competition specials. Loved big motorcycles. A speed nut, in fact. Like his father, he also loved beer, and the two together were the end of him. He was younger than I and moved in a circle of boys I didn't know, most of them from other villages, but after he was gone, they all had the same thing to say about him: "Big and powerful as he was, nobody could make him angry. He never raised his hand against anyone no matter what they said."

Well, one night, very late one night, young Dave was coming in Putnam Avenue in his overtuned V-8 Ford, heading home from a party somewhere, and he missed a curve and hit a tree head-on. His chest was most horribly crushed by the steering column, but he "walked away from it." Walked home, a mile, in that condition to get his father to tow in the wreck before the cops found it. Dave, of course, rigged the proper equipment on the Chevy truck and went and towed in the wreck, and the ruins of the tree while he was at it, while Mary cleaned the boy up and called in the family doctor.

Now the ultimate horror begins. I see here a classical tragedy with all Aristotle's qualifications, for Dave Senior was as much a king as Oedipus or Caesar or Lear or Hamlet or anyone in this degenerate age, and he had a king-size flaw which slowly, and while he watched, undid him. The family doctor was Andrew Jackson Rice, who had been through his own tragedy. A Hyannis doctor with a police record which he acquired like this: Late one night there came to the doctor's office, which was in his home, a young couple who had driven down from Boston. The girl was pregnant and she had tried, maybe with amateur help, to abort herself, and now she was dying of toxemia. Far too late for Dr. Rice to do anything for her, and she and the young man refused to go to the hospital, so the doctor gave her what medication he could, wrote a couple of prescriptions, and they got back in the car and drove back to Boston. At some point she died and it all came out, and the doctor, whose only crime had been neglecting to report the evidence of a crime (attempted abortion), went to jail. Just as bad, in the eyes of the law, as attempting the operation himself, which he had not done.

So his family suffered the loss of his income as well as the ignominy. Mrs. Rice taught for years in the Cotuit Cooperative Nursery School until the doc got out and resumed the practice of medicine. Here the law was more merciful than the profession; he regained his license but was never again permitted to admit his patients to the hospital. This was the doctor the Lelands called in, and Dave's tragic flaw, and Mary's, I see as their misplaced and overemphatic loyalty to Dr. Rice. He begged, he pleaded with them—they told me so themselves—to get another doctor so their son could be admitted to the hospital, but they persisted in their loyalty until young Dave died, as Dr. Rice had told them he would. The tragedy had many victims; people who hadn't heard the true story, who would not hear it, still blame Dr. Rice for young Dave's death.

And of course, Dave and Mary spent their remaining years blaming themselves for it. I can only imagine what their life together must have been like; they had for years been out of the way of communicating with each other, and they had pride that kept them from showy mourning. Dave talked to me and to other friends about his boy, but it was obviously only froth off the surface of his deep, bitter draught. On rainy evenings his old Chrysler would be parked in our comic cemetery, Dave sitting in it looking at the grave. He told me one time that what he was thinking about was how cold Dave must be out in the ground in the rain. He recalled, over and over, the final scene: the father came home from somewhere and the doctor was there.

"'How is he?' I asked, and the doctor said, 'He's dead.'" End of story. Dave was silent, and you realized all he was feeling.

In this condition, poor Dave had not many days left, but they were slightly, painfully prolonged by my busybodiness. We had done business for years in the old-time way: he would fix things for me and nothing said about money, then one day he would feel the need for cash and he would hand—not mail —me a bill in his illegible scrawl, numbers clear and plain, and I would write a check. It never was a problem getting the money together; he didn't charge that much. Now I came into the kitchen where he and Mary were sitting by the stove and gave him a check for a hundred dollars, unasked.

"You don't owe me that much," he said.

"No, but you need money at a time like this. I'll owe you

more than that in a week or two." Of course, I knew all about Dave's other weakness; he wouldn't die owing me. Hoped to compel him to live a little longer, have a chance to recover a bit. I was right about the weakness, but I underestimated the pain. He died within the year, free of debt. Poor Mary was less fortunate. Took to drinking, smashed up her car, lost her good job cooking for Matille Wesson. All painful to watch. But meanwhile, she gave me my choice of Dave's tools before she sold them all and closed the shop. One thing I took was his anvil, but somebody stole it while I was getting the shop back after Bobby went bankrupt. Imagine stealing an anvil! For that matter, imagine an anvil having a sentimental value! I know perfectly well who got it — a known thief who had access — but no way to prove it and not worth the legal expense.

Betty Leland had moved away, all the way to Martha's Vineyard, before her father died, even before her brother. She had some sort of job there, and sometime after Dave's death, she died too, I believe of complications connected with her obesity. I never knew Betty Leland at all well. We smiled and murmured greetings when we met, but I have no notion what was with her at any time.

But I can't drop it here; must remember Dave in happy times. Most times with him were happy. When I went out there evenings with a job for him I always brought a six-pack with me. I would stop in at Harry Crocker's, the Cotuit Grocery-Liquor Store, and ask for "the refreshments for the Engineers Club Banquet." Harry loved any word game. Then Dave and I would do whatever he had to do and whatever I wanted done and discuss whatever free association brought to mind. Sometimes we talked about our friend Thatch Gifford, just up the street, who presided in the Cotuit version of "Tobacco Road." Thatch and his lady wife, far too good for him but loyal in the

Yankee way. Fierce only in protecting her two daughters from the moral standards of their two teenage sons, retarded Maynard and fierce and unruly William, Ralph Baker's friend. Respectable women avoided William; he had a lecherous and predatory eye. Of Thatch, Dave would say "He could do anything if he wasn't so in-fer-nally lazy."

Dave and I would talk about the two classes of people: those whom we both knew and those Dave knew before he came to Cotuit. Friends from his down-Maine childhood, men he had been shipmates with. Of two comical brothers in the fo'c'sle of a pogy boat where each bunk had a little door so a sleeping man could shut out the light and the noise of the others. The cook on this boat had an attack of stomachache, terrible cramps, when the boat just happened to be in port somewhere. (Or because she was in port, and he ate in a shoreside restaurant.) So Dave went ashore in the middle of the night to fetch a doctor, told me all the turns he had made at intersections, all the strangers of whom he had asked directions, all this in a dark town I had never seen, of his finding a doctor and bringing him back, of the cook's subsequent recovery. The next day, one of the brothers asked Dave, "Chief, was that a real doctor you brought aboard?" and how one of the bunk doors popped open, the other brother popped his head out and said, "No. He was a teamster."

"He was a teamster!" Dave thought this one of the funniest things he had ever heard. To me it was just another example of "you had to be there." But Dave laughed at the recollection in his enormous way, a shaking that began at his middle and shook his whole body and the cracked cement floor he stood on and went up the posts to the rafters and the shafts up there until the whole building shook. If you look, you can find all sorts of real-life examples of this sympathetic response of nature and objects. Like those poplar trees that sighed like a character in an El Greco painting. When I was working in Russell's Garage in Swarthmore, Pennsylvania, I had a Packard car with hypochondria. Anything I fixed on anybody's car, next day my car came down with it and I had to fix it again. In Cotuit, my Mercedes knew the way home as well as any horse. For years after we moved into our grand new house in Mashpee, it kept taking me home to the old place on Piney Road. I know a tugboat that can moan with passion, but Dave Leland's was the only machine shop in the world that would shake with laughter. One more thing in this village that is gone forever.

XVI
THE LAST GIANT OF ALL

Now, to reach the dearest friend of all, turn around and head south again on Main Street, back to the corner of Main and Putnam, formerly Maple, where so many of my memories are centered. Here on this tee-shaped corner were, during my lifetime, the Cotuit Grocery and Loring's Garage behind it, the house of the Holdsteins and the house once occupied by Captain Phinney and after him by his daughter Hattie. Hattie lived on for twenty or so years, a sour spinster. She had for years a handsome lodger named Marshall Potter, whom everybody (except the hopelessly prejudiced) liked. Well, one day after they had been sharing the house for at least ten years, Hattie and Marshall up and got married, to everyone's astonishment. Less likely candidates for marriage can hardly be imagined; such disparity in age, beauty, sexual orientation, everything. And, to prolong and intensify the astonishment, they "made a go of it." Marshall may have, as everyone assumed, married Hattie for her valuable house on its corner lot, but all agreed he earned it. He made Hattie's last years easy, maybe even pleasant, smiling, asking how she felt and what she would like to eat, showing that he cared, always in that precise, clipped, high-pitched voice. He earned his bequest from Hattie and his respect in the neighborhood by being a genuine nice guy. But it is not of the Potters I sat down to write. As soon as Hattie died, he sold the house, and I never heard anything of him since. Thereafter it was occupied by two or three families. Remember Miss Nellie Crocker's protégé "Miss Nancy Parker"? Her family lived there. After them, there was a rarely handsome young couple who did folk-singing gigs. She had the most beautiful long blond hair and went out of her mind. Finally the place passed into the hands of my number-one best friend, Frank Minot, and his wife Bernice.

This couple, not as mismatched as the Potters, but almost, had moved to Cotuit and rented one of the few year-round houses maybe ten years before. For one who was so close a friend for so long, I know only the roughest outline about his background. He was almost the tail end of a Boston family as grand as the Lowells. No doubt they were related, by marriage at least, somewhere back among the generations. They had the same physique, big but not fat, the same handsome face, straight prominent nose. The Minot family summered in Falmouth; Frank's father or grandfather was one of those rich Falmouth folk who endowed the New Haven's private train daily between Boston and Woods Hole. There is a Minot Street in Falmouth. That's nothing; there is a Minot's Lighthouse in Boston Harbor. It marks the approach from the southward and is unique among lighthouses—a cylindrical sheet-iron tower set on a submerged rock—and in storms the spray leaps up as high as the lens. Also, it says "I love you," that is, flashes in groups of one, four, three, over and over. Frank bore the weight of all this family lightly; he proclaimed himself the black sheep, named one of his boats that, told wry tales of his childhood spent in defying this or that group of relatives. A delightful story of sneaking Seidlitz powders into a spinster aunt's commode. He and Bernice moved to Cotuit; I think now that they had made Falmouth too hot to hold them. They owed everybody in town and everybody from New York to Boston.

I'm trying to remember when they first came here. Had to be in the 1940s. I was between college and graduate school and had to take a year off because education grad school was full, so I was working nights as maintenance man in a cement plant. Every night I was supposed to grease all the fittings on all the rollers on the long conveyor belt which moved the aggregates from the piles and bins to the top of the tower, where they dropped into the mixer trucks. That, by barely numerical math, was the winter of 1949 to 1950.

But we had, by then, known the Minots for some time (again the maddening vagueness of that word "some"). There were four of them: Frank and Bernice, Betsy, his daughter but not hers, and Muriel, her daughter but not his. Bernice was Frank's third wife; he had two grown-up children by his first, a Boston society lady, and Betsy by his second. Her mother — I never met her, but I heard of her — was of Quebec French background and had little in common with her rakish society husband. Their marriage didn't last, and after Frank came home from the war, he got a divorce with custody. All this was before we knew them. Little Betsy was a charmer, just about the most beautiful child I have ever seen.

Frank put a lot of thought and effort into flouting the morals of his ancestors, but he was the most straitlaced man I ever saw concerning a man's responsibility to his children and to all children. "None of it is the kid's fault," he'd say of his failed marriages. Straitlaced but clearly unfit to bring up a beautiful daughter, so before they came to Cotuit, before we met them, he met Bernice and married her. They had one thing, at least, in common: a little daughter to bring up single-handed. And both were capable of loving a spouse, a child, a friend with the whole soul, though both were a little shy of showing it.

Here's an anecdote about the Frank Minot few people saw. I said he was, in some ways, straitlaced. One night when Bernice and the kids were out of town and I was supposed to be working, I had a slight industrial accident climbing around that ramshackle plant in the dark and came home early. Betty thought that was occasion for a party; she called Frank and invited him over. She hung up looking puzzled; he had declined, sounded embarrassed and ill at ease, which was not normal with Minot. Didn't take us long to figure out what was wrong with him; he knew my schedule, thought I was at work and she was making a proposition, and he would have none of it, but such behavior from Betty caught him off guard. Once we had figured that out, we had to put it right at once. Couldn't have him go on thinking that. She called him back and mentioned two details she hadn't bothered to tell before: "Leonard got home early and I just made an apple pie."

"I'll be right there," said he.

I had decided by then to stay in Cotuit, make my living here, but there weren't many people here in winter with whom I could have a conversation of any depth. Plenty of Harvard men in summer, but even your usual old grad is hardly fit to talk to. To most of them, Harvard is the name of a football team, and they are interested only in the drunken fellowship of fandom, while I think even fielding a team named Harvard is a disgrace. Never mind. Talk about straying from the subject. I didn't realize that I missed intellectual conversation until Minot came along overflowing with it. He had been through not only Harvard but MIT. We had plenty in common right from the beginning, for he was a marine engineer of international repute, knew great volumes of technical stuff on ship design as well as yacht design. He had been a partner of the renowned Professor Owen, designer of a "J Boat" built to compete for defense of America's Cup. The firm of Owen and Minot designed the ketch *Atlantis*, a sailing research vessel for Woods Hole Oceanographic Institution and, up to the time of Minot's death, still at work for the institution. Imagine a ketch with mainmast so high she can't get under the canal bridges, has to go round the Cape like the pre-canal schooners every time she is going or coming, north or east.

So, still sidling up on a date I can't remember, they must have moved to Cotuit in the 1940s when I was an undergraduate. At least one of their little girls was enrolled in Betty's co-op nursery school, so Betty and the hyperenergetic Bernice met, and through her, Betty met Frank and got us together. At the time, and right up to this day, my friendship with Minot reminds me of what T. E. Lawrence wrote of an English officer who visited him during the first war: "he was the only fully-taught man in Arabia and . . . our minds had ranged over. . ." Not quite the same, to be sure. Lawrence's deep thoughts seem to have been in Greek; ours were in Maritime.

Minot was patient in bringing me up to date in shipbuilding and ship-designing techniques, ship construction problems. We went abstractly but thoroughly into problems of tanker design and operation, the danger of carting oil about the world in thin, tin buckets barely floating, bigger and bigger ones. Cleaning tanks after every voyage and disposing of the wash water overboard. Tanks must be washed between cargoes; oil, as the public does not know, is corrosive. The oil we at home use to combat corrosion is nothing like tanker cargo, much of which is crude oil with all the acids and pollutants still in it, and more of it partially refined but still corrosive to steel hulls. In the less than a century that tankers had existed, there had grown up in the maritime community a tradition of careless, thoughtless disposal of contaminated wash water and bilge water and even pure oil directly overboard. Tankers, Minot told me, right through World War II and after, were built with "wing tanks" which carried oil only when rough seas were not likely to be a problem, and owners might send ships out into the North Alantic with these tanks full on the slim chance of their not being caught in any storm. If the weather turned bad, which it usually did, they just pumped that excess oil overboard in thousand-barrel lots. Standard procedure!

All this discussion, plus news of the sinking of the liner *Andrea Doria*, her instability the result of keeping certain deep tanks empty to ease her roll, make her motion more comfortable for the passengers, got us thinking what could be done about slop oil. The original inspiration was mine, from a mind not bound by maritime tradition: tank liners of plastic film. Frank found out that it could be had, or made to order, in any reasonable strength or thickness, and we built a model of a section of a tanker's hull and fabricated a plastic liner for it. The idea was that the cargo would never come in contact with the ship's structure at all, thus would not corrode it, and the liner, when empty, could be hoisted out through a hatch (larger hatches would have to be fitted) and disposed of ashore. (Like everybody else to this day, we begged the question of disposed of how?) The increased life of a ship whose steel was so protected should make shippers and shipowners willing to pay us for our process. We never got anywhere with our invention; Frank got too busy with the new ship Woods Hole was planning to build and then he died, and it was so way beyond my knowledge technical, and required admission to the councils of professionals who had never heard of me—I had zero credentials—that it just died along with Minot. Today I think there are other ways of accomplishing the same thing.

Minot deplored these oil-dumping practices, but even he, with his grasp of the facts of marine life and marine procedures, did not foresee the environmental disaster that is now ensuing. Today, relative to the number of mouths to feed, there are no more fish at all. They have been fished out, their habitat destroyed by modern deepwater trawls, or they have been poisoned by deepwater oil drilling. Tons of oil are spilled, bringing it ashore. Minot, in fact, collaborated in writing a book entitled *The Inexhaustible Sea,* prophesying a time when most of the human food supply will have to come out of the ocean, as farmland stops producing and gets filled up with condos. Based on aquaculture and fish-farming techniques being developed in Japan, the coastal seas will be farmed like the land. I suppose one could take comfort in the thought that he didn't live to see his arguments turned upside down by other human practices of which he was all the while aware.

Anyway, the details of tanker operation I learned from Minot brought me minor distinction after he was gone. I was writing for that weekly paper, supposed to be the paper's maritime authority, though the editor would always print anything I wrote, and when a blundering Greek-flag tanker, the *Torrey Canyon,* went aground on Nantucket Shoals, there was consternation. There were meetings, official statements, all sorts of fuss, and I was, for the occasion, a member of the "press corps." Went to a meeting in Boston where speeches were made by Senator Kennedy, Senator Chafee of Rhode Island, all sorts of big shots, Coast Guard salvage officers, executives from the big towing and salvage firms, the whole first team reassuring us land-based reporters about their plans to keep her cargo of oil from leaking into the ocean. It was all bullshit; all those discussions with Minot when he was alive had made me indeed an expert on tanker operation and oil pollution. Seas were breaking over the wreck. It took the Coast Guard three days just to put a man aboard. Haste was called for; the ship was about to break up. How to put a barge alongside? They knew perfectly well that the oil couldn't be pumped even if they got that far. Oil of that grade is a solid until it is heated, and she was long since a "cold ship," boilers underwater.

So I came home and wrote my article. Said "I will make a prediction right now: The Coast Guard and the best civilian salvage men in the world aren't going to make it. That oil is going in the ocean." My deadline was Monday, and the paper would be on the streets Wednesday. My editor told me later, "My heart was in my mouth, but I told myself, the man knows what he's talking about." He printed it just as I wrote it, and of course, it fell out just as I said. *Cape Cod News* and I scooped the world, but the world didn't know to read us. Those five hundred or however many thousand tons of oil did indeed go in the ocean, but they didn't cause much disaster. That kind of oil, that cold, just makes lumps kind of like asphalt that sink to the bottom or wash ashore in chunks about the size of cowflops on the beach. All this I learned in those long conversations with Minot. And all those talky press conferences I traveled to were nothing but PR. No professional, from the Coast Guard or from the industry, believed there was a chance of saving the oil; it was all for us, the press, to pass on to We the People. Still a puzzle to me is which group the politicians belonged to. Did those senators know it was all phoney, or did they believe, like their constituents, that there was any chance?

Following this thought brings one to the conclusion that, for a senator, there is such a thing as being "too smart by half." He is better off not knowing that the cause is hopeless; then he can hold out hope to his constituents without lying.

By now it must be apparent that Minot was the fourth of what one might call the *quadrumvirate* with whom I was on a last-name basis. Except that two of the four were not *viri* but *feminae*. (I can write like Lawrence, if not in classical Greek, at least in schoolboy Latin.) I loved the man above all others I have ever known. Loved the way he talked, aphoristically the way I do, with a Harvard accent so broad, and a word choice and word order that seemed somehow British, even when talking absolute nonsense. "On Fridays I either fish or . . . cut bait." Always pronounced "either" and "neither" in the British way—eyether, neyether. Everybody loved him, the whole yacht club, old and young. He did all kinds of things to make his rare technical training of use to us. He raced skiffs, not victoriously but enthusiastically. He had *Black Sheep* built for him at Bigelow's and, in a year or two, sold her to buy one of the new boats I was building. Called her *Minot's F'light*; he played with words the way I do. That was in 1957, when Minot himself was pushing seventy and too frail and slow-moving to be attempting anything so strenuous and abrupt. He capsized frequently and once broke a couple ribs on the coaming when she was righted. I was there with *The Big Wheel* to take care of such emergencies, for adults as well as for kids, and we rescued Minot forthwith, but he healed slowly and never curtailed any of his activities.

The Big Wheel, now. I had some sort of notion of grandeur and converted her from an open navy whaleboat into a miniature tug. Following, maybe, in the footsteps of my friend Chet Crosby senior, who was a world-class tugboat nut. Now the navy twenty-six-foot whaleboat is tough; she was designed to bang against the side of an armor-plated warship and, in the words of Minot, "to do it all day long." And, in the words of Dave Leland, "hell for stout." Without being too heavy to hoist aboard and overside again quickly. To which end, she had two watertight bulkheads, ahead of the engine and astern of it, double-diagonal planked and steel framed. I was aware of the importance of these bulkheads for strength in a boat that I ran always in shallow water and frequently right onto the beach, so, not to compromise them, I built my decks and my tugboat house over top of them. Made my little boat very high in the air. She looked beautiful to me, but to anybody else she looked God-awful top-heavy, and my employer, the Association whose children I was hired to protect, asked Minot for his professional advice. Should they continue to hire a craft which seemed so unstable?

My ideas were different; I had fallen in love with the steam tugs in the port of Philadelphia. Was always cadging rides on them, and they looked just like *The Big Wheel.* But of course, these contained like fifty tons of engine and upright boiler. To have equaled their stability, my tug would have needed like two tons of ballast and a tugboat shape that would have drawn over six feet of water, altogether useless working among skiffs sailing where it was only three feet deep. But the whole question put poor Minot on a terrible spot; he was a professional with deep integrity, and his responsibility here was for all the children in this society. And he was my friend. He handled it, with vast diplomacy, by convincing me that my boat could indeed be unstable. Not by talking; he came aboard representing my charterers, with a stopwatch, and showed me how to time her roll and apply a formula in which one variable was the time it took her to make a complete cycle, starboard to port and back to starboard. All sorts of abstruse engineering things were thus revealed, for we were measuring her "metacentric height," establishing the length of her "GM," the vertical distance between two theoretical places inside her, all sorts of abstruse shit like that. The formula applied to the liner *United States*, the battleship *New Jersey*, to *Minot's F'light*, as well as to *The Big Wheel of Cotuit*. Look at the company we're in! We all had metacenters and GMs. G is the theoretical center of gravity and M is the metacenter, an even more unfindable point around which she pivots when she rolls, and it must be higher than G or she would float upside down. How much higher determines how fast she rolls, the faster the more stable, but too long a GM results in a vessel that rolls so rapidly that she is not comfortable. She "snap rolls." He convinced me that I understood, and based on such a belief, I had no choice but to agree; she was not stable enough. There might arise an occasion when she could roll over. (Another factor which neither of us mentioned but of which we were both aware was my custom of carrying like five hundred pounds of girls on the pilothouse roof, where they could see more and be seen more.) One of the figures in the formula is the ship's beam or width at the waterline, and Minot told me a tale of how the navy had ruined a class of warships of respectable design by adding heavy top hamper. And had cured the problem by welding buoyant blisters out to the sides of the hull at the waterline, thus making her wider, therefore faster rolling. That's what I ended up doing to *The Big Wheel* after we had discussed and figured and considered the notion of adding ballast, finding that ballast wouldn't be sufficient.

M 2123 J

Photo by Dorothy I. Crossley

The author aboard *The Big Wheel* in 1968. Note the cypress bow rail, the high house, and the stability blister along the side of the hull.

I had (you will pardon the digression) a great store of secondhand cypress boards which I had acquired from a deal
with Hayden. He had the contract to demolish the old two-
room Cotuit elementary school, and it turned out there were
miles of prime cypress boards in it. The cornices were one
board under, fourteen inches wide, and one board up, eleven
inches all the way around. All a full inch thick, finished one
side, and not a knot or imperfection all the way twice around.

Cypress is the finest boat lumber there is, strong, lightweight, rot resistant. Only trouble with this lot was its age; it
was dry. You couldn't bend it or it snapped, but it made ideal
framing for those blisters. Evie Jackson, Gardner's second
son, had worked a couple years for Fisher-Pierce, manufacturer of the latest innovation in plastic boats, and had
learned to mix and "blow" flotation foam into cavities. He
was full of this new technique and never hesitated to share it
with me. It was a complicated process, involving seven ingre-
dients which must be precisely proportioned by weight using
a gram scale, under controlled climatic conditions. Also,
working with the stuff was later found to be hazardous to
your health. Some of the components were toxic, one was
formaldehyde, if that means anything to you. Evie and I sim-
plified, adapted his knowledge to conditions we had to work
with. We were the first to try to blow foam outdoors; for controlled environmental conditions, we waited for good days.
As a result, some of the compartments turned out more
buoyant than others; foam of varying density. Our job did not
require precise control of the total amount of mix; we blew it
into open compartments, trimmed the top with a saw and
decked them over after it had hardened. I must explain here
that we filled the "blisters" with flotation foam as an easier
task than trying to make those blisters watertight where they

came against the planking, at an ever-changing angle. Water was kept out since they were already full of foam.

Result was unchanged tugboat profile but a sort of pontoon built unobtrusively into each side. Like the sponsons on a sailing canoe. Worked fine, and after we launched her, Minot came aboard again with his stopwatch and pronounced her stable. I am sure his relief was even greater than mine. He even asserted that the design was beautiful!

Two balls in the air are not enough for a word juggler like me. Let us now bring in Bernice — Bunnice, Bill called her. This story contains the four women that, now that three of them are dead and one a hundred years old, I remember as being most full of life. Marianna, Dodence, Sophie (plus her daughter, Margot) and Bernice are, of all the people I have known, the ones most alive, who lived every moment at the most frantic, breakneck pace. Each of them had her individual way of expressing her individuality. Marianna flaunted her Lowell snobbery. Sophie played up her flamboyant Britishness. Dodence showed her love for everybody in a way that was genuine, not played up at all. Margot flaunted her elfin beauty through her expressive legs. Bernice acted the tough New York career girl.

Beyond that, Bernice was an accomplished pianist. I have no music, but it appears, from what I have been told, that her playing approached professional, concert quality. She would say, if she were still alive, that it surpassed it. Some said that she played too emphatically, too loud, which is certainly the impression it made on me. And on Minot; I remember once, when we had all drink taken, his shouting above the piano, "Darling, play 'I married a man who had no testicles whatsoever.'" Which might apply to any man who thought to "make it" with such a package of energy as Bernice. Evie Jackson made it; I'll come to that.

My old love Helen Cobb was married to a New York lawyer named Lester Solomon, and they came here summers to the Cobb house way up the Narrows, among the Almys. So they had some people in, old friends like us, and we brought the Minots, and it turned out that Bernice and Lester knew each other from an earlier existence. Lester was one of those who, as those humorless liberals I knew at college put it, "made a buffoon of his race." So now occurred an effusive greeting such as you might encounter on the Lower East Side. Or in the ethnic Yiddish theater. Bernice was a big woman, though not particularly tall, but she towered over Lester. From his knees upward, he was invisible, out of sight in her ample flesh. Her husband was tall and very handsome, with a big Lowell-type face, a droll wit, a slightly British way of speaking, but Bernice became the focus of any group, and Frank didn't mind. I suppose that having such an unacceptable wife was another way of irritating his Brahmin relatives.

So, to draw together this account of what went on in Minot's life before I knew him, it appears that he came home from the war, where he had served in some secret civilian capacity connected with all he knew about ships and shipping, to try to put some sort of life back together. I never knew his second wife (never knew his first one either, until we met at his funeral), but evidently number two was the sort you had to get rid of. A boatbuilder who worked for me spoke of her "cruising" along the docks, bringing the child along in her baby carriage. So Minot got rid of her, hanging on to their baby daughter. He had no veteran's benefits because he had not been in the service, and after the divorce, he had no money either. One unsuccessful attempt to make a living involved buying a used Nova Scotia lobster boat and taking out charter fishing parties. But that didn't pay because he didn't run the boat himself. He hired a captain, so he could work at his profession. He designed a new trawler which included some European ideas novel in New England. He had a connection with Burmeister and Wain, ship and engine builders of Copenhagen, one of the two or three great shipyards of the world. His trawler had some B & W patents in her propulsion and control systems, from her engine to her reversible-pitch propeller, and I guess she fished successfully, but scarcity of parts was always a problem. Finally, things were looking up; the Woods Hole Institution was ready to replace old *Atlantis* with a new modern research vessel, the navy was buying in on this ship and Minot was employed there to represent the institution in her designing and building. She became *Atlantis II*, and she is still working there; I see her picture often on public TV tending the ultra-deep submersible *Alvin*.

Minot did not design this ship; to design a vessel of this size and complexity requires a whole firm of designers, technicians, draftsmen, specialists. He was the "owner's man" in the planning and negotiating. He was, I say again, a "fully taught man" who could communicate between draftsmen at Rosenblatts' and the visionary scientists at Woods Hole and the "Buships" admirals in the Pentagon. He spoke all their languages. With style. He used me and my profound interest in these things so far above me to discuss his ideas on the layman's level. If I could understand them, anybody could. A special problem, which he dealt with as his own, was the requirement of making her absolutely silent when some of the acoustical instruments were working. Another goal was the nearest approach yet envisioned to absolute motionlessness of a body floating on a sea in motion. My kindergarten suggestion was a catamaran, but they required something far more motionless than that. Such a vessel is still far from attainment, but they seem to have made some progress in that direction; evidently the ship does what was expected of her. Another problem, anticipated before the contract for her design was even signed, was the relationship of the institution with the navy, which was putting up a lot of money, which was sure to restrict the institution's freedom in how it chose to employ her. Don't know how they settled this either, nor even how much input into the controversy Minot had.

But the result for me was heightening of our friendship. Numberless long evenings spent in discussion not only of *Atlantis II* and her problems but of all manner of marine-related tales, anecdotes, history. Minot loved to make fun of himself. Told a tale of taking a New York society girl out sailing at the New York end of Long Island Sound, of being becalmed there, a frequent occurrence on that body of water, and of sitting on the tide washing out of the East River, bearing its uncountable cargo of spent condoms, sitting there still while the tide swept back in with the same cargo. And the girl so naive she didn't know what they were and Frank embarrassed what to tell her. I think he finally convinced her they were squid.

Which led to another tale of going to dinner at the home of some society family whose name he didn't even know and drinking too much wine and acting foolish. After dinner, the party went to the opera, where Minot, still full of wine, made loud and disparaging remarks about what a lousy opera it was. Finally he was pulled aside by his friends and enlightened: his host at dinner and the opera was Mr. Music himself,

Walter Damrosch, conductor of the New York Symphony Orchestra; his date was Damrosch's daughter. The opera was the opening performance of Damrosch's latest composition.

That was one of a thousand and one such tales Minot told on himself. But how could he have known what a chord it would strike in me? Damrosch was conductor also of the NBC Symphony Orchestra on radio, and one of the busy-busy things he did was every Friday he conducted "The NBC Music Appreciation Hour" over WJZ. And my parents and the school administration ganged up on the helpless kids and made sure every child in school marched down to the auditorium to hear that section of the hour (which lasted all morning) selected for his age group, to listen to the music played on the school's huge radio-phonograph and hear Damrosch explaining it in his oily voice with his unctuous foreign accent. Patronizing! Nauseating! Beyond endurance! Bierce once quoted Disraeli as describing Bishop Wilberforce as "unctious, oleaginous, saponicious." That is how Damrosch came on. I blame him for turning me altogether off music of any kind for life. My parents and adult conformism had a lot to do with it as well, but the sugary voice of Damrosch was the ultimate unendurable. How could Minot have sensed this prejudice of mine? How could he have known to choose this anecdote from all his vast, self-deprecatory repertory?

All his anecdotes had similar personal appeal; he was a master at choosing which tale would reach which audience. Mindful of my addiction to tugs, he selected one about sailing home on a foggy night from Martha's Vineyard to Falmouth in his catboat, about the time I was born it must have been, hearing foghorns all around him from every direction. "Suddenly," he said, "I saw this great telephone pole rise horizontally from the water just abaft my rudder." He had sailed, all unknowing, right over the catenary, the submerged part of the hawser between a tug and its tow. "Never saw either the tug or the barge." If you don't know what a hundred percent certain death it would be to have snagged that hawser and ridden down it till you were under the barge, just think about it. Probably no trace of you would ever be found.

He had a Lowell story too. Seems someone called the office at Harvard asking to speak to Mr. Lowell and got this reply: "The President is in Washington visiting Mr. Wilson."

But his favorite Lowell story he learned from me. And, of all ironies, it is the one which his daughter Betsy best remembers. Cousin Lawrence was walking about his vast estates on Cape Cod when he met a man fishing in a ditch. Full of joie de vivre, the president addressed the peasant, "Good morning, Piscator."

To which he got the reply, "Hello, shitface." Notable about this tale is its provenance: I heard it from a communist, a radio op in the merchant marine, whom I met in Philadelphia in 1942 or 1943, and goes to show how thoroughly the Marxist underground hated Lowell all those years ago, all those years after Sacco and Vanzetti. Relevant to all the forces that have whirled, almost unnoticed, by me in my long and useless life.

Minot had one story to top them all. For some reason he told it in the third person, as something a friend of his did, but it really happened to Minot himself, as you were supposed to suspect. He (this friend) went to the Harvard-Yale game in New Haven and Harvard won, and the party was as soggy as such parties traditionally get, college-age people determinedly learning to drink and to pretend to enjoy it, and in the small hours he climbed into his berth on the New York train, took off and neatly folded his clothes and laid them down just outside the open window. He failed to wake up in Pennsylvania Station, and the train crew failed to arouse him. The heat roused him toward noon in the sun-baked yards somewhere out on Long Island, surrounded by tracks with other parked rolling stock, without either clothes or the money which had been in the pockets, all scattered along the tracks from here to New Haven, and no idea how to get out of there, never mind which direction out was. He walked at random through the yards, draped in Pullman curtains, till he found a taxi which he could not pay. The way he told it, you were yourself this wild, rebellious rich kid digging, as fast as he could dig, one pit after another to fall into.

As I say, most of Minot's stories were self-deprecatory. His Christmas lament went like this: "Everybody else buys his cards in October, spends November addressing them and gets them in the mail by Thanksgiving. Not I! I remember them on Christmas Eve and then phone, long distance, everybody I know all over the world and wish them Merry Christmas!"

Our son Bill called Frank "Minotz," and Minot forthwith took to calling Bill "Pecks." The two of them had their own thing going. Bill, learning to talk and talking this time like his mother, said once, "I like Minotz. Minotz nice person." But early in the 1950s Minot's life changed; Bernice took up with Evie Jackson. Evie was then working for me in my early location in front of Coolidges' garage, almost next door to Minots' house on the corner. Evie and a lot of younger kids worked there, some of them not on my payroll but there working on their own boats. Bernice would vibrate by, and she and Evie would go off together. All these teenagers whispered and giggled about such behavior. They were old enough to know such things went on; just they had never observed them. Neither Bernice nor Evie were ever bothered with what society thought. Evie was his own sort of screwball. A vile temper and a vile vocabulary; he never outgrew the childish thrill of using naughty words. Pat's big skull and Dode's small pelvis combined to give him a not uncommon minor birth injury—gave his head a slightly grotesque shape—and he had what seems to go with this trauma: a loud, rasping voice. He was the fiercest, angriest skiff racer of us all, and he used his loud profanity to scare smaller kids out of his way. He appropriated his family's standard Bigelow skiff for his exclusive own, and she was one of Bigelow's faster creations anyhow, and he equipped her with one of my C & P sails, this one of Orlon, and he cleaned up. I could beat him in my souped-up Butler, but not so often as he beat me.

We were best of friends. Like me, and like hardly anybody else I ever knew, he went to college and carried college—what he learned in his studies, the interesting content of the lectures—around with him all his life. Evie went to Colorado College, where the Jacksons had a family connection. There he specialized in philosophy and music. Whether he was painting a skiff, racing *Gatherwind*, courting Bernice, his hands were always in motion conducting something from Beethoven that was playing inside his head. He loved also Tolstoy and Dostoevsky. He loved Bernice's playing. With all his oddities, Evie was energetic enough to match the life and fire of Bernice. As soon as they could afford quarters, she moved in with Evie.

The financing turned out to be mostly taken care of by her, with the energy she had left over. She went into real estate, not just brokering for others but buying and developing on her own account. She had nada capital but *mucho cojones*. And nada ethics. She sunk her shaft in the gold vein of Cape Cod land, built on the borderline between subdivisions and retirement communities, took ore from the vein of approaching old age. She would make a down payment on a defunct estate or farm, parlay every bit into down payments on more. To this breathless gambling she brought all that pep plus her New York ruthlessness. She sold a house lot to Betty and me, and on it we built our first home. Then she built, yards from the door, a road that was on an old layout, which she had promised us would never be built, to get at other lots behind us. We were enraged at this behavior. We had made a deal with her as though it were with Frank, unbreakable. Like a verbal contract with Hayden. But it wasn't with Minot or Hayden; it was with Bernice and worthless. She was so New York ruthless that soon nobody would take her word for anything, nor her paper. Her deals fizzled, and she and Evie ended up where they had started, penniless and landless. Too much gall and not enough capital.

She put Evie to work building and repairing houses, but this was another failure; he would apply his standards of yacht quality to spec houses or homes for himself and Bernice. In neither place were they appropriate or appreciated, and he didn't have any practical knowledge of wood and how it acted, how it aged. Only too much theory. He helped build two houses for the two of them, one in Cotuit and the other in Concord, but neither of them really cared about their surroundings, and the Concord house, where he and Bernice finally settled when they went bust here, remained unfinished. They went on living in it half done until Evie died of that familiar heart of the hefty, and Bernice went on living in it for years thereafter. Frank gave her a divorce so she could marry Evie, who seemed to have energy enough to keep her entertained but not much left over. His skiff racing tapered off and his work got so slow you couldn't see any progress after he had been on a job for a year. Evidently his other talents were enough; never heard any more scandal about her.

So Minot had, once again, sole custody of Betsy. It wasn't easy; she wasn't an easy child. She had been exposed at the wrong age to Bernice's morals and a little to Evie's vocabulary. Too beautiful for her own good; she attracted boys like chum. She had never in her life had a mother, and there was a lot of tut-tut talk about her among the society mothers. Because I was always around with her dad and because all the kids liked me, I was once or twice able to protect her. I once took her home from a beach party. She had been honing her drinking skills when I snatched her from the very claws of a gang of boys whose ganging-up instincts were stirring, took her home to her dad and took myself right back to that party so they'd all know I hadn't grabbed her for myself.

As I say, I was the friend of all these square-dancing, skiff-racing kids. Went to all their parties, drank their beer, kissed their girls, made an unmistakable point of stopping right there. They told me their triumphs and failures, and a couple of the boys told me right out that Betsy was fun to kiss and fondle but that was as far as she'd go. Not from their want of trying. And all the scandal was made up by jealous old biddies from Cleveland to titillate themselves.

As a parent, Minot must fall into the category of "permissive." Never heard him give either of his daughters an order, never heard either of them ask his permission to do anything or go anywhere. (Unless, of course, it required money.) Muriel was not Frank's daughter but she chose to spend at least half her time in his house rather than with Evie and Bernice. Muriel was an affectionate child, but with her mother's effusive management, it seemed phoney, Shirley Temple cute. It wasn't at all. She was (is) talented, but Bernice's management made her seem posy, like the typical daughter of any New York upwardly mobile young couple. Betsy, a few years older and with her generations-old class and beauty and with the merciless meanness of her whole insecure life, was hard to live and impossible to compete with. Muriel triumphed over this bringing up. She matured later, but then she showed class of her own, beauty of her own, right through a face disfigured in a car accident. Today she looks from this distance to be a successful singer and actress out on the coast and a good wife to a very nice guy.

Frank made a big point of treating these two daughters, one his own the other no relation, with absolute equality. His will made no distinction between them, but that was a small part of the story; much of what he "died possessed of" was family stuff, and much of the rest he owed money on. His will listed lots of small personal things—*Minot's F'light,* for one —which were left to Muriel outright to balance the family things Betsy got. By the time he died, Minot had something to write a will about. Had a good job in charge of all the engineering on half a dozen big, modern research vessels at Woods Hole, a partnership in a separate little oceanographic firm dealing with a narrow phase of undersea study which I don't even understand.

Minot was the world's worst driver. By himself, he would get to thinking and not pay enough attention; in company, he would get to talking with the same result. He had a huge car, 1950-something, one of the last Packards ever built, and coming home from New York or somewhere with Bernice and both kids, he got into a head-on collision in Taunton, and all four of them spent time in hospital. He and Betsy were soonest out, not visibly damaged. Frank broke ribs, as usual. Bernice's face was marred, not badly, but poor Muriel will always have a reconstructed look. They all got on with their together and with their separate lives.

There were a few good years then. Minot's new subject for rollicking conversation was his Portuguese housekeeper, Mrs. Rose Condinho, whose behavior and conversation he found hilarious. She had her own way of pronouncing American names and, like many strong personalities, she was not to be corrected. Called him "**Mister** Myatt." Called Shyzee and Hatta "Mrs. Lopes and Mrs. Cabin." Called Mary Leland, her best friend, "Mrs. Leon." Called me "the man with the truck." She had a daughter married to a state policeman, and this cop's lucky child was nicknamed by his mother and grandmother "Trooper." Much of the gossip she talked about unceasingly involved pseudo-confidential police undercover work. She had imaginary dirt on most of the leading citizens in her end of town; they had, she would report, mob connections. Miss Rose had a whisper you could hear a block away, and in this whisper she would report confidential police matters like, "There's going to be a raid." Seldom did any raid take place, but the expectation, wherever it originated, provided adventure in Miss Rose's dull day. Telling about it was every bit as good as seeing it. Minot took it all down in his memory and repeated it with glee. Rose was, Minot always explained, illiterate, "except for numbers on a check."

Meanwhile, Minot's specialized and detailed work for the institute built up and up with the preliminary design for *Atlantis II*. He prepared an enormous list of specifications and represented the institution in negotiating with worldwide firms like M. Rosenblatt and Gibbs and Cox, names to conjure with in leading-edge ship design, for the voluminous set of structural drawings. He was getting a lot of recognition in his profession now that he was too old to perpetuate the image he had cultivated of the rich young man in rebellion—Betsy picked it up where he left off—and could concentrate his great talent and erudition. When he spoke as a dilettante I could follow his shop talk; when he got numerically professional, he left me behind. But we had a happy social life, Betty and me, Minot and his girlfriend Judy, a few years younger than I, a divorcee with two kids living year-round in the family summer place on Ocean View, a girl I had much admired when we were kids for her beauty, daintiness and pep. She and Minot had a close relationship, close but platonic, as they took pains to let everyone know.

The four of us drank, partied, did impulsive kid-type things. One Hallowe'en we made spur-of-the-moment costumes and went out trick-or-treating among friends of our own generation. Got a "decidedly mixed" reception from those who had less drink taken. Like Mr. and Mrs. Mark Bryan. Mark, a widower well over seventy, had recently married Dulce, half his age, recently divorced from my friend Richard Ryder. The whole village was gabbing about this odd marriage, taking sides, and we called on them to show our support, which they hadn't asked for and didn't need. Mark was a sour old poop anyhow; today my joke is to say that now he's gone, I have inherited his title of Village Grouch. Anyway, we didn't carouse long in their frigid atmosphere, and Mark showed his contempt for gossip in his own way: got Dulce with child not once but twice in the next couple years. Didn't stop the talk but made it far more respectful! And the final result is two very bright boys.

After this cold reception, we trekked over to Barnstable village and dropped in on Kurt and Jane Vonnegut. You were always well received there, and so we had a hap hap happy Hallowe'en after all.

Minot's growing reputation got for him a trip to Europe, to Italy in particular, to lecture to some marine society. He went by liner, which was still an unremarkable way to get there, and we made a party of his departure from New York. We all moved in on Sally, a pretty friend of Judy's who had an apartment overlooking Central Park. By "we all" I mean Betty and I, Frank and Betsy. Judy wasn't with us; for one thing, she had her children to look after. For another thing, I speculate she was making advertisement of the fact that she was not Frank's mistress. As if anybody cared. For another thing, I speculate, she was trying to keep Minot at arm's length by setting him up with Sally. Clearly she didn't see him as either a husband or a lover. Frank's idea of sex remains, after all these years, still mysterious to me. Most mod and explicit as a subject for rollicking conversation but strangely straitlaced and reticent when it came to participation. I speculate, based on a lot of casual, accidental evidence, that he suffered from life-long feelings of inadequacy.

Betsy was in the phase of rude and rebellious teenager, scowling and not talking, saying sarcastic things. We all worked on her, and one or another of us made her smile from time to time. Sally told us later that Betsy had whispered to her, "Take care of my old man."

Minot, having totaled the Packard, was now driving a wee, sma' foreign car, a Simca I think, and when he totaled this, he totaled himself too. There was a party one Saturday night in January 1960 in Woods Hole to celebrate the final closing, signing of the contract to build the new ship Frank had had so much to do with designing. For all the years of practicing, Minot was not a much better drinker than he was a driver. On the way home through the snow, he and his insubstantial car were wiped out.

XVII
MINOT AND *MINOT*

IKNOW FEW details of this disaster, for I didn't hear of it until Frank Junior called me Sunday morning. I have made no attempt to find out anymore; what good would that do? But Frank Minot's influence on me and on everybody didn't end with his life. His son, from his first marriage and a little older than I, a borderline nut interested only in wildlife and nature, who was trying to support his wife and baby daughter small farming in North Falmouth, planned a worthy funeral with the help of ideas and suggestions from the oceanographic institution and from Bernice. She swiftly took charge of all the festivities, as usual, crassly unaware of the incongruity of his ex-wife, now married to somebody else, managing his funeral and reception. At least Evie didn't show. Minot was maybe looking down in tolerant amusement. There was a High Episcopal funeral at St. Barnabas in Falmouth with the ritual for burial at sea and six formal pallbearers: the five captains of the Woods Hole research vessels, in uniform, and me. I had until this moment no idea that Minot thought so much more of me than any of his host of other friends, but it seems his family knew. And I have never felt so distinguished before or since.

It took me eight years, but I have returned the honor, "in my fashion." In 1967 I saw an illustrated article in *Maine Coast Fisherman* about a miniature working tug, designed by my old friend Bob Rich, the same who had, almost twenty years before, built a lobster boat to my order for Joe Mattison. I went to see Bob, looked at drawings. He would build one of these tugs of his design, any length, any stage of completion you want. So I ordered one, twenty-eight feet long, hull only, finished as far as deck beams, top timbers and covering boards. She was to be my ultimate committee boat and yard workboat. And hobby. When the hull was ready, Johnny and I took our shop truck and our biggest trailer down Maine and loaded her up, in her pine cradle, brought her back to Cotuit. Made a stop in Searsmont for a load of fresh-cut white oak on the empty truck, then drove all night, stopped to recradle her when she shifted. John was not yet old enough to drive on the road, but he manhandled that heavy hull back into place when it shifted going over the road, with no tools but a pry bar and a hydraulic jack. We off-loaded her New Year's afternoon, skidded the boat, cradle and all, over greased planks and greased floor, right into the new carpenter shop which Hayden's crew had just built us, a lean-to addition, doubling the size of that original twenty-four by sixty railroad building. All the skills and Yankee ingenuity which I had spent my life acquiring and which Johnny was born knowing, skills patiently imparted by Dave Leland, Ralph Baker, Deak Crosby and the crews at both Crosby yards, and by Dave and Arnold, the technical specialists at Automarine, Inc., were now put to work.

All that spring, my whole family and the whole shop crew, three men, worked on her. I had Bob's drawings, but I made my own changes. Like I had to be high enough, standing in the pilothouse, to see over the heads of the Race Committee on the foredeck. So, perhaps still under the influence of the steamer *Priscilla*, I made her look top-heavy. She wasn't at all. Bobby had told me that to bring her down to her design waterline, she would need three thousand pounds of ballast, and even with that much, in the form of Hayden's second-hand iron window weights in the bilge, plus five hundred pounds of batteries and fifteen hundred of engine, she was no way top-heavy. She snap-rolls uncomfortably in any sort of sea. Long GM, as Minot would have said.

There is a saga to be written about that spring's work. I had never bored end-grain oak for a propeller shaft, never seen it done; I borrowed the strange tools from Chet Crosby's and taught myself to use them. That secondhand diesel out of *The Big Wheel* (now defunct) I fitted to engine beds we built in the new boat. Had the engine in and out three or four times before we got it lined up right, and each attempt was frightful, for the engine weighed fifteen hundred pounds and the electric hoist we lifted it with was rated for five hundred, and it rode on a track which was attached to the rafters by brackets I had welded onto it, and it was only some old barn-door track to begin with. No way of knowing what it would carry except to test it. So that's what we did: tested it almost to destruction. The whole building creaked and shuddered every time I picked up the engine, and everybody but me got right out of there.

Everybody included the best kids I ever taught to sail or fix boats. Most of them, of course, were like Johnny, gifted to begin with. Bobby Boden, who in spite of his shortcomings as boss was an unsurpassed shop man; John Murray, Anna Mattison's son, who worked by understanding the whole theory of whatever he was trying to accomplish and was therefore unexcelled at carpentry; Bill Peck, who was as good as he, better at repetitive jobs; Bill St. Coer the outboard mechanic, who was just a beginner with heavy diesel power but enthusiastic about the whole project. None of these guys was much over twenty. Johnny Peck was away at prep school. He came down weekends and solved all our problems with hardly more than a glance.

To build the high pilothouse, we had to move the almost finished hull outdoors, and just about then I broke my ankle stepping from the shop to the truck. John Murray took over the out-front things I had been doing. I remember with delight his astonishment, his utter disbelief, when he saw how green oak would bend U-shaped around a small radius when it came out of the steam box. He had heard of this well-known procedure all his life but never before seen it done. I hobbled around the shop and around the job in my "walking cast," always getting the plaster wet in puddles, driving the doctor crazy. "Walking cast" is a relative term, and I tested it to destruction as I did my overhead hoist, and neither let me down. We launched our new boat and had her working in June. Chet Crosby lifted her off the trailer with his crane and set her in the water. We found we couldn't shift or steer; the manually powered hydraulic linkage which I had designed while Johnny wasn't home was altogether inadequate. Took Johnny several days to straighten it out, and we have gone on improving it since and it still isn't perfect. But we had the most beautiful workboat of any yard within miles. Perhaps in the world.

Anyhow, as you have already figured out, I kept her name secret until the annual meeting of the yacht club on Fourth of July 1968, when Betsy Minot christened her *Francis Minot* alongside the yacht club pier. Betsy had been through a lot since her father's death. Remorse, no doubt, for having been so bratty to him. Bernice turned out to be as good a mother to her as Frank had been a good father to Muriel. Betsy was now into folk music, and into a sort of "coffeehouse culture" the kids had going. Folk music is the only kind I have ever understood or cared for, and Betsy hooked up with a singularly accomplished banjo player named Bob Siggins, who is today a singularly accomplished biochemist. Anyway, she got it into her pretty, unpredictable head that she wanted a High Episcopal wedding. Altogether out of character, but that's what she wanted, and Bernice gave it to her in grand style, the only style Bernice recognized. Another outrageous thing she wanted was that I should give her in marriage! I guess I really was Frank's best friend, as he was mine. Maybe Betsy remembered how I had stood between her and all those rapacious boys. Like a "father figure," it must have seemed.

But if she indeed thought of me as a substitute father, it was a singularly loose relationship. As we started up the aisle all dressed up, she in a long gown showing the appropriate area of to-die-for bosom, me in striped coat with tails, I leaned over to her and whispered, "Hey, Betsy, I can't give you away."

She looked up at me with eyes as round as Orphan Annie, "Why not?"

"Haven't ever had you."

The rest of the way to the altar, I was getting the elbow in the ribs, mutters of "Dirty old man! Wicked old man! Evil old man!"

Betsy had four bridesmaids, all lovely and one a celebrity: the folk singer Joan Baez. Wedding breakfast was at the Wayside Inn in Sudbury, made famous by (ugh) Longfellow, and the bridesmaids rode there with Betty and me in our old Mercury. Joan expected to perform and she was practicing her selection, getting her voice up, in our back seat. A private rendition just for us, though she had no such thought. Some voice! What luck I have had!

Betsy and Bob produced, before they broke up, "one daughter, passing fair, " Leah (Leo, my sons called her), who, like her mother, loved me passing well. So here is my anecdote about Leah: When she was still not much more than what conformists call a "toddler," she went with me to the Cotuit Grocery to pick up some last-minute refreshments, really so I could show her off, as the child well knew. Miss Nellie, installed at the checkout counter, wanted to know who this was. "This," crowed I, "is my granddaughter Leah. Betsy's little girl." Leah had by now had her fill of adults making a fuss over her. She took me by the hand and started out the door. "C'mon, Poopface," said she. And to this day, now that Leah is grown up with a daughter of her own, we still call each other Poopface.

As I said, Betsy and Bob broke up while Leah was still a baby. Betsy acquired a second husband, Benno Schmidt Junior, a gentle, pleasant scholar, later for a while president of Yale, vulnerable to all sorts of nutty ideas. This marriage didn't last either but I mention it because Betty and I were once again involved. Ceremony took place at our new home in Mashpee, in Betty's lovely garden overlooking Popponessett Bay.

My lifelong, undeserved, unexplainable good luck has become my theme now that I am old enough to look back. Long about 1970 or so I was asked to address my classmates at a meeting at the Downtown Harvard Club in Boston. Among other profound and revealing things I said was, "I am the luckiest man I ever heard of." One thing I hoped to convey was my supreme luck in not having to decide what I wanted to do. I wanted to live in Cotuit and play with boats and never had to waste all that time looking for a career. I told my classmates, the guys I went to school with, they didn't have any idea what they wanted in life, so instead they worked their asses off, made a lot of money. They figured that when they found out what they wanted they'd be able to buy it. They made the money, but they never found out what it was, so all the work and all the money did them no good. So at Harvard I studied what interested me rather than what I imagined would pay off later on, and most of what I studied, the geology, the history, above all, the poetry, is still right there in the front of my head, to be enjoyed forever. Not to work at; just to enjoy. That is the big thing, and in the little things, too, I have been lucky like that all my life, already a long one. Too long, I think on bad days, but everything has worked out for me.

If all these blessings are consciously bestowed, if it is the will of "Somebody up there," that is, to me, further proof that Somebody is inexcusably random and capricious in handing out the blessings without regard for merit. I have done nothing, ever, to deserve all the good showered on me. The prettiest, classiest wife for miles around, to whom I have been faithful only when it suited me, a mistress almost as pretty and classy. And finally, the ultimate in class: motor vessel *Francis Minot*. I used without fail to take her to Newport whenever they were racing for America's Cup, and we got our picture taken more often than the twelve meters. Took her there to join the world's tall ships in 1976 and signed on to tend the schooner *Gladan*, the Swedish tall ship and also the American brig *Unicorn*. Everywhere we go, we are on camera. Not only does she get me attention, her very name gets for Frank Minot some of the prestige he deserves. It's enough to turn one's head. Couldn't get enough of it. This was at least part of the reason I set off on that longest possible inland voyage. People taking our picture and interviewing me for the local paper at every lock. On national TV eight times. We went single-handed through 215 locks and at every one a crowd looking at us, and it is a law of nature that half of every crowd is girls. No problems with the boat in the almost ten thousand miles.

But this close account of a single insignificant village, calling a lot of its people by name, must have more to teach me than just how undeservedly lucky I have been. Most of the good people I have known have done some evil unaware. Most individuals I have ever known are good people; most organizations, groups of the same individuals, from groups of two on up, are disgusting. There is something about humanity, which Minot and I used to talk about, which might be called social mathematics. Two good people joined together make a bad pair. Combining invariably works out for ill. If I thought in numbers the way Minot could, I would put it this way: Three good people plus three good people makes not six but nine bad people. That's the cause of organizations like WOE.

The Creator that Dave Leland saw behind "all things created" saw fit to create this idyllic village and then to destroy it by creating holy acquisitiveness as the diety of its people. More precisely, with enough brain to think up for themselves this justification of greed, but not enough brain to realize its absurdity. People learned to harness their own greed as an awesome engine to produce plenty, and before they were through, it had harnessed them. Greed, profit, they have made into the God they worship. Nothing may stand in His way. Neither land nor beauty, neither all the trees of the forests nor the fish of the seas. There is the real meaning of the suit brought by the Wampanoag, lost, of course, since it was brought in the white court.

Most of the effects people cause, in this helpless village as everywhere on earth, are unintended side effects; we are all on earth doing, unconsciously, things we do not intend and of which we are not aware. Filling up the world with people until soon there will truly and literally be no room for more. Then retroactive abortion will be an option, not a wisecrack. Then indeed, as Bierce foresaw, man's underlying savagery, automatically multiplying, will take charge. With the luck that has never yet deserted me, I will just miss this apocalypse.

INDEX

ABOUT THE AUTHOR

Most of the facts can be found in the text: born Philadelphia 30 July 1918, of Leonard Adolph Peck, a former teacher turned salesman, and to Genevieve Richmond Peck, M.D., who had as a young girl been the wife of Reid Carradine, London correspondent of the Associated Press, by whom she had a son, my half brother John Carradine, the actor. After the death of Carradine the elder, she became a nurse, to convince her crusty old father she was serious about it so he would pay her tuition to Women's Medical College in Philadelphia. Mother never practiced medicine; on graduation day she married my father and a year later had me and five years later had also my sister, Genevieve Anne.

My maternal grandfather, Horace Richmond, fought as a very young recruit in the Union Army and was wounded in the knee. I never knew either grandfather. Grandfather Richmond seems to have been a tough old soldier; from him I may have inherited my cynicism about everything. I was told that the city of Richmond was named for one of his forebears, but never heard any specifics or detailed substantiation. He had a farm near Cooperstown, New York, and sent his youngest daughter to a convent school in deference to the last wish of her immigrant Irish mother. Those nuns did a fantastic job with her; she was one of the most thoroughly educated people I ever knew. From her I got my love of poetry.

Grandfather Peck was likewise supereducated. He was from Vienna, where his family were prosperous weavers of fine linen. I always imagined that he came to America to avoid serving in the armies of Franz Josef. He settled in Gloversville, New York, where he became the only teacher for all twelve grades and still had time to found and operate the free library. "Professor" Peck is still honored in Gloversville. Another family myth is that he was one of those who worked with and shaped the library endowments of Carnegie. He brought here with him his Viennese *Kultur*, sent both sons to Yale, and even his daughters went to college. His wife was Klara Sperling of Berlin, who seems to have lacked the fierce qualities of Prussians and had no claims to intellect. She was the only grandparent I ever met and I was a very small boy when she died.

From this mishmash of love and intellect, part of the assimilation of immigrants in the nineteenth century, I somehow came to the surface like a bubble of gas in a swamp and, unlike any of these ancestors, I elected to specialize not in great causes and great ideas but rather in the petty concerns of which this book is a sample.